HARPOON

HARPOON

INSIDE THE COVERT
WAR AGAINST TERRORISM'S
MONEY MASTERS

NITSANA DARSHAN-LEITNER
AND SAMUEL M. KATZ

NEW YORK   BOSTON

Hachette Books
Hachette Book Group
1290 Avenue of the Americas
New York, NY 10104
hachettebooks.com
twitter.com/hachettebooks

First Edition: November 2017

Hachette Books is a division of Hachette Book Group, Inc.
The Hachette Books name and logo are trademarks of Hachette Book Group, Inc.

The publisher is not responsible for websites (or their content) that are not owned by the publisher.

The Hachette Speakers Bureau provides a wide range of authors for speaking events. To find out more, go to www.hachettespeakersbureau.com or call (866) 376-6591.

Library of Congress Cataloging-in-Publication Data

Names: Darshan-Leitner, Nitsana, author. | Katz, Samuel M., 1963– author.
Title: Harpoon : inside the covert war against terrorism's money masters / Nitsana Darshan-Leitner and Samuel M. Katz.
Description: First edition. | New York : Hachette Book Group, Inc., 2017. | Includes bibliographical references and index.
Identifiers: LCCN 2017027731| ISBN 9780316399050 (hardcover) | ISBN 9781478923442 (audio download) | ISBN 9780316399029 (ebook)
Subjects: LCSH: Terrorism—Finance. | Terrorism—Economic aspects. | Intelligence service—Israel.
Classification: LCC HV6431 .D285 2017 | DDC 363.325/16—dc23 LC record available at https://lccn.loc.gov/2017027731

Printed in the United States of America

LSC-C

10 9 8 7 6 5 4 3 2

For the victims of terror

CONTENTS

PART III
Legacy

AUTHOR'S NOTE

This is a story of a new and unconventional method of fighting terrorism—financial warfare against the extremist organizations, their leadership, and the rogue regimes that support them. It plays out in Israel's cloak-and-dagger world of espionage and counterterrorism. The concept was initiated and developed by a small band of innovators—members of a secret unit in the intelligence services of Israel. As with any new start-up that seeks to disrupt, at first nobody believed that this new path could be effective, but today it has proven itself as one of the most potent means to fight terrorism globally. This book chronicles the close-knit relationship between Israeli intelligence and elements of the United States government as well as lawyers from the private sector that joined forces to fight the financial infrastructure that enabled terrorists to blow themselves up inside cafés and buses in the name of the Jihad.

Like any good spy story, there are heroes in this tale, and there are villains. But this is also a recounting of an alliance forged by historical ties and inescapable necessity. Much of this story has remained secret until now. Operationally, as well as politically, secrecy was a requirement. It remains a requirement to this day. Even the name of the unit, Harpoon, was classified for nearly twenty years.*

---

* That codename was first publicly revealed by Israeli journalist Ronen Bergman in a 2008 book he authored about Israel's war against Iran; the name passed the military censor's scrutiny, although only in English, while in the Hebrew-language media, he referred to the unit

Israel's lead in fighting terrorism on a financial front, as well as on the battlefield, established an operational precedent that the United States would follow in the aftermath of the September 11, 2001, attacks; other western nations, noting the nexus between money and bloodshed in their cities, would also use the Israeli example of financial warfare as a new dimension in which terrorism can be fought and vanquished.

This new form of warfare was largely the vision of Meir Dagan, a legendary Israeli warrior and spymaster. Dagan spent most of his adult life with a weapon in his hand, and a dagger at his hip, fighting terrorists behind their lines in spectacular operations. He realized that money was the oxygen that allowed terror to breathe, and he wanted to use his experience and the forces he led to suffocate every dollar, dinar, and euro from the coffers of organizations that were dedicated to killing innocent civilians. We have had a front row seat in watching Dagan and his team of spies and commandos change the paradigm of the global war on terror. This is their story.**

Nitsana Darshan-Leitner
Samuel M. Katz
July 2017

---

name as *Gilgal*. A reference to the unit's actual Hebrew name, *Tziltzal*, was first published in a book by Orde F. Kittrie in the 2015 book *Lawfare: Law as a Weapon of War* from Oxford University Press.

** The manuscript was reviewed by security sources in Israel prior to publication.

High-Value Targets

The raiders came at night. They always did. The pilots from the U.S. Army's ultrasecretive 160th Special Operations Aviation Regiment (Airborne) were experts at flying in the absolute black of night on missions of the highest strategic importance. The unit, known as Night Stalkers, flew multi-million-dollar MH-60 and MH-47 helicopters outfitted with the top-secret night-vision capabilities. The powerful rotors that provided lift and speed to these armored birds were designed to be silent; they whispered in flight. From Mogadishu to the Hindu Kush, the Night Stalkers had flown America's tip-of-the-spear to targets deep inside the windswept valleys of the countries involved in the global war on terror. In late March 2016, the Night Stalkers were launched into the heart of the self-proclaimed Islamic State in Syria, ISIS, to ferry an as-yet-unnamed special operations unit on one such mission. The raiders' target was Abd al-Rahman Mustafa al-Qaduli.

Abd al-Rahman Mustafa al-Qaduli was hard-core. Known by too many aliases to list, the fifty-nine-year-old physics teacher from Mosul had joined al-Qaeda in Iraq in 2004 and quickly clawed his way up the chain of command to serve as the terror group's deputy commander. The Americans apprehended al-Qaduli in 2003, imprisoning him inside Camp Bucca, the U.S. military's detention center in southern Iraq that was used to hold the most dangerous terrorists seized in the insurgency. But in 2012 al-Qaduli was released in the dust of the U.S. withdrawal from Iraq. He joined the nascent Islamic State, and became a trustworthy and capable deputy to the Caliphate's head, Abu Bakr al-Baghdadi. Al-Qaduli was considered by many to be the most powerful man inside the Islamic State: He was ISIS's finance minister.[1]

As the individual who controlled the dollars and dinars, al-Qaduli decided how the ISIS billions in seized wealth, oil revenue, and Gulf money donations were spent. He was the chief bean counter who made sure that the fighters in Raqqa, the Caliphate's capital, were paid their weekly stipends, and he parceled out cash so that local commanders could purchase the bullets and mortar rounds needed to keep the fight going. Al-Qaduli was in charge of budgeting funds that ISIS used to produce the slick Hollywood-inspired recruitment videos it used to attract fighters from around the world. The financier earmarked resources to ISIS sleeper cells inside Western Europe in order to make sure that the deep-cover operatives had the cash to acquire safe houses, vehicles, and weapons. Al-Qaduli was also responsible for managing ISIS's provincial commands, to coordinate operations in Sinai and the rise of the Caliphate in the swirling chaos that was once Muammar Qaddafi's Libya.[2]

On May 14, 2014, the U.S. Department of the Treasury named al-Qaduli as a Specially Designated Global Terrorist for acting for, or on behalf of, ISIS. The State Department's Rewards for Justice had offered a seven-million-dollar bounty for information leading to al-Qaduli's arrest.[3] But the special operations forces ferried into Syria that black March night had not traveled to the Caliphate to issue an arrest warrant; they weren't in Syria hoping to collect Foggy Bottom's prize. The Pentagon mission was classified as "capture or kill." The commanders who were responsible for carrying out America's secret wars against terror, as well as their liaisons inside the Central Intelligence Agency, had hoped to be able to once again interrogate the wily money chief in order to further undermine ISIS. After all, previous raids against some of al-Qaduli's subordinates had developed the matrix of intelligence that put them on his trail. The

Americans were monitoring al-Qaduli's phones and his messengers. His whereabouts, from safe house to safe house, were followed by drones and by satellites. The ISIS chief financial officer traveled with a large security package of men and vehicles. Once located, he was an easy target to track.

The American assault team's plan was: stop al-Qaduli's convoy, eliminate the bodyguards, and subdue and secure the target so that he could be extracted and the helicopter flown back to base. But al-Qaduli likened himself to a warrior. He was often seen inspecting forces in Raqqa wearing the traditional pale green outfit, *shalwar kameez*, that barely contained a bloated belly, a relic of his days with al-Qaeda in Pakistan; his AK-74 assault rifle was always slung across his shoulder, and his load-bearing pouches were crammed with hand grenades just in case the Americans had any idea about taking him into custody again. He had no intention of being captured alive on a darkened stretch of a Caliphate side road.

When the assault force swooped in from the air, al-Qaduli's men responded with a fusillade of machine-gun fire that illuminated the thick black sky. The battle was one-sided and brief. Within minutes of the first shot being fired, al-Qaduli and his bodyguards were dead; the Toyota 4×4s they drove had been chewed to pieces by armor-piercing rounds and shrapnel. The American operators rushed into the flames and twisted metal to retrieve cell phones and other personnel effects of the ISIS operatives. The material was spirited back to the analysts and the spymasters for examination.

At the Pentagon, Defense Secretary Ash Carter and U.S. Marine Corps Major General Joseph Dunford, the chairman of the Joint Chiefs of Staff, discussed the raid with the press, careful not to disclose details of the covert operation. "We are systematically eliminating [ISIS's] cabinet. Indeed, the U.S. military killed several key [ISIS] terrorists this week including, we believe, Haji Imam [a nom de guerre for al-Qaduli] who was an [ISIS] senior leader, serving as a finance minister and who is also responsible for some external affairs and plots," Ash explained. The removal of al-Qaduli as leader was presented as a severe blow to ISIS's ability to conduct operations both inside and outside of Iraq and Syria."[4]

The termination of the financier was a major blow to ISIS. Al-Qaduli knew where the bank accounts were and what the balances were and the interest rates; he knew the PIN codes and the passwords to access ISIS's portfolios. Al-Qaduli was the number cruncher who divvied up the profits from oil and the sex trade. The money that he managed enabled ISIS to threaten much of the Middle East and target Europe and even the United States. The intelligence that led to him had been assembled, in large part, by previous operations that had targeted money changers, bankers, and the men responsible for turning the oil that flowed underneath the Caliphate into hard currency.

One operation that yielded a gold mine of actionable data in May 2015, a raid by some twenty-four members of the famed and ultrasecretive Delta Force, had targeted Abu Sayyaf, the man in charge of ISIS's oil revenues. The raid, carried out in the heart of ISIS-controlled Syria close to one hundred miles southeast of Raqqa, resulted in Abu Sayyaf's death. But the Delta Force had also seized computers and mobile phones, along with the dead man's notebooks and personal effects. The American operators had also captured Abu Sayyaf's Iraqi-born wife. When questioned, she provided an in-depth insight into the secret world of ISIS revenue. The Abu Sayyaf operation, like the raid that targeted al-Qaduli, had been ordered at the direction of President Barack Obama.[5]

The raids in Syria were a clear indication that the strategic emphasis of the United States' war against ISIS—and other transnational Islamic fundamentalist terrorist groups—had shifted like seismic plates moving underneath a troubled earth. Financiers were never considered priority targets—the men who handled the money were never marked for death. The distinction of being on a kill list was for those who ordered and ran operations. But now the money men were not only high-value targets, they were considered the highest value. There were no longer any white-collar jobs in the terrorist organization. The U.S.-led war on ISIS had become one of follow the money, devalue the money, seize the money, and kill the money. America, well into its second decade in the global war on terror, had learned that one of the most effective and long-lasting counterterrorism tactics was to suffocate the funds that were used to buy weapons, pay for explosives, rent safe houses, train recruits, and orchestrate and market catastrophic destruction on a global stage.

The new emphasis targeting terror money did not originate in the West Wing of the White House, though. The blueprint for this war plan was drawn up in the West Bank of the Jordan River some twenty years earlier. Well into the fourth decade of its own global war on terror, one man inside Israel's security hierarchy came to realize that the phenomenon of Palestinian Islamic fundamentalist, a wave of suicide bombings and death that combined nationalistic aspirations and religious fervor, was fueled and financed by a complex underground economy that had a global outreach. Stop the money, the idea followed, and the oxygen that stoked the fires of terror could be suffocated. The individual responsible for popularizing that notion was a man named Meir Dagan.

Using ledger books and bank accounts as a weapon in the battle against terror was out of character for Dagan. He had spent a military career serving the State of Israel in the up-close-and-personal world of deadly special operations. From the alleys of the Gaza Strip to the sweeping hills of southern Lebanon, Dagan had left his mark—and the bodies of his enemies—on the battlefield. He realized that heroics and daring were essential in the day-to-day fight against terror, but Israel needed an outside-the-box solution with long-term and game-changing results. As a major general and as the prime minister of Israel's advisor on counterterrorism, Dagan pursued and targeted terror financing as a course of national policy, creating a special task force of intrepid spies, accountants, experts, and military officers, as well as attorneys who were able to mobilize the resources of all Israel's security and intelligence services in the effort to bankrupt the terrorist organizations that threatened Israel. Later, as the director of the Mossad, Israel's famed espionage service, Dagan turned this task force into a global team of hand-picked agents who traveled the world to dry up the funding for the bullets and bombs that, over the course of the Palestinian intifada, killed more than one thousand Israelis and maimed more than five thousand.

Meir Dagan dispatched his operatives on daring missions around the world in the effort to fight terror money. But Dagan's most effective weapon was the close-knit alliance his team built with the highest reaches of the U.S. government, primarily in the Department of the Treasury. This alliance used espionage tradecraft and the overwhelming power of seizures and sanctions to coordinate full-fledged assaults against the banking systems that enabled Hezbollah to launder its narcotics profits and Iranian stipends and pay for the largest terrorist army the Middle East had ever seen. Dagan's asymmetrical form of financial warfare was ultimately used to target the Islamic Republic of Iran in order to prevent Tehran from realizing its nuclear ambitions.

The task force that Dagan created was called Harpoon.[6] This is the remarkable and untold story of this secret unit and how they redefined the way that Israel—and the United States—waged war on terror.

PART I

THE PALESTINIANS

CHAPTER ONE

The Tourists from the Windy City

All beginnings are difficult.
—*Rabbi Shlomo Yitzhaki (Rashi)*,
Mekhilta de-Rabbi Ishmael, *on Exodus 19:5*

It was roughly 4:00 AM on December 13, 1992, when Nissim Toledano walked into his young son's room to softly kiss the two-year-old on the forehead. The kiss, and the proud gaze that focused so lovingly on his young son, was routine for the twenty-nine-year-old sergeant in the Border Guard, the paramilitary arm of the Israel National Police. Nissim lived and worked in Lod, a mixed Jewish and Arab town near Ben-Gurion International Airport. He made the twenty-minute stroll to the Border Guard headquarters every morning, and often walked home in time for dinner. The young father felt blessed to be able to go home every night and spend time with his family.

Toledano walked briskly in the morning cold, an hour before the winter sun would appear. The morning's first traffic whizzed by him as those forced to be up at such an ungodly hour made the most of the mostly empty thoroughfares, and Toledano didn't notice the 1973 red Subaru sedan with Israeli license plates inching up behind him. As Toledeno crossed the street the car sped up and knocked him to the ground. Four young Palestinian men, all in their early twenties, emerged from the vehicle, beating the young sergeant, and then gagging him. They took his gun, handcuffed him, and threw him into their vehicle. The car sped toward Jerusalem.

The policemen who worked with Toledano knew that something was wrong when the always punctual officer failed to arrive for morning inspection. Repeated calls to his pager went unanswered. A patrol car was dispatched to look for him. The General Security Service, Israel's domestic counterintelligence and counterterrorism agency known as the Sherut Ha'Bitachon Ha'Klali, or Shin Bet for short, was also alerted. Toledano's disappearance bore the telltale signs of foul play. Hamas, the Palestinian Islamic Resistance Movement, had kidnapped soldiers in the past and buried their victims in unmarked graves, never telling the Israeli authorities where the slain soldiers lay.

The four young men who kidnapped Toledano called themselves the "Secret Squad."[1] They carried out the operation in order to prove their worth to a local Hamas commander, hoping that the deed would be enough to earn acceptance into the group's military wing. The kidnapping was done completely on spec: The perpetrators even pooled their savings to purchase their getaway car. The four planned to carry out an operation in the capital, but Jerusalem's streets were too well protected. They chose the city of Lod instead. Toledano was targeted at random.[2]

The Shin Bet received confirmation of Toledano's abduction shortly before noon. Two of the kidnappers, their faces concealed by kefiyyehs, or Arab headdresses, walked into the Red Crescent office in the West Bank town of El-Bireh and handed over a copy of Toledano's police identity card, along with a pledge that the sergeant would be killed at 9:00 that night unless Hamas founder Sheikh Ahmed Yassin was freed from an Israeli prison. "Our group kidnapped one of the officers of the occupation on Dec. 13, 1992," the communiqué proclaimed. "We are demanding the occupation authorities and Israeli leaders release Sheik Ahmed Yassin in exchange for releasing this officer."[3]

Sheikh Yassin was a quadriplegic Islamic scholar who had created a Palestinian version of Egypt's Muslim Brotherhood in Gaza and the West Bank, an organization that would become known to the world as Hamas.

The Israelis imprisoned Yassin in 1984 for stockpiling weapons in his home, but he was released a year later as part of an exchange of 1,500 Palestinian prisoners for three Israeli POWs captured in Lebanon. He was arrested again in 1989 and sentenced to two life terms for ordering the kidnapping and murder of two Israeli soldiers, and attempting to use the bodies as leverage to free Hamas terrorists jailed by Israel.[4] Yassin was also convicted for approving the torture and murder of an Arab man suspected of collaborating with Israeli security forces in Gaza.

Toledano's kidnapping sparked a political crisis in Israel. Prime Minister Yitzhak Rabin convened an emergency security cabinet session, demanding action. Israel had just endured close to five years of bloody violence during the Palestinian intifada, or uprising. Hamas, along with the Iranian-funded Palestinian Islamic Jihad (PIJ), had successfully injected the zeal of fanatical Islamic fundamentalism into Palestinian nationalism, making the most of a thirst for catastrophic bloodshed. Israel was at the time involved in delicate and covert talks with the Palestine Liberation Organization. The abduction of Nissim Toledano was a brazen attempt by Hamas to disrupt those tenuous negotiations and trigger a wave of rage and violence.

Rabin had no intention of negotiating with Hamas for Toledano. The prime minister realized that Toledano was probably already dead, and he understood the political ramifications of terrorists kidnapping a police officer off the streets of an Israeli city and murdering him in cold blood. Rabin was a seasoned politician, but his background was military, and he knew that a decisive battlefield statement was needed to send a clear message that there would be consequences for Hamas. Like many of Israel's commanders at the time, Rabin was a chain smoker, and a cloud of smoke engulfed the stormy cabinet meeting of angry strategizing. Rabin had vowed to break the bones of Palestinian protesters during the intifada, and now he wanted to break the back of Hamas. A no-holds-barred measure was required, the prime minister explained. He ordered the heads of the intelligence services, and the commanders of the Israel Defense Forces (IDF) to take immediate action.

Led by the Shin Bet, IDF special ops units and Border Guard counter-terrorist teams raided multiple locations throughout the West Bank and the Gaza Strip. The raids yielded high-ranking operatives from Hamas and the PIJ. These men ran the Hamas and PIJ political wings, controlling the charitable funds that were the groups' financial lifeline; they were also all active commanders in terror operations against Israeli civilians. The detained men included doctors, lawyers, and engineers; some were even American green card holders. In all, some 1,200 were arrested and detained. Prime Minister Rabin wanted to sever Hamas's civilian spine, which fueled and provided safe haven for its military component. He wanted the terrorists relocated far from the territories. Rabin ordered that the top leadership of the two terror organizations, 415 operatives in all, be deported to the no-man's-land of southern Lebanon. Lawyers for the deportees took the matter to the Israeli Supreme Court to plead for the expulsions to be halted.

On the morning of December 16, 1992, as the Israeli justices wrangled with the legalities of expelling the suspected terrorists, Fatma Abu Dahuk, a twenty-five-year-old Bedouin girl, made a grisly discovery in the West Bank. Fatma set out from her family tent near Kfar Adumim, halfway between Jerusalem and Jericho, to search for a lost camel that had strayed during the night. The desert hills and wadis were deep and cavernous but easy terrain for an experienced Bedouin. As she walked through the steep valleys, in a ravine made colorful by winter flowers, Fatma stumbled upon the badly mutilated body of a man clad in military olive, his face covered by a matching green parka. His hands were bound high behind his back and he had been stabbed repeatedly. It was Toledano. Investigators believe that he was savagely tortured and murdered shortly after his capture.

News of Toledano's murder sparked riots in his hometown of Lod. Jewish protesters marched toward the Arab neighborhoods screaming "Death to Arabs." The fate of the 415 was sealed.

At a little past midnight on December 17, the 415 Hamas and PIJ leaders were ushered from their holding facilities throughout Israel. They were blindfolded and placed on buses, the windows of the vehicles covered by blankets to prevent the prisoners from knowing their destination. The buses drove north, toward the Lebanese border. Israel occupied a security zone inside southern Lebanon, and the buses pushed deep into Lebanese territory, until they reached lines patrolled by the Lebanese military. The deportees were ordered off the buses and told to make their way to the nearby village of Marj al-Zuhur, several miles from the Israeli lines.

Rabin's move drew international condemnation. Even U.S. President-elect Bill Clinton saw the deportations as counterproductive to the success of the ongoing negotiations. But the men forced into a tent encampment inside the freezing wasteland of southern Lebanon were the brains, muscle, and—most important—the accountants of the Hamas underground. These men knew the intricate details required to keep an illegal and covert organization functioning on a daily basis. It was a severe hit to the terror groups. While the 415 shivered around their South Lebanon campfires, assault rifles weren't being purchased on the West Bank black market; terrorists' widows weren't receiving their stipends; and there was no money to rent Gaza safe houses. Hamas operations in the Palestinian territories had come to a dead halt.

Mohammed al-Hamid Khalil Salah was one of the thousands of passengers landing at Israel's Ben-Gurion International Airport on the afternoon of January 15, 1993. Salah, a Palestinian native, was a naturalized U.S. citizen who sold cars for a living in Chicago. He appeared nervous as he stepped onto the tarmac after his flight from London. Plain-clothed Israeli security officers were everywhere, conspicuous in their safari jackets and mirrored sunglasses. These young men were designed to be a visual deterrence, and they kept an eye on anything out of the norm as travelers entered Israel. The security services had received information that a Hamas operative would arrive from the United States, although they did not know his identity or his mission. Salah found himself under the gaze of border policemen patrolling around the aircraft; the shuttle from the tarmac to the arrivals hall provided little relief. The Chicago resident readied his American passport for the inevitable scrutiny. It wasn't easy for West Bank natives to return to the region, and especially not through Ben-Gurion.

Salah was nervous when he handed over his passport. "I am here to visit family and friends," he said in a soft and shaky voice when the young customs official asked what the purpose of his visit was. His travel documents were studied. The entry process took much longer than usual. Men in uniform, and some Arabic speakers in plainclothes, questioned Salah intensely. Finally, after a very long delay, Salah's passport was stamped. His suitcases were the last ones rotating on the baggage carousel.

Salah hurried outside from the arrivals hall and into the winter's cold in search of a taxi. Agents from the Shin Bet were already on him. Salah's name was not on any terrorist watch list, but he sparked some curiosity and the agents at the airport decided to follow him. The Shin Bet had tossed Salah back into the sea, hoping to catch bigger fish.

Salah traveled the forty minutes up the twisting Highway One toward Jerusalem. The Israeli capital had been cut in two in the armistice agreement that ended hostilities in 1949 between Israel and Jordan. The western half of the city was Jewish, and the eastern part, including the Old City, had been held by Jordan until Israel captured it in the 1967 Six Day War. Salah headed to the eastern section of the city, to the YMCA, a sprawling complex that occupied a city block on the Nablus Road just outside the walls of the Old City. A room had been prepared for him. Salah kept to himself, barely leaving his accommodation.

The Shin Bet maintained close surveillance on the YMCA, and additional resources were provided for the operation. The security services even summoned the assistance of Unit 33, a secretive undercover police unit assigned to the Jerusalem District. Unit 33 fielded policemen from all backgrounds, speaking a Tower of Babel of languages and using a variety of disguises as they blended into the Jerusalem landscape. Salah had no idea that a large-scale surveillance operation was monitoring his every move.

A few days after his arrival, Salah was joined by a friend from Chicago. Mohammed Jarad was a thirty-six-year-old Palestinian green grocer from the Windy City's Albany Park neighborhood. His arrival worried the Shin Bet. Were the two men sent to Israel on a terrorist mission? Did their bags hold weapons or explosives? Shin Bet Director Ya'akov Peri, a veteran of the terror wars inside the Palestinian areas, ordered his agents to seize the two men. On January 25, Unit 33 received its orders to apprehend the suspects.

The police approached Salah's room cautiously. Terrorists had traveled to Israel before, posing as tourists then building bombs inside their hotel rooms in the hope of mounting a catastrophic attack. An entry team positioned itself at the door and readied for the push inside; one of the operators used his skill in picking the lock to open the door, cautious due to fears that the room was rigged with explosives. But when the officers burst in, they found the two men unarmed. A police bomb disposal unit was summoned to open the suitcases, concerned that the luggage held Semtex or another military-grade explosive. But when the bags were opened, the Shin Bet agents and policemen stood in surprised silence. Salah's luggage contained a huge amount of American dollars. Some of the policemen joked that they had uncovered Aladdin's treasure.[5]

Salah and Jarah were ushered to the Russian Compound, the Jerusalem Police District's operations center for questioning. If there was a simple explanation for the money—a down payment on a business, perhaps a wedding dowry—then the men would have to pay the customs fine and be sent on their way. But the police knew that there were regional—even transnational—criminal enterprises run from the West Bank that reached all the way to the United States. Guns, drugs, and auto theft were rife in the territories, and some of the Palestinian gangs involved ran international fraud operations in the Midwest. But if the money was destined for a terror faction, the Shin Bet wanted details.

Salah was questioned by the security services, who called him by his Hamas nom de guerre, Abu Ahmad. The Israelis would discover that Mohammed Salah was much more than a bag man, delivering bundles of cash like a common courier. He had been recruited into the ranks of

Hamas in 1987, by Musa Abu Marzook, the Gaza-born Colorado State University–educated political head of Hamas. Abu Marzook operated out of Falls Church, Virginia—well out of the reach of the Israeli security services. Salah was trained by Hamas and began working as a covert financier for the organization in 1991. He opened several accounts in his name at the First National Bank of Chicago, LaSalle Bank, and Standard Bank and Trust, all for use by the Islamic Resistance Movement.[6]

Salah was carrying $97,000 in U.S. currency when he was arrested; the money came from his American account that had boasted a healthy balance of $650,000.[7] Salah couldn't initially explain where the funds came from. He argued that he was a simple man who had done well living the American dream. But under intense questioning, he confessed that the money indeed belonged to Hamas.

Salah recounted the instructions he received from Abu Marzook before he embarked to Israel:

> "It is necessary to organize the military activity in Hebron, Ramallah, Nablus, Bethlehem, Jericho and Jerusalem. It is also necessary to check the situation in Gaza and the requirements of the people there, since the dominant feeling is that Gaza was not hurt by the deportations, neither politically or militarily. It is necessary to allocate funds as follows:
>   Ramallah: $100,000
>   Nablus: $130,000
>   Hebron: $100,000
>   Gaza (military activity): $300,000
>   The rest: according to the military and general requirements."[8]

In the past these monies were disbursed to Hamas cells through the offices of *halfanim*, or money changers. The money changers were an essential thread in the fiscal fabric of the West Bank following the 1967 War, when the proper banking system all but disappeared. They exchanged foreign currency in kiosks, and brought cash of all currencies to and from the Arab world, transporting it across the Allenby Bridge between the West Bank and Jordan. The money changers were reliable and could often handle large transactions using a network of contacts in cities around the Middle East. They were ideal conduits for the illegal movement of money, as their transactions were untraceable.

Salah knew the names of the money changers that Hamas generally worked with throughout the West Bank, but he had been instructed to stay in his room and await telephone instructions from Abu Marzook. Abu Marzook had traveled to Lebanon before the New Year to meet with the deportees at Marj al-Zuhur. He also met with Hamas leaders in Sudan, and Palestine Liberation Organization officials in Tunisia.[9] Abu Marzook called his messenger several times from his pit stops across the Middle East.

Salah confessed that he also made a previous trip to Israel on behalf of Hamas. Passport records revealed that Salah was in Israel months earlier, in August 1992. At that time he delivered $96,000 to Saleh al-Aruri, the Hamas commander in the West Bank city of Hebron. That money was later used to purchase black market weapons and ammunition, including assault rifles, an Uzi submachine gun, pistols, and a significant supply of ammunition. These weapons were later used to murder an Israeli reservist soldier in Hebron and a Border Guard police officer in Jerusalem. Abu Marzook, Salah admitted, was angry that some of the money delivered in August went to charitable causes and not completely to the Hamas military wing.[10]

Salah's connection to al-Aruri was troubling to Israeli authorities. Saleh al-Aruri had launched his Hamas career in Hebron University where he studied sharia law and rose to lead the student union's Islamic faction. He had an uncanny gift for recruiting reliable operatives and was adept at handling money.[11] Al-Aruri developed and maintained links between Hamas military cells in the West Bank and in the Gaza Strip. He also was one of the conduits for Palestinians living in the United States who collected money, ostensibly for charitable purposes, and then funneled it into the territories. As someone inside Hamas who dispensed the money, al-Aruri was one of the most important—and dangerous—members of the terror organization's hierarchy.

The Shin Bet arrested al-Aruri in 1992 and charged him with terror offenses. He was sentenced to more than fifteen years in prison. Yet although he was incarcerated in a maximum security facility, al-Aruri continued to act as a Hamas military commander from behind bars. Few inside Hamas possessed his comprehensive vision for armed resistance against Israel. Fewer still, even on the Israeli side, understood the absolute link between money and blood.

Salah was a thorny problem for the State of Israel. He was ultimately charged and convicted in a military court for involvement in a terrorist entity and sentenced to seven years in jail.* His case led Israel to press the United States to have its law enforcement agencies look deeper into the underground economy of Palestinian charities that supposedly collected nickels and dimes for orphans and food kitchens, but ultimately funded the bullets, bombs, and bloodshed.

This was the first significant case in which terror financing was placed center stage by intelligence, security, and law enforcement agencies. Somewhere in the Israeli security apparatus, a light switched on as they realized that a war on terror financing could be a tool in disrupting the activities of terrorist groups. This was where it all began.

The Israeli government was eager to make an example of Mohammed Salah, labeling the Chicago resident as the "World Commander of the Hamas military organization."[12] After months of questioning, Salah admitted that the money he and Mohammed Jarad had brought to Israel was intended for Hamas, but he maintained that the cash was to be distributed to the families of the 415 deportees to Lebanon. The cash, Salah stressed, was raised legitimately through charities in the United States and Europe, for legitimate charitable purposes. After all, charity, or zakat, was

---

* Jarah was released after several months and allowed to return to the United States.

one of the five pillars of Islam. The Israelis, somewhat belatedly, were concerned that Hamas was actually controlled from the United States, and that the freedoms afforded by due process, and the success of many Palestinian immigrants who found a place in the American dream, enabled the organization to serve as a remote operational command center.[13] The United States had become an ATM of terror for Hamas.

But despite Salah's arrest and subsequent revelations, there was growing tension between Israel and the United States over the deportees. United Nations resolutions were passed to condemn the expulsions by Israel. From London to Lagos, foreign ministers contacted their counterpart in Israel to demand that the men trapped in a southern Lebanese no-man's-land be permitted to return home. The Lebanese winter was harsh, and reporters from CNN and other international networks held sympathetic interviews with the men as they huddled around campfires wearing tattered blankets. But at night, as those same reporters returned to Israel or Damascus for a hot meal, the deportees were visited by representatives from Iranian intelligence and from Hezbollah, Lebanon's Shiite "Party of God," which had been at war with Israel and the United States, in Lebanon since 1982. Hezbollah introduced the revolutionary Iranian leader Ayatollah Ruhollah Khomeini's philosophy of martyrdom into the vernacular of the Middle East. During his country's war with Iraq, Iranian military commanders had ordered thousands of schoolchildren to go out along the borders to dig up mines placed by Saddam Hussein's soldiers. The students were given plastic necklaces with keys on them and told they were the "keys to paradise."

Iran exported its Islamic revolution to Lebanon, where young Shiite men, eager to earn a spot in heaven, volunteered in droves to strap on explosives and blow themselves up. Hezbollah destroyed two U.S. embassies; they blew up barracks of both U.S. Marines and French paratrooper peacekeepers. They rewrote the terrorism handbook.

Imad Mughniyeh represented Hezbollah at the meetings with Hamas in Marj al-Zuhur. Mughniyeh, a south Lebanon native, was the thirty-one-year-old diabolical mastermind behind Hezbollah's meteoric rise as a terrorist army powerful enough to force the United States out of Lebanon, an army that was also waging a bloody guerrilla campaign against Israeli forces in the country. Iran's representative at the meetings with Hamas was Ali-Reza Asgari, the commander of those Islamic Revolutionary Guard Corps based inside Lebanon.[14] Asgari was instrumental in transforming Hezbollah into a formidable terror power, and now he had similar hopes for Hamas. By January 1993, as the deportees were working with their new strategic allies, Iran began budgeting $30 million annually for Hamas.[15] That stipend would increase tenfold in the months to come.

The Iranians and Hezbollah schooled the deportees in the A to Z's of terror tradecraft, in bomb building, suicidal terror tactics, and intelligence gathering. But U.S. President Bill Clinton and the leaders of the European Union pressed Yitzhak Rabin to take the Hamas commanders back. The deportees were out of range and out of sight of Israeli intelligence, who didn't know what was going on once the news cameras left at night. American and European political pressure on Israel was enormous, especially as the winter's chill gave way to the warmth of spring and then the broiling heat of summer, and the secret talks with the Palestine Liberation Organization intensified. Rabin would ultimately yield to this foreign political pressure.

The Israelis allowed some of the deportees to return months after they were dispatched to southern Lebanon. A trickle soon turned into a steady stream. The men returning to the West Bank and Gaza were searched for explosives or incriminating paperwork, but there was no visible evidence of the intense schooling they received. The formulas for homemade explosives and the methods and means for recruiting an army of martyrs were committed to memory. Hamas and Hezbollah, like the two things they told you to never mix together in high school, were primed to explode on Israel.

According to then military secretary to Yitzhak Rabin, General Amos Gilad, allowing the deportees to return was a fatal mistake: "Deportation in and of itself is a good tactic. You can either kill someone or you can expel him, but in both instances he has been removed from the territory.

The problem here was not the deportation but that they connected with Hezbollah and we should have prevented this. Hezbollah hates the Sunnis but they hate us Israelis even more. When they returned from Lebanon they were much more dangerous than when they left. They were unified and now they were big heroes to the Palestinians. This was a war of symbols and in such a conflict you cannot permit your enemies to become heroes."

The returning deportees also learned the details of bank accounts to be at their disposal upon their arrival home. Iran had vast resources that it pledged to Hamas. The tens of millions of dollars that the Islamic Republic would invest in Hamas would rival the funds raised by the charities in the United States and elsewhere in the world Palestinian community. Hamas military commanders would soon have their hands on generous amounts of funds.

Weeks after they kidnapped and murdered Toledano, members of the Secret Squad traveled to the West Bank town of Yamoun to meet a certain Hamas military commander. Mohammed Issa, the twenty-three-year-old squad leader who shot Toledano, presented the Hamas commander with the Israeli policeman's service weapon to prove that they were the ones who seized and murdered him. The Hamas commander was impressed. He gave the kidnappers 4,000 Jordanian dinars (approximately $7,000), along with a pistol and an Uzi submachine gun purchased on the black market, and urged them to continue their work on behalf of Hamas.[16]

That money went far. The squad purchased a white van that they used in an attempt to run over two hitchhiking soldiers one evening in central Israel, but they crashed into a guardrail after slightly injuring one of the young conscripts. The squad's Hamas handler gave them an additional $1,000 to fix the van so they could use it for future terror operations.[17] On March 30, the squad shot and killed two Israeli policemen in a drive-by ambush. It was to be their last operation.

Early in the morning hours of June 6, 1993, the Shin Bet, supported by special Border Guard forces, apprehended the four East Jerusalem residents behind the bloodshed. The arrests happened as the Secret Squad was planning a series of potentially devastating car bombings throughout Israel. A bomb factory, with components to make several powerful improvised explosive devices, was also uncovered in Nablus.

The four men were charged with Toledano's abduction and murder, as well as a slew of other terror offenses. They were tried and convicted in an Israeli military court, and sentenced to multiple life terms.* But their crimes, and the deportation of the 415, set in motion a chain of events that emboldened Hamas and gave it access to more funding from the United States, the Persian Gulf, and Iran.

In the early 1990s, a new and highly lethal form of terrorism had emerged against Israel, one that weaponized Islamic fervor thanks to a multitude of money streams. Veteran Shin Bet agents knew that the paradigm had changed. The worst was yet to come.

---

* The four men were released, along with 1,023 other terrorists, as part of a 2011 prisoner exchange between the State of Israel and Hamas. In the highly controversial exchange, Israel released 1,027 terrorists, including many with blood on their hands for their active role in terrorist attacks including suicide bombings, in exchange for one soldier, Corporal Gilad Shalit, who had been seized in 2005 just outside the Gaza Strip. The release of so many terrorists with "blood on their hands" was political dynamite in Israel; the families of those who had been killed by the terrorists protested. On behalf of the families, Shurat HaDin, the Tel Aviv–based civil rights center, petitioned the Israeli Supreme Court in the attempt— unsuccessful—to block the prisoner release.

CHAPTER TWO

Da'wa

Many Israelis found it hard to contain their disbelief. Some wept as they huddled around television sets with grainy images broadcast live, via satellite, from the American capital. It was 1993. Prime Minister Yitzhak Rabin, a founding father of the Jewish state and the army chief who was one of the architects of Israel's amazing 1967 Six Day War victory, was in Washington, D.C., standing on the same grass as Yasir Arafat, the PLO chairman and, in most Israeli eyes, a man who embodied cold-blooded terror.

Up until that moment it was illegal for Israelis to maintain contact with the PLO. Now, on the White House lawn with U.S. President Bill Clinton bursting out of his suit with joy, Israel and the Palestinians were moments from signing an accord that would ostensibly end hostilities between two sides locked so intractably in a deadly fight over a small patch of land. The unthinkable happened on September 13, 1993, when Yitzhak Rabin and Yasir Arafat shook hands.

Palestinians also watched in disbelief. It was unfathomable to many in the towns in Gaza and around the major West Bank cities that Abu Ammar (Arafat's nom de guerre) would make peace with the hated Jews. The Israelis monitored the mood in the territories, not knowing if the handshake in Washington, D.C., would trigger new violence. Virtually every arm of Israel's military and intelligence services thought they understood what was going on in the territories, but they could never control the mood on the street.

The West Bank of the Jordan River captured from the Hashemite

Kingdom in 1967, called by its biblical name Judea and Samaria by the
Israeli security forces, consisted of more than 2,100 square miles and more
than a million inhabitants living in eight major urban sprawls, smaller
towns, and villages, as well as nineteen refugee camps. The West Bank
also encompassed East Jerusalem; the city was divided in the armistice
between Israel and Jordan after the 1948 War of Independence. The Gaza
Strip, 140 square miles in size and one of the poorest and most heavily
congested locations on the planet, was captured from Egypt in the 1967
war. Both the West Bank and Gaza were under Israeli military control,
and it was the army that had the daily contacts with the Palestinian
themselves.

The large conference room in the IDF Central Command Headquarters
in the West Bank was overflowing with high-rank officers, senior Shin
Bet agents, and intelligence officials. They gathered to analyze the situation after the now-famous White House lawn handshake and deter-
mine how it could impact on the terror activity in the region. There
had already been other vociferous debates among the generals and the
heads of the security services. The officers and commanders who ran
security operations thought themselves expert in the day-to-day lives of
the residents of the West Bank and Gaza. The commanders viewed the
areas under their control tactically. The Shin Bet had human assets deep
inside the various terrorist groups that staked a claim to the resistance
against Israel. The Shin Bet agents were Arabic specialists; they spoke
the language, immersed themselves in the culture, and understood the
nuances of Islam. Each agency and unit went around the table speaking
its piece.

Toward the end of the meeting a young army officer by the name of
Uri L.* serving in COGAT, the Coordinator of Government Activities
in the Territories, asked permission to speak. He started to explain and
analyze the development of a new terror phenomenon—the civilian

_____

* Uri L. is a pseudonym.

infrastructure being constructed by the terror organizations. This phenomenon was known as *da'wa*, which in Arabic means "the call to the believers to shelter beneath the faith." It also meant a return to the faith, a way where those who lived outside the struggle could give something back to the community and to the greater cause.[1] In essence, *da'wa* covered the enormous Hamas civilian infrastructure in the West Bank and Gaza. Its objective was to imbue every aspect of Palestinian life with a fundamentalist message. The *da'wa* was life: It was food, medication, and schoolbooks. But it was also triacetone triperoxide—the homemade witch's brew of store-bought materials that could be turned into the explosives used by suicide bombers to attack Israeli targets. The *da'wa* was funded globally.

Uri focused on the financial basis of this growing threat. The money poured into the territories from all over the world—ostensibly to benefit the daily lives of Muslim Palestinians. The Holy Land Foundation, a not-for-profit group in Richardson, Texas, was one of the primary conduits of funds from the United States. Hamas leaders—including Musa Abu Marzook, the group's Virginia-based political chief—sent fiery clerics from the territories on speaking tours of the American heartland to raise funds for the people back home. Palestinian communities thrived in Brooklyn, New York, and New Jersey, as well as in Virginia, Michigan, and Florida. But there were also vibrant Palestinian communities in the Midwest—in Missouri, Oklahoma, Texas, and Indiana—where stores always had a small collection jar so shoppers could help those "under occupation." Money was also collected in mosques, and millions of dollars were sent back to the territories via a multitude of charities and nongovernmental organizations (NGOs).

The al-Aqsa Foundation funneled money from Germany; Interpal, with posh offices in London, as well as Birmingham, Manchester, and Leicester, raised money from the Palestinian communities in the United Kingdom.

The monies brought in overseas were sent to the West Bank and the Gaza Strip via bank transfers, money changers, and transnational IOUs. There were even barter arrangements, where goods were shipped free of charge to merchants in the territories and the money earned from their sale was given to the charities—minus a small cut for the merchant.

Uri described the perilous implications that would arise from this threat and urged his assembled colleagues to find ways to crush it in its infancy. He explained that if the IDF did not prioritize undermining the escalation of this dangerous development it would be come back to haunt Israel for generations. Most of the participants were already packing up and leaving as Uri spoke, and the meeting was adjourned without any meaningful resolution of the matter.

Despite their lack of interest in Uri's words, the only real experts, those who truly understood what was really going on inside the schools, mosques, and hearts and minds of the Palestinian people, were the officers and administrators assigned to COGAT. The unit was part of the Ministry of Defense and attached to the IDF General Staff. It is the official Israeli agency for one-on-one interaction with Palestinian civilian entities. COGAT made sure that homes and hospitals had water and power; COGAT helped to build and maintain infrastructure and enable a semblance of normalcy for the Palestinian population; COGAT ensured that Palestinian merchants could continue to ply their livelihoods.

Virtually all the officers and administrators assigned to COGAT had something of an intelligence background, and virtually all spoke flawless Palestinian-accented Arabic. These men and women sat with Palestinian mayors, clerics, human rights leaders, shopkeepers, and teachers. They spoke to Palestinian family heads and tried to help settle all sorts of disputes—from clans at odds with one another to businessmen fighting over a failed deal. COGAT personnel knew what the Palestinians ate, and whom they admired. They knew the currency of day-to-day life better than anyone.

Uri L. was one of the most capable officers serving in COGAT. Uri was very much a field man. A large, bald, and warm-spirited man with an appetite for humor, Uri wore his smile like a badge of honor. He was the kind of spymaster who could be fatherly to those human assets who needed reassurance, and brutal to those who had to be thrown out to the wolves. Uri could wrap his bearlike arms around a Palestinian recruited to be an informer and convince him of the importance of the intelligence he provided, but he could also use his large forearms to apply pressure when pressure was called for. The intelligence specialists in COGAT as well as the Palestinians they dealt with all liked Uri: Whether the conversation was in Hebrew or Arabic, he always paid attention to those he talked to and gave them his interest and respect.

Working alongside Uri was Lavi S.* Lavi was a charismatic intelligence officer: Gentle and unassuming, he was careful with every word. He was very much like John le Carré's legendary character George Smiley— every move he made on the chessboard was made knowing what he'd do twelve steps later. There were many men like Lavi in Israel's security services: men of medium height and unassuming physiques who didn't look like spymasters. Lavi, whose parents had come from Europe, was a master Arabist: He was fluent in Arabic—including the all-important Palestinian colloquial—and possessed an ideal mix of academic and field work, enabling him to understand the Arab street like few others. From COGAT, Lavi went on to head the Palestinian Affairs Division of the Israeli Ministry of Defense.[2]

Uri and Lavi were very typical of the men and women who worked for COGAT: dedicated professionals with very specific areas of expertise. Each developed an intimate understanding of Gaza and the West Bank. They traveled to Palestinian cities, villages, and refugee camps on a daily basis, seeing the facts on the ground, and listening to the unfiltered Palestinian narrative. They knew the landscape: what lay on the surface and the tensions that simmered beneath.

Both men saw the terrain was rapidly changing. A religious storm had swept the territories.

More and more children were attending religious schools across the West Bank and Gaza. Women who once wore tight jeans and who worked to help support their families now wore the niqab and stayed

---

* Lavi S. is a pseudonym.

home. Neighborhood mosques could barely contain the worshippers who flocked to daily prayers. More mosques than could be counted were under construction. There were new buildings everywhere. Medical clinics and food banks sprang up inside refugee camps and small villages as Muslim benevolent societies filled a vacuum that was not served by the Israeli authorities or the various Palestinian resistance movements based on nationalistic struggle and socialist ideology. There were pan-Arab communist groups, like the Popular Front for the Liberation of Palestine. Others, like the Democratic Front for the Liberation of Palestine, were Maoist; some, like the Palestine Liberation Front, were pro-Iraqi Ba'athists.

The commanders of these factions used to meet in coffeehouses and in universities. The men of the new Islamic movements met in the mosques and in the Islamic schools. Uri and Lavi felt the ground shifting under their feet.

The changes were obvious, but the new Islamic fervor did not correlate into a marked increase in security-related incidents, and those were what concerned the generals. The Shin Bet was in the intelligence-gathering and threat-mitigation business; the motivations behind the violence mattered little. The spies were concerned about locating, undermining, apprehending, and targeting the men who led terror cells. "There were many Shin Bet agents and army officers who believed that the Palestinians were simply targets and nothing more," an Israeli intelligence officer who worked the territories at the time said. "These men made no attempt to get into the heads of the people and to immerse themselves with the mood on the Palestinian street."[3] Understanding the territories fell to COGAT's experts, and the reality of a Palestinian society fueled by religious fervor and lavish investment of cold, hard cash worried men like Uri and Lavi. They tried to alert their colleagues—anyone who'd listen to the threat before it began to further metastasize.

Hamas takes its name from the Arabic acronym for Harakt al-Muqawama al-Islamiya, or Islamic Resistance Movement, and it also means "zeal." It was created in 1987 in Gaza as an offshoot of the Egyptian Muslim

Brotherhood Society. Under Great Britain's rule of Egypt, the Brotherhood was intent on instilling Islamic law into the fabric of Egyptian society. The movement also became a national liberation force that used fanatic displays of barbaric violence to prove their intent and to illustrate their ambitions. In 1936, during riots that engulfed the British mandate of Palestine, elements of the Brotherhood came to Gaza to inspire the inhabitants with the call to Islam.

Various Egyptian regimes outlawed the Brotherhood; the dreaded Egyptian secret service, the Muchabarat, sent many of its founders and top commander to the gallows. But the movement took root in Gaza. The year 1978 saw the opening of the Islamic University in Gaza, considered by many to be a base of operations for the Brotherhood. Gaza was poor and desolate—woefully neglected by the Egyptians who ruled the strip from 1948 to 1967. Gazans were traditionally religious, and more in line with the fundamentalist form of Islam that many preached in the mosques of Cairo and the Nile Delta.

In 1987, Sheikh Ahmed Yassin founded Hamas. Yassin was a quadriplegic since childhood, yet he did not allow his disability to interfere with his pursuit of religious studies. Although his spinal injury affected his voice, turning his words into a squeaky whisper, Yassin became a charismatic preacher and an Islamic scholar. His Hamas was billed as a religious organization dedicated to charity. Its message of religious piety and fierce nationalism found a receptive audience in the Palestinian communities in the United States and Europe, as well as among the tens of thousands of Palestinians who lived and worked in Saudi Arabia and the Persian Gulf, and their money flowed into the Strip. Hamas built schools and clinics, employing thousands of jobless in Gaza and later in the West Bank.

Hamas styled itself as a religious and political organization, but it was also a military force and a terrorist army. The funds it raised internationally paid for widows and orphans, as well as fighters and their weapons. The money went to the Hamas military wing, the Izzedine al-Qassam Brigade—named for an Islamic preacher who attacked Jewish civilians in prestate Israel. Its members trained for war, and they adopted the principles of Jihad, martyrdom, and self-sacrifice.[4]

The Hamas military arm was directed by the organization's political wing—the same wing that controlled all of the charitable donations flowing in from the United States and Europe, as well as the apparently endless stream of cash from Saudi Arabia and the other Persian Gulf states. According to conservative estimates from Israeli intelligence at the time, Hamas military networks in the West Bank alone operated on an annual budget of over $1 million. The funds were filtered through the front offices of foundations and charities, and through the back doors of schools and mosques. The money, doled out in dribs and drabs, was laundered through an extensive criminal conspiracy that was virtually untraceable to Israel's prying eyes.

The territories themselves, men like Uri and Lavi knew, were not awash with money. The local economy was primarily agricultural; laborers, when the security situation allowed, ventured into Israel to work at menial jobs. Much of this money, as well as earnings sent home by Palestinian laborers and professionals working in the Persian Gulf and subject to a PLO tax, paid the salaries of local commanders and their men in order to keep the resistance going. Other funds, from the terror factions' budgets, paid for the widows of men killed and stipends for the families of those with husbands or sons jailed in Israel for terror offenses.

Uri was the first Israeli officer to consider how Israel could insert itself into the flow of money, into the Hamas *da'wa*. In 1992, as a consultant in Arab Affairs to the West Bank military governor, he wrote an in-depth intelligence briefing examining the civil infrastructure of Hamas in the territories, where the money was coming from and how it was spent. "I knew we were dealing with a monster," Uri remembered, "and that the only way to deal with this monster was to wage war against the intertwined threads that connected the Hamas military wing with all its benevolent components. The civil infrastructure, the complete *da'wa*, had to be defeated."[5]

Uri's report, coupled with the arrest of the Chicago tourists and other events, was considered groundbreaking enough to launch a wave of military raids against Hamas-run schools, mosques, and clinics. The Israeli effort, known as Operation Destruction of Leaven (named for the Jewish ritual of ridding homes of bread before the Passover holiday), was far-reaching: Community leaders were arrested, and weapons, explosives, and piles of money were seized. So many documents were confiscated that intelligence officers found the paper trail overwhelming.[6] Much of what was seized ended up in the trash bin. The intelligence value of the find was not yet appreciated by the military and political echelons. Uri's thesis was largely ignored. It was back to business as usual.

But Uri continued to lobby the IDF hierarchy to take the issue of the *da'wa* seriously, and view it as a strategic threat. Uri traveled to bases throughout the West Bank, giving presentation after presentation, to local commanders. One general working out of IDF headquarters in Tel Aviv seemed very interested in what Uri had to say: Their meeting, slated for fifteen minutes, turned into a three-hour discussion. But the end result was the same—the IDF wanted to go after men who commanded cells and knew where the weapons were. Uri began to despair. He felt like he was hitting a dead end. However, there was one high-ranking IDF officer who saw promise in Uri's work.

Meir Dagan was born Meir Huberman on January 30, 1945, on a train to the Soviet Union as his family fled war-torn Poland. The train, it is believed, was traveling through the Ukraine at the time. The family settled in Novosibirsk, in the middle of the Siberian wasteland. His parents were survivors of Hitler's death camps and Meir was raised on tales of suffering and resilience. He arrived in Israel in 1950 at the age of five; his family first lived in a temporary camp for new immigrants before settling in suburbs south of Tel Aviv. Life in post-independence Israel wasn't easy for the Huberman family. There was a new language to learn; the country was poor, struggling to pull itself out of a costly war of independence and into a functioning state that could absorb the millions of immigrants flooding to its shores from all around the world.

Meir's father was an administrator in a technical school. His mother was a cashier in a supermarket. The family settled in the beach town of Bat Yam, located a few miles south of the Tel Aviv city limits. Most of the kids in the neighborhood were like Meir, refugees and newcomers. Dagan recalled that in his family's inner circle many had different last names. The family wasn't one of blood ties but rather a common thread of surviving the horrors of Hitler's Europe.[7] For Meir and other youngsters like him, their upbringing was molded by the horrors of the Holocaust.

Meir's grandfather, Rabbi Dov Ehrlich, was photographed in 1944 moments before German soldiers shot him dead. That image haunted the family, Meir in particular. Ehrlich was wearing a prayer shawl and his hands were raised; he was on his knees. The murder of six million Jews, especially for those whose families escaped the horror, created a uniquely Israeli form of determined defiance. "The notion," one of Meir's dearest friends, Major General Yossi Ben-Hanan, remembered, "was that we were not going to be one of the flock walking meekly to the slaughter."[8] Meir Hebraicized his family name to Dagan and became, as Ben-Hanan recalled, "more Israeli than the native born Sabras."[9]

The young Meir was a troublemaker. He was a handful for his teachers and his parents, and his older brother often had to go and search far and wide for the adventurous young boy who had a passion for exploring. Rumor was that he even made it to the famous Red Rock in Petra, Jordan, across the then enemy border, all by himself.[10] He liked to visualize knowledge by seeing or by reading. He was always surrounded by books. He loved to read histories and biographies; he even read a few science fiction novels.

Meir Dagan was conscripted in the Israel Defense Forces in August 1963. Highly motivated, the eighteen-year-old volunteered for Sayeret Mat'kal, the elite General Staff Reconnaissance Unit that was Israel's most secretive commando force. Dagan was determined to make it in, to prove his mettle to everyone at the IDF recruitment center. Danny Yatom, a future commander of Sayeret Mat'kal and future director of the Mossad spy agency, was also there. Seeing Dagan, Yatom felt out of place. Dagan enjoyed removing a commando dagger from his pocket and, for kicks, throwing it at a block of wood ten yards away. "I don't know how to do these things," a young Yatom said to himself, watching Dagan. "I don't belong here."[11]

Dagan's hopes of joining this most elite club came to nothing. Mat'kal was the bastion of Sabras, and the unit's ranks were primarily filled with the sons of the founding families from the Kibbutzim (Israel's collective farms). The IDF was egalitarian, but Mat'kal was the elite of the elite. Only the best could apply, and only those that fit the mold were accepted. The rejection stayed with Dagan, forging the type of soldier—and commander—he'd become.[12]

Dejected though determined, Dagan entered a different elite unit: the 35th Paratroop Brigade. Ultimately, displaying singular tenacity and uncanny leadership, Dagan became a reconnaissance unit officer within the brigade. He was a platoon commander during cross-border counter-terrorist raids that preceded the Six Day War and, as a reservist, led a company that participated in the capture of the Golan Heights from Syria in June 1967. That victory created a sense of euphoria that was infectious. Dagan signed on to make the army his career.

Following the Six Day War, Dagan took charge of an ad hoc reconnaissance unit patrolling the shoreline of the Gaza Strip. The unit operated in the shadows to stem Palestinian terror cells that sprang up in the wake of the war. A friend recalled seeing Dagan in Gaza one day dressed as a native, surrounded by soldiers also dressed as indigenous Palestinians, and sitting atop a camel talking Arabic to locals. The Gaza Strip was home to over one million Palestinians and almost twice as many weapons. At the time, most of the Palestinian violence was directed at fellow Palestinians who worked in Israel, but in January 1971, an Israeli family was killed when a grenade was tossed in their car. Major General Ariel "Arik" Sharon, the commander of IDF Southern Command, summoned Dagan to his headquarters, ordering him to ramp up his force of plainclothes men to end the violence once and for all.

The unit that Dagan formed was known as Sayeret Rimon, or "Grenade Recon"; the unit's IDF codename was *Zikit*, Hebrew for "chameleon."[13] As the bodies began to pile up, many viewed it as nothing more than a hit squad,[14] but the unit developed into a special operations force that would revolutionize how Israel battled terrorists. "We always acted according to military standards," Dagan was quoted as saying in one of his rare interviews. "The Rimon era was not the Wild West where anyone could shoot anyone he wanted. Indeed, we never thought it permissible to eliminate women and children. But it's correct that the rules of engagement were different. There were few limitations."[15]

Dagan's men were all volunteers, all combat veterans from various commando units.

Some were Arabic speakers. Those who weren't were subjected to a crash course in Arabic and Palestinian culture. Dagan's own Arabic was impeccable. His commandos used disguise and cunning to infiltrate every corner of the terrorists' world. Dagan himself masqueraded as a beggar and a fisherman on more than one occasion.[16]

The dangers of the work in the field, even a battlefield injury, didn't deter Dagan. He was seriously injured when his jeep ran over a land mine in the Gaza Strip, resulting in his hospitalization for eight months. Dagan's legs were wrapped in plaster, and his body was damaged by the powerful blast, but it didn't prevent him from returning to the unit faster than the doctors would have liked, in order to lead his operators through the murky world of Gaza counterinsurgency. He was decorated for valor for an encounter with wanted terrorist Abu Nimer, from whose grasp Dagan personally wrestled a hand grenade with its pin already pulled during an arrest operation.[17]

The unit's use of strength and guile made Dagan a legend. The Palestinians called him a bastard; unit operators under his command were known in Arabic slang as Abu Ali, men of violence. And their methods were effective. Sayeret Rimon neutralized the outbreak of full-fledged violence in less than two years. There were 850 wanted terrorists in Gaza when Sharon ordered Dagan to clean things up. By the time Dagan was through there were only nine fugitives left.[18] The relative quiet he brought to Gaza would last for nearly twenty years.

The Gaza Strip was the perfect proving ground for Dagan's brand of brilliant innovation. He devised operations that were so daring and diabolical they sounded more like spy fiction than real life. One unit officer proudly told Israeli television that there was little point in talking about the Gaza operations because nobody would ever believe him. In one instance, Dagan and his men impersonated a group of high-level PLO officials who had sailed from Lebanon to meet with operatives in the Strip. At the meeting, Dagan accused the local Popular Front commander of being a traitor and summarily tried him on suspicion of being an Israeli imposter. The Palestinian, frantic to avoid a firing squad, did everything in his power to prove that he was indeed loyal, and to rest his case, he provided intimate details about his cell commanders—including names, addresses, codenames, and upcoming operations. Within days Dagan managed to destroy the entire network.[19] In another instance, when Dagan learned of a shortage of hand grenades in the Strip, his men arranged for a special sale of former Egyptian military grenades from a secret stash prepared by Bedouins in Sinai. Dagan's engineers booby-trapped the grenades, and within days reports of "work accidents" in the Palestinian ranks filtered up the IDF chain of command.

Ariel Sharon loved Dagan's wild imagination and courage—and his capacity to turn outside-the-box thinking into success on the battlefield. It was said that the two men were cut from the same cloth; some said that the two could communicate telepathically, carrying out entire conversations without ever uttering a word. It is clear that Sharon viewed Dagan as his prodigal son, and their great admiration and friendship lasted a lifetime.

Meir Dagan was a loyal man who remained close to the childhood friends he had played with as a youngster on the streets of Bat Yam. And he would be a loyal husband. He married his wife, Bina, in 1972. He had met her in 1968 in Sinai, when she was a nurse at a local hospital, and the two dated throughout his service in Gaza. "He was very charming," Bina remembered. "He was quiet, but interesting. He always liked to tell funny jokes."[20] Finally, after four years of courtship, she gave the Meir the ultimatum: Marry me or it's shalom! Dagan ran out and bought a suit in a market in Gaza City.

Married life wasn't easy for military newlyweds. Dagan came home every two or three weeks for a quick Sabbath, but the army was his calling. He served as a combat officer in the 1973 Yom Kippur War, in the armored division that Sharon commanded, where he saw extensive combat and witnessed many of his friends getting killed. Following the war he was stationed in northern Israel. The family moved to the town of Rosh Pina, close to the 1967 demarcation lines with Syria and a quick drive to the Lebanese frontier. He built a home with Bina; they raised three children. When Meir was home, he was a loving husband and a doting father. The family made a point to explore the Israeli wilderness every Sabbath. There were always officers and soldiers in his house, though. His men meant everything to him.

Dagan enjoyed a meteoric rise up the IDF chain of command. He commanded a battalion of tanks in Lebanon in 1978. He was named the commander of the South Lebanon Theater of Operations shortly thereafter, where he handled covert operations for the General Staff and Israel's intelligence community. As a colonel, Dagan commanded the 188th Armored Brigade during Israel's 1982 invasion of Lebanon. His tank columns advanced all the way to Beirut. His brigade suffered heavy casualties in the bitter fighting. The losses of friends and subordinates would haunt him for the rest of his life. The carnage he witnessed weighed heavily on his mind. When Dagan returned from Lebanon, he became a vegetarian, vowing never to eat meat again. His family was forced to follow along.

Following the 1982 war, Dagan served as commander of Ya'kal, the secretive liaison unit to Lebanon, which ran much of Israel's intelligence efforts against the Palestinians, Hezbollah, and the Iranians. It was here, in his dealings with Christians, Sunnis, Druze, and Shiites, that he learned the value of human intelligence (HUMINT) in the war on terror. "The Arabs don't hide honor," a former comrade remembered, "and the locals revered him, treating him as a sage or a well-respected elder."[21]

In 1991, Dagan was appointed the chief of staff's counterterrorism advisor. In 1992, he became the head of the IDF General Staff's Operations Brigade—effectively running special operations and counterterrorist missions. It was here that Dagan first met Uri. Before a mission to target a wanted terrorist cell leader in the West Bank, Dagan asked to be briefed by men who knew the territories like the back of their hands. COGAT sent Uri.

Many officers dreaded being summoned to an audience with Dagan. He was as no-nonsense as they came—even by Israeli standards—and he had little patience for anyone who wasted his time. Dagan often butted heads with fellow officers, including his superiors. During the 1991 Gulf War, IDF Chief of Staff Lieutenant General Ehud Barak did all he could to oust Dagan from the military, but the defense minister at the time would have none of it.[22]

The first meeting between Dagan and Uri took place shortly after Operation Destruction of Leaven, in Ramallah, in the office of the COGAT governor of the city. Dagan authorized nightly missions carried out by some of the top-tier units in the IDF and Border Guard arsenals. The missions, requested by the Shin Bet, apprehended hard-core fundamentalists with blood on their hands or at least blood in their plans, but the operations did little to dent Hamas capabilities and influence. To the contrary, under attack by Israeli special operations units, the mystique of Hamas spread, and new recruits converted to the fold as the street credentials of the Islamic Resistance Movement spread with greater fervor. Dagan understood that the State of Israel needed a new and not necessarily tactical approach to ending the terror.

Dagan and Uri were kindred spirits—both larger than life, gregarious souls with a dry sense of humor. Both looked like knuckle draggers, but each relished academia and art. Dagan enjoyed the company of professionals who were sharp and dedicated, who could combine courage and innovative thought to create battlefield solutions. If you won his respect, you had it forever.

Dagan and Uri hit it off the first time they met. Dagan saw promise in

Uri's theory on waging financial war against the terrorists, and he asked if the two could meet regularly. Their encounters would blossom into a lifelong friendship and working relationship.

Both understood that if Israel could disrupt the money, the bloodshed would stop. They pondered how to change the minds of the powers that be, who often viewed outside-the-box thinkers with skepticism and suspicion.

Hamas perpetrated its first suicide bombing in an Israeli city on April 6, 1994. It was the eve of Holocaust Memorial Day, a somber day when Israelis fall silent to commemorate the six million Jews killed by the Nazis. At just after 11:00 AM, a nineteen-year-old Palestinian drove a car straight into a crowd of students about to board a bus in the center of the northern city of Afula. Infamous Hamas bomb maker Yehiya Ayyash (aka "the "Engineer") had fitted the car with seven gas cylinders, antipersonnel grenades, and 1,100 rusty carpenter nails. Detonation resulted in a quick and blinding flash of fire followed by black, acrid smoke and widespread devastation; fire and shrapnel spread across a horrific kill zone. An eyewitness was quoted as saying that two boys were burning like torches.[23] Eight people were killed in the bombing and close to one hundred others were seriously wounded.

The Afula suicide attack elicited half-hearted condemnation from Arafat. The 1993 Oslo Accords gave his Palestinian Authority control of Gaza and the major urban areas of the West Bank. For Oslo to work, Arafat's iron fist had to pound the radicals inside his own organization, as well as hammer the Islamic fundamentalists. But the Palestinian leader merely gave his standard condemnation of the violence; he had no intention of embarking on a civil war in order to preserve Israeli favor.

A week after the Afula bombing, a Hamas suicide bomber blew himself up on a bus at the Central Bus Station in the small central city of Hadera. Five were killed in the attack and dozens wounded. This time, the bombing took place on Memorial Day, when Israel honors its fallen soldiers and innocent victims of terror.

*   *   *

Most Israelis were never under any illusions that the Oslo Accords would bring peace in their time, but they had hoped for a de-escalation of violence. The numbing images of the dead and wounded at suicide bombings in the heart of Israel were almost too much to bear. There seemed to be no end in sight to the bloodshed.

CHAPTER THREE

Closed Accounts

Three more suicide bombings took place in Israel in 1994. The worst of the attacks was on October 19, on the No. 5 bus in the center of Tel Aviv. The attack coincided with the signing of a peace treaty between Israel and the Hashemite Kingdom of Jordan. At just before 9:00 AM, a young Palestinian male detonated nearly ten kilograms of homemade explosives and prepackaged shrapnel as the bus passed by the bustling Dizengoff Circle. The blast was so powerful that shards of glass and body parts were strewn hundreds of feet away; a bus passing in the other direction was also hit.

First responders, even hard-nosed combat veterans who had seen war close up, were paralyzed by the extent of the carnage. Once bomb squad techs determined that no more threats existed at the crime scene, the dead, including the driver, were removed from the blackened skeleton of the red-and-white bus. Orthodox Jewish volunteers hunted with tweezers for human remains that required burial under Jewish law.

Twenty-two people were killed and fifty others were seriously wounded in what was the worst terrorist attack in Tel Aviv's history. Hamas claimed responsibility just as they had for the other bombings that year. The terrorist came from the West Bank town of Qalqilya, and Hamas erected a celebration tent outside his home so that his family and much of the town could celebrate his martyrdom. Lambs were slaughtered for the feast that would come, and women cooked rice and vegetable delicacies to feed the throngs of well-wishers; sweets were purchased by the truckload. The refreshments provided were expensive—costing more than the raw materials he used to build his lethal device.

The bloodshed continued into the New Year.

On the morning of January 22, 1995, hundreds of soldiers gathered at Beit Lid Junction, a series of bus stops and transit points for rides to bases throughout northern Israel. Just as many Israeli civilians huddled behind bus shelters to protect themselves from the winter winds. The junction, especially on Sunday, the start of the workweek, was always busy. Soldiers were returning to base after weekend leaves; commuters were waiting for buses to take them to their jobs in Haifa to the north and Tel Aviv to the south. Beit Lid was also near Tulkarm, a West Bank city under full Palestinian Authority civil administration and security control.

Many of the soldiers were huddled around a snacks kiosk while awaiting their buses when the young Palestinian, disguised as an Israeli soldier, detonated fifteen kilograms of high explosives. The massive blast ripped the kiosk apart. Bodies, army boots, and a rainbow of colored berets were blown in all directions. Military policemen on security detail at the bus depot warned others to be wary of secondary devices.[1] But many soldiers ignored the warnings, eager to help those who were still alive. But they were cut down by a wave of fire and a storm of shrapnel that came three minutes after the first blast, when a second suicide bomber, also disguised as an Israeli soldier, detonated his own lethal payload. Twenty-two troops and one civilian were killed in the bombings; one hundred more were seriously wounded. Military rabbis were busy all day knocking on doors to bring the grim news to parents that their sons and daughters were dead.

The Beit Lid Junction massacre was one of the worst attacks in Israel's long and bloody history of terror. This time, though, Hamas did not claim responsibility. The group behind the carnage was the Palestine Islamic Jihad. The PIJ was similar to Hamas in its desire to establish an Islamic state in all of Palestine. It was considered more radical than Hamas and less political, more about armed struggle than any coherent political vision. The PIJ was founded in Gaza in 1981 by a pediatrician named Dr. Fathi Abdel-Aziz Shiqaqi. The doctor learned the art of terrorist compartmentalization and covert tradecraft during his days at Egypt's Zagazig University, a nerve center for the outlawed Muslim Brotherhood.[2] Copying the Egyptian Brotherhood's tactical setup, Shiqaqi established small, secretive cells drawn mainly from clans, where blood was stronger than religious and political affiliation. Shiqaqi was imprisoned by the Israelis in 1985 and deported to Lebanon several years later.

Unlike Hamas, the PIJ did not offer social services of any kind.[3] Much of its command structure was based in Damascus, Syria—far from the long arm of Israel. Much of the PIJ's funding came from Iran, which over the years would assume the lion's share of the PIJ's operational budget. The PIJ also had a very strong connection to the United States. One of its founders was Gaza-born and British-educated Ramadan Abdullah Shalah, a professor at the University of South Florida in Tampa. From there, Shalah continued to serve the PIJ.[4] He planned violent operations, earmarking cash, and making political decisions as he marked papers and enjoyed a State of Florida paycheck.

The PIJ struck again just after midday on April 9, as the No. 36 bus from Ashqelon navigated roads connecting Jewish settlements dotted around the Palestinian Authority–controlled Gaza Strip. As the bus neared the Kfar Darom settlement, a van moved alongside it, as the Palestinian driver detonated close to twenty kilograms of high explosives. The blast blew out the bus windows and peeled its side open. Passengers were thrown into the air, and the dead were everywhere.[5] The acrid black smoke made it difficult for first responders to remove the injured and the dying. Later that afternoon, the PIJ released a statement identifying the bomber as a twenty-four-year-old from a Gaza refugee camp.[6] Eight people were killed, including Alisa Flatow, a twenty-year-old Brandeis University student from New Jersey who was visiting Israel.[7] Flatow was the first American to die in what would be the opening wave of Palestinian suicide terror. Another American citizen, Seth Ben-Haim, was grievously wounded. Flatow's murder would ultimately get the Federal Bureau of

Investigation involved and surreptitiously establish new, covert levels of cooperation between the United States and Israel on fighting terror. It also created new avenues for victims of terror themselves to fight back.

The bloodshed of the day was not over. Hours after the Kfar Darom attack, Hamas also struck in Gaza, though there were no fatalities in the suicide bombing against a convoy of Israeli civilian vehicles. Prime Minister Yitzhak Rabin convened an emergency security cabinet meeting. There had been a sense inside the government that they were due a respite from the violence. Rabin had staked his political future on a go-for-broke end to the stalemate between the State of Israel and the Palestinians. Israelis were persuaded there would be an end to the bloodshed and the start of a new reality of cooperation and coexistence. Instead, the fanatics had assumed control of the narrative. The blood flowed, more than ever.

It was dark when the ferry between Malta and Tripoli, Libya, docked in the Port of Valetta on the night of October 28, 1995. One passenger, Ibrahim Shawish, clean-shaven and dressed to look like a middle-aged professor, carried a brand-new Libyan passport. He cleared immigration and customs easily and hailed a taxi. His destination was the Diplomat Hotel in the waterfront Valetta suburb of Sliema.

Ibrahim Shawish wasn't his real name, and the passport, while genuine, was provided by Libyan intelligence. Shawish was in fact Dr. Fathi Shiqaqi, returning to Syria allegedly following a cap-in-hand visit to Libyan strongman Colonel Muammar Qaddafi to ask for money. The PIJ had escalated its war with Israel, and Shiqaqi needed money for more weapons, more explosives, and more stipends to the families of suicide bombers; paying monthly allowances to the families of dead operatives was a financial drain, costing hundreds of thousands of dollars annually. It isn't clear how much money Shiqaqi managed to extract from the Libyan dictator, if any. He had traveled to Libya with three representatives of other Palestinian terror organizations, also seeking cash.[8] The oil-rich princes, emirs, dictators, and despots were used to such visits, usually handing out a few million dollars to make the supplicants go away.

Malta was an island crossroad connecting the Middle East and North Africa with Europe. Like Casablanca during the Second World War, it was also a hub for spies of all stripes. Upscale Sliema, known for its shopping district and cafés, was far from the bars and brothels of Valetta and an easy place to monitor any surveillance. The Diplomat was a modest hotel on the corner of the Tower Road. In a small sitting area at the front guests could enjoy a drink while watching people pass by.

Shiqaqi left his hotel for a shopping excursion early on October 29. As lunchtime approached, he started walking back toward his hotel, still unaware of the constant surveillance teams that kept him in sight every step of the way. Shiqaqi failed to detect the man of Middle Eastern appearance behind him as his hotel came into view, nor did he pay attention to the two men on the motorcycle, and he certainly did not see their hidden submachine gun.[9]

Policemen from the Pulizija tá Malta, the oldest police force in all of Europe, were soon standing over the body of the man with the Libyan passport. A sheet had been thrown across his face, hiding the multiple shots to the head. His body would be back in Damascus by nightfall; President Hafez al-Assad had sent a military plane and an honor guard to retrieve the body. On October 30, 1995, the Palestinian Islamic Jihad formally announced that Ramadan Abdullah Shalah, a thirty-eight-year-old academic, had been unanimously named as Shiqaqi's successor, during secret consultations between leaders of the Islamic Jihad in Gaza and Damascus.

As a matter of policy, the State of Israel neither acknowledges nor denies any involvement in overseas assassinations. When asked, government ministers and intelligence chiefs might opine that the world was better off, but would never publicly admit culpability even as specifics were often leaked to the Israeli press in intimate details.[10] Numerous sources attributed the killing of Fathi Shiqaqi to the Mossad, Israel's foreign intelligence service, in particular its elite special operations unit known as *Kidon*, or Spear. Although great secrecy shrouds the unit, it supposedly consists of a small group of men and women trained in combat, intelligence, and covert action.[11] The Shiqaqi operation must have taken months of planning, apparently involving a dozen people[12] and a motorcycle stolen in Malta months earlier. What is clear is that those behind the operation were professionals. Maltese police couldn't find a single spent shell near Shiqaqi's body.[13]

When asked about Shiqaqi's death, Prime Minister Yitzhak Rabin merely said, "I would not feel sorry about the killing of a man whose existence could not be tolerated by civilized societies."[14] According to *Der Spiegel*, Rabin had personally ordered the hit in the wake of the Beit Lid bombings.[15]

Any celebrations in Israel over Shiqaqi's violent end would be short lived, however. Ten days later, Rabin himself was assassinated by a Jewish zealot's bullets as he departed a pro-peace rally in the heart of Tel Aviv.

Meir Dagan was in one of the former Soviet republics in Central Asia when Rabin was assassinated. He had been racing up and down dunes with his dear friend Yossi Ben-Hanan, on a long-planned jeep trek in the far reaches of the Silk Road, over unchartered hills and stretches, that fateful night when Rabin was shot and killed. Dagan had retired from active duty months earlier, ostensibly following in the footsteps of his mentor Ariel Sharon and hoping to be named the head of Southern Command.[16] But when Dagan was not among the generals slated for promotion, he put in his retirement papers. After thirty-two years in uniform, spending more nights in Lebanon and stuffy command posts than he did at home with his wife and three sons, Dagan entered the civilian world, retiring with the rank of major general.

Those closest to Dagan knew that retirement wouldn't be an easy transition. At fifty he was still at the top of his game and by no means ready to fade away. He also wasn't ready to don a new uniform of white shirt and slacks to become a senior manager or, worse, a salesman, at one of the country's bustling defense and high-tech firms. The general still had a lot to contribute to his nation's defense—and if it wasn't going to be on the front lines it would be somewhere his decisions mattered.

Veteran Labor Party leader and Rabin heir Shimon Peres, who assumed the office of prime minister and defense minister following Rabin's assassination, inherited a nation rocked to its core. To help the country's military, intelligence, and law enforcement entities effectively battle terror, Peres created the Prime Minister's Counterterrorism Bureau. The bureau was designed to coordinate all government agencies involved in combating terrorism and establish closer cooperation, as well as contain the egos of the men who led them. Peres tapped Ami Ayalon, the decorated former Navy commander, to lead the bureau. Ayalon was a no-nonsense special operations veteran, an analytical thinker with a far-reaching—and many have argued left-leaning—view of Israel's predicament vis-à-vis the Palestinians. Peres named Meir Dagan as Ayalon's deputy.

The sense at Shin Bet headquarters following Rabin's assassination was one of failure. The famed service had failed in one of its most important missions. They had failed the prime minister and the state. Officers in military intelligence and the police felt the same despondence, wondering if they could defeat the next threat. Meir Dagan, however, thought of Fathi Shiqaqi.

For its part, the PIJ announced forty days of mourning to honor Shiqaqi, its slain leader, vowing a wave of terror the likes of which the State of Israel had never seen before. Communiqués from Damascus, distributed in the mosques of Gaza, warned: "This ugly crime will make every Zionist, wherever he may be on the face of the earth, a target for our amazing blows and our bodies exploding in anger. We shall take revenge and set the ground on fire under the feet of the Zionist criminals."[17] But retribution never came. The Gaza-born doctor might have been a potent terrorist commander, but he proved to be a terrible manager. Shiqaqi took many of his secrets to the grave, including details of the banks and accounts where the PIJ kept its operational funds.

The PIJ had dozens of bank accounts in Lebanon and Syria, as well as in Iran. PIJ accounts also existed in financial institutions in the West Bank and the Gaza Strip. After Shiqaqi's death, Israeli intelligence learned, PIJ operatives in the field weren't receiving their salaries. Weapons and explosives weren't being purchased, and safe houses weren't being rented. The parents and wives of suicide bombers and jailed terrorists also began to complain that their monthly stipends weren't being paid.

Shin Bet chiefs monitoring the PIJ in the territories couldn't understand how could Shiqaqi be so operationally agile yet so logistically haphazard. Some hypothesized that Shiqaqi must have been embezzling funds; others thought he believed that his survival was best secured by being the only one to know where the money was. Either way, when Ramadan Abdullah Shalah rushed to Damascus from Florida to assume command of the PIJ, the organization had virtually no access to its money.

Meir Dagan read the intelligence reports from Gaza and Hebron, and from outside Israel's frontiers. He understood that regardless of intentions, cash was vital for continuing terrorist attacks. Dagan understood that if Israel focused on the money that fueled the organizations that dispatched the suicide bombers, it could achieve long-term tactical and strategic results. "Hamas and the Jihad were definitely not like the classical national liberation terrorist armies who waged war in Europe, Latin America, and the Middle East in the 1970s," Lavi S. recalled. "It was important at that stage, in fighting the Islamic organizations, not to think of fighting terror simply as a struggle to kill a mosquito here and there. If you wanted to end of infestation, you had to dry out the swamp where they lived and multiplied."[18]

Dagan was determined to change the paradigm. He viewed the money as the air that the terrorists breathed, and he was determined to strip them of every dollar, dinar, and euro he could. It was a hard sell.

Hamas for its part continued to build explosive vests and convince young Palestinians to strap them on and detonate themselves with promises of earthly glory and heavenly bounties. The West Bank–born Engineer was still Hamas's chief bomb maker and asset and, as such, the number one fugitive hunted by the security services. The Shin Bet eventually removed the thirty-year-old Ayyash from the equation in early January 1996. Ten grams of military-grade explosives hidden inside a Motorola cellular phone killed "the Engineer" as he spoke to his father. The death of Ayyash was as much an act of preemptive deterrence as it was of vengeance. The brilliantly executed operation was a desperately needed confidence booster for the Shin Bet.

More than 250,000 mourners flooded the streets of Gaza City to express their grief over Ayyash's assassination and swear revenge. There was a forty-day period of mourning and then the suicide bombers returned to the streets of Jerusalem and Tel Aviv. Other bomb makers picked up where the Engineer left off.

The first catastrophic attack came on the morning of February 25, 1996, when a Hamas suicide bomber blew himself up on a bus on Jaffa Road in the heart of Jerusalem.* Twenty-six people were killed and more than fifty were wounded. Exactly one week later, the same bus route was hit at the exact same time. This attack left nineteen people dead, and close to one hundred wounded. On March 4, 1996, Hamas claimed to take revenge again for the Engineer's death. At 4:00 PM that day, a twenty-four-year-old suicide bomber from Ramallah, Abdel-Rahim Ishaq, detonated himself outside the Dizengoff Center, Tel Aviv's largest mall. It was the eve of the Purim holiday, and the stores were particularly crowded with shoppers, many accompanied by children dressed in costumes for the holiday. The bomber sought to enter the mall but turned back because of the armed guards on the doors. Instead, he stepped into the busy intersection where a large number of pedestrians were crossing the street and set off his twenty-kilogram nail bomb. Thirteen people were killed and 130 were wounded. One of the victims, Tali Gordon, was a twenty-four-year-old student from the Tel Aviv suburb of Givatayim. She was standing in line at an ATM machine, waiting to withdraw some cash before she went out to celebrate that evening with friends. Her mother, a tour operator, was in Jordan that day on business. She heard the news about the Dizengoff attack but had no clue that her daughter was nearby, much less one of the victims. "Two hours after the attack," she said in an interview,

---

* A Hamas suicide bomber had been killed earlier in the day attempting to blow himself up inside the central bus station in the southern city of Ashqelon.

"I suddenly saw Tali in the sky. The entire sky filled up with her image. She was all over it. I stopped breathing. I realized then that Tali was one of the victims. She came to me to say good-bye."

It was the fourth suicide bombing in a ten-day period.

The Rabin assassination, the bombings, and the sense of paralyzing fear that ensued had brought Israel to the brink. Israel went to the polls on May 29, 1996. It had been a traumatic two years for Israel, with hopes of peace dashed by suicide bombers and an assassin's bullets. Election polls and the Hebrew press were predicting Peres would be returned to the prime minister's residence. But Israeli voters opted for stability and security, and the close election saw Benjamin Netanyahu, the head of the Likud Party, become the twenty-seventh prime minister of Israel. On June 18, 1996, Netanyahu formed a right-wing coalition between Likud and some smaller fringe and religious factions.

Netanyahu was elected on a promise of security. One of his first steps was to promote Dagan, whose genius and tenacity he appreciated, to head the Counterterrorism Bureau. Dagan's first phone call as the head of the bureau was to the COGAT headquarters. "I was a colonel, working at my desk when the call came in," Uri recalled. "Dagan asked me what I was planning to do with my future. Before I could reply he asked if I'd like to come and work for him."[19] Shortly after, Uri was in Jerusalem as Dagan's deputy.

One of the unit's first acts was to establish an informal task force to focus on terror financing. Finally, there would be a real effort to cut the means of terror off at the source—its funding. For the newly appointed Bureau Chief, it was like Sayeret Rimon all over again. It was pure Dagan—rogue and revolutionary. Prime Minister Netanyahu didn't even know it existed.

CHAPTER FOUR

The Head of the Table

M eir Dagan's detractors liked to say that he shot first and aimed later. His rivals in the IDF believed that the man was all about brute force, the ends justifying the means. The depiction was inaccurate and, ultimately, insulting. Dagan possessed a tactical gift to analyze strategic threats and create daring ways to mitigate them. He analyzed every military objective, and was never scared to make a tough call or venture into harm's way to do what had to be done.

Planning to create a financial intelligence task force in the mid-1990s, Dagan envisioned an all-hands-on-deck effort. He wanted to chair a roundtable comprising a representative apiece from the IDF, military intelligence, the Israel Police, the Ministry of Finance, the Israel Tax Authority, the Israeli Customs Directorate, COGAT, the Bank of Israel, and the Foreign Ministry. Joining them would be one of the prime minister's legal advisors. Of course, for Dagan's experiment to work, both the Mossad and Shin Bet had to send representatives of their own.

As the director of the Prime Minister's Counterterrorism Bureau, Dagan should have had little difficulty in getting the various government agencies to cooperate and send a representative to the monthly meeting. But the opposite was true. None of the intelligence, military, or security chiefs wanted anything to do with the venture.

The Mossad had little interest in cooperating. They were battling Hamas overseas, as well as attempting to gather intelligence on Hezbollah, Iran, Syria, Saddam Hussein's Iraq, and the multitudes of other enemies that kept the director of the Mossad awake at night. The Shin Bet, shepherded by Ami Ayalon, also had more than it could handle. The PA, Hamas, and the PIJ were all waiting for an opportunity to launch a war against Israel. The zealots, like Rabin's assassin, were still out there— still determined to make the next prime minister pay with his life for the unpopular agreement with the Palestinians—and the Shin Bet's Jewish Affairs desk had to recruit personnel from other divisions just to protect Netanyahu.

The Mossad director did all he could to ignore Dagan's constant stream of calls and e-mails. The Shin Bet displayed an equal dose of contempt for the repeated requests to assign a senior staffer to Dagan's task force. "Many in the organization," a senior Shin Bet official confided, "simply hoped that Dagan would forget about the nonsense and go away."[1] But Dagan didn't take rejection well. The more the Mossad and Shin Bet chiefs resisted, the more persistent he became. Dagan possessed an ample supply of a uniquely Israeli personality trait known as *davka*, a word that loosely translates as "stubborn spite." Ultimately, the spy chiefs relented, overwhelmed by Dagan's full-court press insistence, and dispatched representatives to the monthly meetings.

Most of the task force's early work was to establish a true forensic analysis of how the terrorist groups funded their activities.

The financial warfare unit was plagued by politics and ego. Jealousies, a trait very apparent in ambitious Israelis in prominent positions, hampered Dagan's attempts to formalize and unify this element of Israeli counterterrorism. The various representatives bickered and dragged their feet; some were reticent to share intelligence. The spies didn't like being told whom to snoop on, the military didn't like being told whom to target, and the police didn't like being told whom to investigate. Reluctance and confusion reigned.

The new unit had no clue where to begin or whom to target first. There were also political considerations to take into account because of the peace process, not to mention a separate financial effort directed against the PA.

*   *   *

Prime Minister Yitzhak Rabin had staked his political legacy—and, ultimately, his life—on a lasting peace with Arafat, and the establishment of
the Palestinian Authority. The United States and countries in the Middle
East and Europe weren't willing to go all in just yet, so they sent money—
billions of dollars intended to improve the lives of the Palestinian people.
The donations were meant to fund schools, build hospitals, and establish a national infrastructure—everything that Hamas was already doing
with its own separate network, the *da'wa*.

But corruption inside the territories was rife. Arafat had built a feudal
empire of nepotistic grandeur, where funds intended to help the impoverished were diverted into Swiss bank accounts and secret stock portfolios, and sent to Parisian real estate brokers. While ordinary West Bank
Palestinians struggled, the BMW and Mercedes dealerships in Ramallah
did a stellar business. Cronies close to Arafat, along with those related to
his security chiefs, built palatial hilltop villas around Ramallah and Nablus. The money provided the Palestinians with just enough confidence to
work with the Israelis, but they always made it clear that they could easily
halt the relationship and unleash more horrific bloodshed.

One of the officers working the COGAT desk near Ramallah liked a
political cartoon so much that she hung it at her work station. A former
member of COGAT remembered the sharp daggers of the illustrated edi-
torial. The lampoon depicted Arafat, at his desk in the president's office
at the helm of the Palestinian Authority, taking a call on why the garbage
hadn't been collected and why the mail hadn't been delivered. Arafat, the
drawing showed, turned to a comrade, lamenting, "Hijacking airplanes
was so much easier."[2]

Jet-setting around the world as a guerilla leader and fighting in the
trenches of Beirut were simpler affairs than building a state or meeting
the enormous expectations of his people. The PA was supposed to be a
transitional step in the establishment of a sovereign Palestinian state. The
PA's true power was evident primarily in what was known under the 1993
Oslo Accords as Area A. This designation—the Gaza Strip and the eight

West Bank cities of Hebron,* Jericho, Bethlehem, Qalqilya, Tulkarm, Nablus, Jenin, and Ramallah—was where the PA held full security and civilian control. The Palestinians enjoyed political autonomy there— political control that Arafat maintained with an iron grip courtesy of thirteen security services, intelligence agencies, a Praetorian guard, and a police department. All were led by sycophants and Arafat loyalists. He even had a Coast Guard. The PA was not allowed to maintain a standing army under Oslo, but Arafat's security services were firmly in charge. Israeli citizens and, crucially, Israeli military and intelligence personnel were forbidden to enter Area A.

Meanwhile, the money also kept flowing into the Hamas coffers. The group perpetrated three suicide bombings in 1997, the deadliest of which were the July 30 twin attacks at Jerusalem's busy Mahane Yehuda Market. Both bombers entered the outdoor market dressed in black business suits and white shirts, masquerading as attorneys; reportedly, the bombers smiled at each other before detonating themselves moments apart.[3] Sixteen people were killed in the double bombing and more than one hundred were wounded.

The Mahane Yehuda attack put Hamas squarely in Israeli crosshairs. Experts like Lavi S. did their best to argue that in the case of Hamas the money was both a tactical and a strategic target. "The *da'wa*, the long-term investment in the fundamentalist education of children from cradle to grave, was more important to Hamas than military operations," Lavi argued. "The *da'wa* was everything for Hamas. The money paid for schools and teachers to indoctrinate future generations. The *da'wa* paid for bread for the hungry and care for the sick; if you were sick, the *da'wa*

---

* Because of Israeli bastions inside Hebron as well as immediately surrounding the city, the Palestinians were in charge of 80 percent of the city. An international monitoring group, the Temporary International Presence in Hebron, consisting of observers from Denmark, Italy, Norway, Sweden, Switzerland, and Turkey, was established in 1997 at the invitation of the Government of Israel and the Palestinian Authority to help maintain peace and a sense of security for the residents of the city.

funded your medical treatment in Israel, in Jordan, or even in Doha. The *da'wa* housed the homeless."

And, Lavi argued, "The *da'wa* not only paid for the salaries of military commanders but it paid for the bullets and for the explosives. The *da'wa* paid the salaries of those in the field and it paid salaries to those arrested by the Israelis. The *da'wa* paid for the funerals of suicide bombers; the *da'wa* paid the widows and the bereaved families. Without the *da'wa* Hamas couldn't attract recruits nor could it function."[4]

The infrastructure and proselytizing wasn't something that could be taken down with an assassination or air strike. It was a complicated process that required a slow and methodical approach—something that the Israeli public, dealing with daily threats, did not have the patience for. The men sitting around Dagan's roundtable didn't want to take their focus away from targeting Hamas commanders and working with the PA on joint security operations. Secretly, and with naïve overreach, many Israeli security and military chiefs still had hoped that the PA would do Israel's dirty work for it.

Despite all of his efforts and all of Uri's analytical studies, little progress was made on the task force.

In the spring of 1999, Netanyahu's government lost a vote of no confidence in the Knesset, setting the State of Israel on the path of yet another election cycle. On May 17, 1999, the voters resolutely showed that the status quo was unacceptable, voting Netanyahu out in a landslide. The new prime minister was Ehud Barak, Netanyahu's former commanding officer in Sayeret Mat'kal and a protégé of Yitzhak Rabin. Barak had an impressive résumé: Israel's most decorated soldier, a former commando, IDF chief of staff, and foreign minister. He promised to go above and beyond, to once and for all reach a peaceful accord with the Palestinians. He won the elections with 56 percent of the vote—an unprecedented victory by Israeli standards. Dagan was not immune to undercurrents of politics and ego, and he wasn't interested in a clash of wills. "Dagan always said that Barak was incredibly smart, but also very dangerous," Uri recalled.[5] Meir

Dagan resigned as head of the Prime Minister's Counterterrorism Bureau shortly after Barak's election.

Old soldiers didn't fade away, however, and Dagan became an ad hoc advisor to IDF Chief of Staff Shaul Mofaz. Uri remained at the Counterterrorism Bureau, working as liaison to the U.S. authorities, aiming to enhance the special relationship between the United States and the State of Israel. He shuttled back and forth between Tel Aviv and the Beltway, where he worked with members of the Department of Justice and other elements of America's intelligence agencies to raise awareness of the Hamas presence in the United States, as well as other regional threats posed by groups such as Hezbollah in Lebanon.[6]

In May 2000 Prime Minister Barak ordered the unilateral withdrawal of all IDF personnel from southern Lebanon; Lebanon had been a quagmire for Israel since 1982, resulting in the deaths and injuries of thousands of soldiers. Many viewed Barak's decision as necessary, but feared that it sent a message of capitulation and surrender to Hezbollah—and Iran. Barak was determined to end the stalemate with the Palestinians at what, to many, appeared to be any cost. Barak was a man who believed in decisive action on the battlefield as well as dynamic all-or-nothing gestures in politics. When in May 2000, the Palestinians launched their annual *Naqba* (the "great catastrophe") protests throughout the West Bank to commemorate the founding of the Jewish state, Israeli counterterrorist officers had a sixth sense of the looming violence. "The protests, the burning tires, and the intensity of the rage and hatred were different this time around to previous years," a team leader in a Border Guard undercover unit said as he stood a safe distance from Palestinian lines in Nablus. "There was an invisible sense that we were on a countdown toward a hellish eruption."[7]

One final last-ditch effort to prevent the collapse of the peace process began on July 11, 2000, when Ehud Barak entered into intense negotiations with Arafat over the final status of the Oslo Accords. The two men met at the American presidential retreat of Camp David, Maryland. Bill Clinton, in the twilight of his presidency, was hoping to secure his legacy by brokering a deal. Barak, according to reports, was willing to offer the Palestinians concessions that were considered unthinkable in Israel, including the partition of Jerusalem. Arafat viewed the negotiations as an attempted ambush by the Israeli prime minister and the American president.[8] For two weeks the parties negotiated in vain, with Arafat obstinately stubborn.

The failed negotiations marked an end to any hopes that the Palestinian Authority could exist in peace side by side with the State of Israel. Barak had offered far beyond what Israelis back home would accept, and Arafat still rejected it.

Israel braced for a status quo, while Arafat prepared for bloody war. The Palestinian leader knew that the world would blame him for the summit's failure, and he planned for a conflict that could give the Palestinians something of a diplomatic initiative.[9] The only question was when to launch it.

The spark that ignited the fires of conflict came on September 28, when Ariel Sharon, head of the opposition Likud Party, led a contingent of party members to the Temple Mount, accompanied by a phalanx of security officers. The provocative visit, telegraphed well in advance, was intended to show Israelis that under a Likud government, there would be no compromise on Jerusalem's Jewish sovereignty. Israeli officials had received private assurances from Palestinian security chiefs that the visit would not be used as a casus belli. But the next day at Friday prayers at the al-Aqsa mosque on the Haram ash-Sharif (the Arabic name for the Temple Mount), Israeli security forces were pelted with rocks and Molotov cocktails. The violence spread across the Old City of Jerusalem and to checkpoints separating Palestinian lines. The second Palestinian uprising, the al-Aqsa intifada, had begun.

Arafat saw his chance, and the violence quickly turned into armed confrontation. Within days Palestinian rioters, Israeli soldiers, and policemen were killed. Palestinian security forces openly engaged Israeli troops in battle. Oslo, as Rabin had envisioned it, was dead. Arafat sought to convince world leaders that the escalating violence and terror attacks were the result of a grassroots uprising spurred on by the disappointment and rage of the Palestinian street against Israel.

General Amos Gilad, serving then as the head of the IDF's Intelligence Research Division, however, asserts that "Arafat waited out the initial five-year period of the Oslo Accords and then opened a bloody and cruel war against us. This was always his calculated plan. His intention was to push us into a corner and he never wanted to pursue the path of peace."

Barak, now seen as a feckless leader, called for special elections for February 6, 2001, to select a prime minister. Ariel Sharon, running as head of the Likud, tapped his loyal friend Meir Dagan to manage his well-funded campaign.

Dagan's job was a relatively easy one. It was almost impossible for Barak and those running on the Labor Party list to argue that the peace process had worked when violence was escalating and the massive PA security arm—lavishly funded by the West to become Israel's partner in peace—was now a hostile Arab army. In January 2001, a failed, desperate peace summit in Taba, a Red Sea resort in Sinai, only reinforced the Israeli view of an inescapable conflict with a duplicitous and fanatic foe.

Election night was little more than a formality. Sharon won a resounding 62 percent of the vote. It was the largest landslide in Israeli political history. Sharon was sworn in as prime minister the following month. His campaign manager was by his side.

Shortly after his victory, Sharon chaired a meeting of his National Security Council. The NSC consisted of three departments—security policy, foreign affairs, and counterterrorism—and was designed to assemble, analyze, and counsel the prime minister on all issues relating to Israel's security. The meeting, held at the prime minister's office in Jerusalem, was meant to review a long agenda of issues. Topping the bill was Meir Dagan's request to transform his old unit on terror financing into a true task force.

The politicians and generals walked into the conference room, some with their own bodyguards, carrying folders and valises; some carried maps. The roundtable included the heads of the Mossad and the Shin Bet. Those who assembled were the most powerful men in Israel, yet each arrived early and, in what appeared to be a middle-aged version of musical chairs, rushed to get to the shiny oak table, determined to secure a seat next to the new prime minister. When Sharon walked into the room, the men of power stood up and then quickly sat down to review the items to be covered at the afternoon gathering.

Moments after the order of business was read and the meeting formally commenced, Dagan arrived late after Sharon was seated, and the order of business had already been read and the meeting begun. He was completely impervious to the generals who expressed their displeasure. Tardiness was unacceptable at a NSC gathering, yet Dagan didn't apologize. He walked slowly to the sole empty chair, far across from the prime minister at the opposite end of the table. The generals and intelligence chiefs raised their eyebrows; some muttered disparaging remarks about his insolence. Sharon, too, seemed perplexed. To the shock of those present, he grinned and said, "Meir, why don't you come and sit up here with me at the head of the table?" The room fell silent. But Dagan didn't get up. He simply replied in his trademark low-key voice and with a devilish smile, "Mr. Prime Minister, wherever I sit *is* the head of the table."[10] Dagan then opened his folder. For him, at least, it was business as usual.

The men in the room were aghast—even by Israeli standards, Dagan's chutzpah was unprecedented. But Sharon let out a hearty laugh and the meeting continued. Dagan, as a friend once said, was never just another one in the room—he was *the* one.[11]

NSC Chairman Uzi Dayan, a Sayeret Mat'kal veteran and major general, wanted the financial task force under his command. Other generals and Shin Bet commanders also wanted to lead the new entity. But the issue had been settled long before the meeting commenced, and Sharon named Dagan as the task force commander, believing in the strategy of going after the money and believing in Dagan. He announced that the new unit would report directly to the prime minister's office.

Every new task force and working group operating within the halls of power requires a codename or numeric designation for bureaucratic purposes: It was how salaries were paid, budgets allocated, and oversight, by the State comptroller, conducted. When Dagan set up the new body, a special computer program delivered a random name for the task force that the retired general liked very much. Dagan's financial warfare task force became known as "Harpoon."[12]

When Dagan first tried to raise the task force under Netanyahu, the heads of Israel's intelligence services and most senior IDF commanders had little interest in adding to their list of responsibilities. Targeting the money, launching operations against money changers or accountants, was unlikely to get combat officers promoted. But under the new Sharon administration, that changed. With the prime minister's full support, Dagan insisted that Harpoon would have the teeth to empower all elements of the Israeli government to go after the money that facilitated the bloodshed.

Dagan once again called on his trusted friend Uri L. to be his deputy. He also brought in experts like Lavi S. and career agents as members of the working group. Harpoon met as soon as Dagan received the thumbs-up from the prime minister. He summoned members of the Mossad, the Shin Bet, the army, the police, and other government agencies to discuss measures that Israel could employ to disrupt, dislodge, and destroy the ways in which Palestinian terror groups financed their operations against Israel.

Most generals and spy commanders knew nothing of the new task force. Dagan loved it. He did his best work in the shadows and without interference.

CHAPTER FIVE

*Khalas**

Meir Dagan was called to Sharon's sprawling Sycamore Ranch home in the south of Israel for their weekly Friday morning meeting. Whenever he had a chance, Sharon would sneak away from Jerusalem and conduct affairs of state from his 1,700-square-acre ranch in the northern Negev Desert. The ranch was Sharon's passion. Before Dagan could even get comfortable in his seat, Prime Minister Sharon looked into his friend's eyes and explained that he had an important mission he wanted Dagan to embark upon immediately. "Meir, your first priority is to target Arafat. I want Harpoon to locate and disrupt all his financial assets. I want you to strip him of everything he has." Sharon explained to Dagan that Arafat's money was used to pay for terrorist activity, and that it was of the highest national importance to relieve the Palestinian leader of as much of it as they could. Sharon knew that Dagan was the right person and would use all means necessary, and then some, to carry out the task.

Dagan was surprised by the request, though. He was convinced that the prime minister would want to focus both on Hamas and the PIJ, as they were the wild cards in the violence perpetrated by terrorist groups whose coffers overflowed with money coming in from the four corners of the world. But Dagan recognized in Sharon's body language that he was transfixed upon destroying Arafat. The prime minister explained to Dagan that the one way to humiliate Arafat and render him irrelevant in the eyes of the Palestinian people was to impoverish him. He explained

---

* Arabic for "enough already."

that he didn't want to harm the Palestinian economy or make ordinary Palestinians suffer. However, the money was the source of Arafat's power and it was how he purchased people's loyalty and paid for blood and misery. Dagan left the ranch meeting and dialed Uri L. on his secure phone. "The PM wants to find Arafat's money and make him lose it." Uri replied that bankrupting Arafat was not going to be easy.

Shortly afterward, Dagan called an all-hands meeting of Harpoon in their secure compound and announced their most pressing tasks. The unit was going to have an important mission, one that had been assigned to them at the highest levels of the state's power. He banged the table and said: "We are going to take away from Arafat every dollar, euro, dinar, and drachma [that we can]."

Many in Israel had held their breath when Prime Minister Rabin shook Yasir Arafat's hand on the green grass of the White House lawn. Many more held their noses. To them, shaking hands with the man who personified the evil of international terror was unthinkable. Prime Minister Rabin had to be coaxed into extending his arm to Arafat by a glowing U.S. president who understood the historic precedence of the event on the White House lawn. When Prime Minister Netanyahu took office, he looked emotionally disgusted by having to sit across from Arafat; he looked physically ill when forced to produce a smile while shaking Arafat's hand in front of the cameras. Prime Minister Barak had, as a commando and then later on as a general, led missions to Beirut and Tunis to assassinate Arafat's friends and lieutenants; at the disastrous Camp David rendezvous in July 2000, his virtual manhandling of Arafat into one of the negotiating sessions was caught by video and went viral.

But Ariel Sharon would have none of this politically correct nonsense. To Sharon, Arafat was someone who should have been dead long ago; he was yet another on a long list of enemies who threatened the existence of the Jewish people.

Sharon had no qualms about upsetting Near Eastern hands at the State Department who urged him to display an optimistic and hopeful peace façade so that negotiations could work. As defense minister in

1982, Sharon was the architect of Israel's invasion of Lebanon that was designed, among other objectives, to remove Arafat altogether; IDF snipers, rumor had it, had Arafat square inside their crosshairs of their rifles, but the political authorization to pull the trigger never happened.[1] It was a lost opportunity, Sharon believed. Arafat's intifada was nothing short of full-scale war. A day barely passed without some sort of murderous incident involving Palestinian security forces—forces permitted by the Oslo Accords, armed by the United States, and financed, in one way or another, by foreign aid, including monies and equipment received from the Central Intelligence Agency. Oslo was dead and Arafat, signed agreements or no signed agreements, would have to be contained or removed—but politically, the Israeli prime minister had his hands tied. The world would not sit quietly by while Israel went to war with the PA. The new American president, many in Sharon's inner circle feared, would be unsympathetic to Israel's actions. George W. Bush's father had been an oil man and was viewed as generally ambivalent, if not hostile, toward Israel; James Baker, his secretary of state, had been alleged to have said, in a private conversation, "Fuck the Jews, they don't vote for us anyway."[2] Sharon feared that if he acted militarily—decisively—to crush the intifada, the new U.S. administration would not stand behind it.

Harpoon was not the kind of unit that could bring about immediate results. The very notion of a counterterrorist task force that focused on money had come a long way since 1996, when Dagan faced endless bureaucratic hurdles dealing with reticent members of the military and espionage communities who believed that the emphasis on finances rather than targets was a waste of limited resources and precious time. "Although they bitched and moaned at times and clearly didn't have their hearts in it," a member of the team recalled, "the representatives from the Mossad, the Shin Bet, and IDF played along."[3] It was, in fact, the participants from agencies never invited to such high-level-security working groups that accepted the challenge with the greatest enthusiasm and with some invaluable insight. The representative from Israel's Tax Authority, because of how it had to coordinate with the PA, knew more facts about the

Palestinian economy than the Shin Bet and A'man, IDF's military intelligence force, did. The police knew intimate details about Hamas and the PIJ from its own criminal investigations of stolen car rings and chop shops in the territories. Yet even in a country as small as Israel, where everyone was supposed to know everyone else, when it came down to working with one another, the various security, police, and government agencies did not like to talk or share information.

Each one of the chairs around the roundtable contributed files, statistics, ideas, and concerns to Dagan and Uri for their meeting with Sharon. The material detailed subject matter expertise on the monies flowing into Hamas and the PIJ; everything was prepared as a presentation.

Yasir Arafat likened himself to an Arab Nelson Mandela. His image—his costume, his persona, the pistol worn on his hip—was all carefully choreographed to depict a man who was a Palestinian Che Guevara, a revolutionary and a freedom fighter who dedicated his entire existence to the liberation of his people. But the propaganda hid the fact that Arafat ran a corrupt oligarchy of stolen billions. Before the establishment of the PA, Arafat's Palestine Liberation Organization had several primary sources of incoming funds: official contributions, some extorted, from Arab states; a 5 percent tax on the income of every Palestinian; stipends from international organizations; extortion and protection fees; arms and narcotics deals, as well as other criminal enterprises; and profits from interest and investments.[4] The revenue streams flooded in after Oslo. Halfway through 2001, the United States had already provided over $100 million to the PA; €250 million flowed in from the EU; and $400 million from the various Arab States. The Accords, for the PA, was like hitting the jackpot in a Vegas casino. But Arafat was always indignant, to the outside world at least, concerning what he did with the money. "I refused and I will never accept!" Arafat said of the conditions imposed for economic aid. "I completely refuse any controls by anybody on Palestinian Autonomy, except the Palestinians themselves. We didn't finish military occupation to get economic occupation."[5]

There were no credit cards in this world of the skim. Cash was always king. Large bundles of neatly packed bills followed the Palestinian chief and his minions wherever he went. In November 1974, when Arafat addressed the United Nations, his entourage paid for coffee and tea at the General Assembly commissary with brand-new $100 bills taken from Samsonite cases. Conservative estimates placed Arafat's personal fortune, at the time, at $200 million. At those numbers, *Forbes* magazine assessed, he was the ninth-richest head of state in the world even though he had no state and most of his citizens lived in abject poverty. According to the head of Israeli intelligence, Arafat had $1.3 billion under his control, which he could use for any needs he had.[6] "He was like a bizarre Robin Hood," said a former U.S. State Department security agent stationed in Israel, who worked with Arafat and his security services after the creation of the PA. "He robbed from the poor and gave to the rich. He also robbed from the rich and gave to the richer." According to reports, Arafat received $50 million from Saddam Hussein for the PLO's support of Iraq's invasion of Kuwait in 1990, the special agent commented.

Cash was everywhere Arafat went. It was in suitcases, bundled into safes and rat holes, squirreled away in foreign bank accounts and in the trunks of shiny new Mercedes-Benzes, but it wasn't in the bellies of the local villagers who wallowed in poverty in the West Bank and Gaza. Nor did the refugee camps scattered across Jordan, Syria, and Lebanon see any of Arafat's appropriated wealth. The Israelis always thought that the disparity between rich and poor, the rampant corruption and nepotism, would be Arafat's undoing. But the Palestinian icon managed to sell himself as one of the people. A former State Department special agent who worked the West Bank reflected, "He had lived in bunkers for most of his adult life and had slept in a different bed every night. He wore the same uniform every day. He didn't have a palace with ornate fountains."[7]

Imagery, the theatrical pantomime of the revolution, meant everything to Arafat. It was the rhythm of his rule. But like all complex political hierarchies where treachery lurked around every corner, Arafat made sure that his immediate underlings reaped the rewards of his vast fortune.

Arafat's lieutenants, their cohorts, and their mistresses lived in palaces that were worthy of an oil-rich sheikh. These men woke up every morning by stepping on floors made of polished marble and illuminated by chandeliers adorned with Czech crystal. Doling out cash was how Arafat governed and how he stayed alive. The flow of money to some very ruthless characters ensured a sense of contentment that few wanted to disrupt. A coup against Arafat would have been pointless because he—and he alone—kept all the bank account information for virtually the entire PA and the Palestinian revolution on his person. "Arafat holds all the financial strings," former PLO executive committee member Shafik al-Hout was quoted as saying. "Only he can sign a check. There is no co-signature."[8] The numbers, the balances, and the passwords to dozens and dozens of bank accounts around the Middle East, Europe, and North America were all kept inside small notebooks with tattered pages that Arafat had scribbled down in different-colored inks in a handwriting that only he could decipher.[9]

Some of the money came from Langley, Virginia. The Central Intelligence Agency invested heavily in Arafat's security services in the 1990s—Palestinians were trained in counterterrorist techniques and in internal security tactics by CIA paramilitary and counterintelligence officers. Jibril Rajoub, Arafat's head of security for the West Bank, and Mohammed Dahlan, Arafat's head of security force in Gaza, maintained close operational ties with the CIA.[10] Wherever Arafat traveled, remembered one former State Department Diplomatic Security Service officer who had traveled to the area extensively during the post-Oslo years, "the forty foot containers of money followed close behind."[11]

Arafat was brilliant in convincing anyone within earshot that he was on the verge of financial collapse. "Arafat for years would cry poor," former U.S. Ambassador to Israel Martin Indyk remembered. "He would say I can't pay the salaries, we're going have a disaster here. The Palestinian economy is going to collapse."[12] Every one of Arafat's squalls of poverty was always accompanied by a request for more money.

According to a PA report, it is believed that in 1996 alone some $326 million, roughly 43 percent of the entire Palestinian Authority budget, was lost to embezzlement by Arafat and his cronies; Arafat took close to another $100 million; another 12.5 percent went to Arafat's own discretionary fund; close to $75 million went to the security services; and the remainder, less than 10 percent of the PA's entire operating budget, went to basic services for the Palestinian people.[13]

One of the unforeseen ugly realities of Arafat's cash grab following the Oslo Accords was that he would never have been able to accumulate his wealth and hide his criminal skim without the assistance of Israelis and Israeli banks. Arafat and his cronies required Israeli business partners who could establish legitimate venues by which goods and materials could reach Gaza and the West Bank. Those Israeli partners, because of their ability to work well inside Israel and inside the PA, had to be those who, in the past, were relatively high up in the security field.

One of the primary Israeli conduits for Arafat's fortunes, Harpoon would learn, was Yossi Ginossar. Ginossar had spent a career in the service of the Shin Bet. Although he was born in Lithuania and arrived in Israel only at the age of eleven, Ginossar mastered a flawless Arabic and joined the ranks of the General Security Service in 1968, in the aftermath of the Six Day War. He quickly rose up the ranks; he served as an investigator in Gaza, and ran counterterrorism in southern Lebanon and security for Israeli installations in North America.[14]

Ginossar was forced to resign from the service in 1984, following an infamous incident where Shin Bet agents killed two Palestinian terrorists who were in custody following a bus hijacking. The Israelis were photographed leading the captured terrorists away, only to have them found dead shortly after. An ugly attempted cover-up resulting in a press scandal and criminal investigation erupted. Ginossar was in the middle of it.

Bespectacled, with a receding hairline and a middle-aged paunch, Ginossar was labeled by some as brilliant; others characterized him as explosively tempered, even unhinged. His gift was being able to develop a vast network of contacts regardless of an individual's nationality or political persuasion. Ginossar went into private business after being forced out of the service. When the Oslo process commenced, Ginossar became a conduit to Arafat and his inner circle and a key player in multiple businesses and monopolies, ranging from imports to gas stations. When Prime Minister Rabin was assassinated, Ginossar helped to arrange Arafat's condolence visit to Leah Rabin. The ex–Shin Bet officer was frequently used by Prime Minister Barak as a go-between with the Palestinian Authority.[15] When Arafat needed someone to help manage his growing Swiss bank accounts—among the $1 to $3 billion in accounts dispersed throughout the world[16]—he selected Ginossar and his business partner, Ozrad Lev, a former military intelligence officer. During the first year of the intifada, when Israelis were dying every day, approximately $300 million of money that should have been destined for the Palestinian people was transferred from a Swiss bank account belonging to Yasir Arafat and Mohammed Rashid, his trusted business partner and economic advisor. The money was held at Banque Lombard Odier, one of the oldest private banks in Geneva, Switzerland, and was administered by Ginossar and Lev.[17] Lev later exposed Ginossar, revealing that the ex–Shin Bet agent had received a handsome cut from Arafat for fronting the account.

Dagan and the Harpoon roundtable were eager to go after Ginossar. He, a Harpoon member remembered, was viewed as a sinister character for his dealings with Arafat and the PA—dealings that made him incredibly wealthy. But targeting Ginossar was easier said than done. He was so entrenched in certain aspects of the peace process that it was virtually impossible to dislodge him from it. But Sharon had no use for Ginossar's meddling, and the prime minister was certainly angered by the fact that Ginossar was making money while Israelis were being murdered by his business associates.

In the months to follow, an exposé in the Israeli daily *Ma'ariv* and a subsequent attorney general investigation of Ginossar failed to result in formal charges of impropriety being filed. He was a bereaved father—his son had been killed in a terrorist attack in the Gaza Strip in 1991—and that held great significance in Israel. Ginossar also knew everyone, on all sides of the political spectrum; he knew everyone's secrets. Moreover, it was revealed that Ginossar was also terminally ill. "Because Yossi was very ill we decided, along with the police, not to investigate him any further," Uri recalled.

Harpoon would have to find another way to get at his money.

There were hundreds of bank accounts that belonged to Arafat that the Israelis could not locate. One very tempting holding, however, was situated only a brisk walk from the Ministry of Defense in the heart of Tel Aviv. Yasir Arafat held a private bank account, number 80-219000 to be exact, in the Bank Leumi branch located on Ha'Hashmona'im Street; Arafat also maintained one of these private accounts in a Ramallah branch of the Jordanian-based Arab Bank.[18] There were all sorts of codicils to the Oslo Accords concerning monies that had to be exchanged between the State of Israel and the PA and into which accounts they should go. Some of this money included tax refunds from the Israeli government to the Palestinian Authority for duties that were placed on imports destined for the PA; these imports had to enter and be processed through Israel's three seaports and one major international airport.[19] Arafat's "economics advisor" Mohammed Rashid asked Israel to pay the Palestinian's fuel taxes into the private Bank Leumi account that had been opened in 1994. Only Mr. Rashid and Arafat had signing authority on that one; Arafat used to identify himself at the bank with his Palestinian passport that was numbered "One."

The Tel Aviv account should have been an easy target for the Harpoon task force. Politically, though, the private account was a trip wire. Arafat, in the spring of 2001, was still considered the sole option for a peace process between Israel and the Palestinian people—even as the fires of the intifada engulfed the horizon. The bank account handled money coming in from the European Union and the United States. If Harpoon were to seize the account, the outcry from Brussels and Washington would have been loud. The account was in an Israeli bank and, from the perspective of the Israeli legal system, completely legal. Bank Leumi was one of the oldest and most powerful financial institutions in Israel, with branches around Israel and throughout the world. They had powerful friends in government and did not want to see a client, even if it was Arafat, be forced by the political powers that still negotiated with the PA, to pull his hundreds of millions of dollars out of their ledgers.

Dagan and Uri realized that it would be difficult to dislodge Arafat's account from its safe perch in Tel Aviv. They also realized that an overt Israeli effort to take away the Palestinian leader's money could have harsh blowback on the front lines of the intifada, especially if Arafat could convey the message to his forces that the Israelis were responsible for them not being paid and for their families not being able to buy groceries. For the time being Arafat's money was safe.

Dagan also began to pay close attention to something new that was taking place in the war on terror: lawsuits filed by private attorneys on behalf of terror victims and their families. This strategy had a two-fold benefit: on a political level, on a moral level, and on a public relations level, high-profile lawsuits could once again equate Arafat with the by-product of his work—suffering and death. For Harpoon's mission specifically, making Arafat pay personally—in punitive damages and for the hiring of very expensive legal representation—would drain his account in Tel Aviv and his accounts around the world better than Dagan and his roundtable could ever hope to achieve. Perhaps if terror cost Arafat money, rather than earned it for him, the violence would diminish.

Uri discussed the dilemma of Arafat and his money with the Americans on many occasions, but as long as Arafat was considered vital he couldn't be touched. One of the men responsible for combating terror finances in the United States with Uri was Juan Zarate. A former prosecutor in the Department of Justice's Terrorism and Violent Crime Section, Zarate was appointed after 9/11 by President George W. Bush as assistant secretary of the Treasury for Terrorist Financing and Financial Crimes.[20]

Dagan and Uri thought of what could be done to expedite the campaign against Arafat. Harpoon was a creature that existed in name only. Harpoon didn't have a physical headquarters; the creation of the task force didn't require that the Israeli intelligence and military commands dedicate even one penny to the acquisition of a plot of land or the construction of a building. There were no recruitment flyers printed seeking young and talented trigger fingers to join this new and mysterious force. No weapons were acquired, no new infrastructure put in place. Harpoon, from a structural level, consisted of Dagan and Uri and one or two clerical workers in the National Security Council.

From an operational level, though, Harpoon encompassed every agency, service, authority, and command of the Israeli government. Each of the agencies represented in Harpoon were ordered to be on the lookout for any blip on their radar that had something to do with terrorist money. Dagan wanted to know anything and everything involving the finances of the terrorists Israel was battling. He wanted the representatives of the agencies assigned to the task force to report when they met and he wanted operations designed around what was happening in the field.

The Harpoon representatives sat down together inside a secure conference room of the NSC. The roundtable resembled a sales meeting inside a corporate boardroom. The representatives, some in uniform, others who had spent a life in civil service and who had never dreamed that they would be participating in an action vital to their nation's defense, sat around a large wooden conference table; cookies and fruit were strategically positioned near the chairs and the coffee flowed freely. The names of the attendees were written on six-inch-wide cardboard placards. Dagan spoke in the low-key cadence that was common for many military men. He smoked a pipe during the meeting. The perfumed plume of his tobacco filled the closed-door session.

Dagan had the authority to, should he see fit, empower the Mossad, the Shin Bet, and the tax office to work together. Dagan could draft and activate civilians, such as attorneys, travel agents, businessmen, and subject matter experts. In many ways—and with Prime Minister Sharon in his corner—Dagan could initiate multiagency operations both in Israel and anywhere else in the world. Representatives from the Tax Authority and the Attorney General's Office loved the skullduggery and secrecy of the roundtable. It was so much more exciting than their usual mundane assignments. Dagan treated each one of these men and women as if they were warriors in a special operations commando unit. Some of the best ideas for what Harpoon could and should do came from people with no espionage experience at all.

Some in the Harpoon roundtable wanted to hit Arafat with a truly outside-the-box operation, one involving a way to defraud him of millions. Others thought of trying to seize the money that came through Israel from around the world that was destined for the PA president. The approach that Dagan settled on was to assemble intelligence and prepare a case, as if going to trial, that the Israeli prime minister could use in discussions with President Bush or when giving a speech at the United Nations. Arafat's corruption had to be documented thoroughly, Dagan realized. Exposing the theft of international good will toward the Palestinian people, good will that ended up in private bank accounts around the world, was a potent tool in Israel's propaganda campaign. Exposing Arafat to be a false prophet, one who embezzled the well-being of his people, was a weapon in Israel's counterterrorism arsenal.

Perhaps the task force's initial operations lacked the explosive, James Bond–ish flair that Dagan was famous for, but Harpoon was slowly but surely taking shape and redefining the way the security services operated. Dagan was able to steer the Shin Bet and the army to focus on the money and to view financial intelligence with the same imperative as the spies, and the soldiers looked at names, addresses, and phone numbers. If a safe house was raided by Israeli special operations units, Dagan wanted the intelligence officers to treat any item connected with money with the same imperative that they would when reviewing information pertaining to weapons or explosives. A terror suspect's bank account was just as important a thread to the fibers of how a specific cell and network operated as were text messages and notes scribbled in code. Dagan was determined to change the paradigm as to how Israel's frontline troops, and especially the intelligence officers and analysts who selected their targets and then reviewed the outcome of those missions, looked at the battlefield.

On an early, rainy morning, at a meeting of Harpoon in an NSC conference room, the representatives removed their jackets and hurried to take their seats around the table, getting ready for the day's briefings and discussions. They knew something big was on the agenda from the excited body language of the NSC director. Dagan started with the biblical phrase "that one who steals from a thief is exempt from punishment." As the plot was explained to them and incorporated into the concept, the assembled group sat riveted. The plot required highly intricate planning and preparation.

The scheme was risky. But all schemes were. This one, though, had two possibilities of reaping enormous dividends. As such, the enticing opportunity was brought to Arafat's personal financier, Mohammed Rashid, by a Palestinian businessman who lived in Latin America. Rashid, with the businessman as a partner, traveled to "the" country in Latin America where he was taken to the plush downtown offices of the investment company. The office was crowded with young and beautiful secretaries, which made concentrating on the matters at hand most difficult. The conference room was ornate and lavish. The managers of the firm were eager to display their profits to the eager investor. Rashid was convinced that the revenues of any investment would be enormous. And of course, he himself was promised a hefty finder's fee for assisting in the project.

After three days of Latin American hospitality, Rashid bid his hosts farewell. He boarded a flight back to Jordan, and he then traveled on to Ramallah by town car. He enthusiastically convinced Arafat to invest in the project. Initially, of course, the investment yielded impressive returns, even more than was promised. Rashid and Arafat's confidence in their new partners as well as their appetites began to grow. Arafat green-lit larger amounts of money to be invested with the company. Soon the Palestinian leader's stake in the venture had hazardously ballooned.

One day, though, the investments suddenly crashed. All the accumulated profit, as well as the principal, was instantly wiped out. The company's plush offices were quickly shuttered and left without a trace. The exact amount of the take is classified. It is believed, however, that Arafat lost more than $100 million in the scheme.

It was a prolific start for Harpoon, but the terror continued.

There was a period in the spring of 2001 when it seemed as if there was some sort of terror attack every day. There were drive-by shootings and there were stabbing attacks; on May 9, 2001, two Israeli teenagers were bludgeoned to death in a cave. Bombs were set off by remote control, and a suicide bomber blew himself up inside a crowded mall in the city of Netanya. There were endless funerals and grieving. Every time Israelis heard an ambulance, they stood motionless, paralyzed by fear, wondering what had happened now. There was a sense of national foreboding the likes of which had never been felt before in Israel. The intifada was in its eighth month and the intelligence services, the army, and the police were overwhelmed and exhausted. Meir Dagan realized that even Israel had a breaking point. It was time to stop strategizing and start making a difference. He pledged to turn the unit operational and ramp up its efforts, throwing everything at his disposal into the mix.

Dagan headed home from his office on the morning of June 1, 2001, looking forward to a peaceful weekend at home with his wife and family. He was tired and frustrated. The Palestinians were waging a total war against Israel's civilian population, and the effort to stem the violence was moving too slowly; the terrorists were well entrenched, heavily armed, and flush with money. The enemy was highly secretive, and the notion of following the money was more complex and moved slower than Dagan wanted. As he left his office, he wished his secretary *Shabbat Shalom*, a peaceful Sabbath. It is what all Israelis say and pray for.

Friday nights in Tel Aviv, the secular capital of Israel, were for partying. The night of June 1, 2001, was no different. The restaurants and the pubs were full of people of all ages enjoying a late meal and a pint of the local lager. Young couples strolled hand in hand into the warm, humid night; older couples, some walking their dogs, walked up and down the seaside promenade listening to the soothing sounds of the Mediterranean surf. And then the first radio calls came in on the police and emergency medical service frequencies. It was 11:27 PM.

One hot spot was the Dolphinarium Discothèque, located along the coastal road in south Tel Aviv overlooking the Mediterranean Sea. The disco had become a favorite hangout for teenagers who had recently arrived from the former Soviet Union; the club, specializing in Russian as well as techno music, offered free admission to girls until midnight.[21] Just before 11:30 PM, a sixteen-year-old suicide bomber had walked into a crowd of teenagers outside the disco entrance before detonating the payload of explosives and shrapnel he carried on him. The blast chewed through the crowd, hurling body parts into the night. The cries of the wounded and maimed, many screaming in Russian, were haunting. First responders, even veterans of previous attacks, were shocked by the devastation. The death toll was horrific. Twenty-one were killed and sixty-eight were critically wounded; nearly all the victims were teenagers.

The bombing was the first catastrophic attack of the intifada. The second catastrophic attack came two months later.

It was hot in Jerusalem on the afternoon of August 9, 2001. The streets of the Israeli capital were crowded; traffic was snarled. Unbeknownst to the throngs of shoppers and tourists seeking shade from the harsh summer sun was the fact that Jerusalem was on the highest state of alert that afternoon. The Shin Bet had learned of a Hamas plot to send a suicide bomber into the city that day, and police units scoured the area for anything and anyone that looked suspicious. Izzedine al-Masri, the twenty-two-year-old son of a well-to-do restaurateur and Ahlam Tamimi, a twenty-year-old university student, passed through at a checkpoint separating the eastern and western halves of the city. Tamimi wore revealing western-style clothes, disguised to look like a young Israeli woman. Al-Masri was dressed like a hippie, one of the many college-aged visitors who flocked to Jerusalem in the summer months. He carried a guitar case slung over his shoulder. The two spoke English to one another and tried to blend into the frenetic, bustling city landscape as they walked toward the center of the downtown area and the Sbarro Pizza restaurant located at the very heart of Jerusalem on the corner of King George Street and the Jaffa Road.

Tamimi bid farewell to her companion a few feet from the busy eatery and walked back toward the eastern half of the city. Al-Masri walked into the pizzeria with the weight of the guitar case causing him discomfort. Abdullah Barghouti, a Hamas bomb building engineer, had inserted five kilograms of explosives, along with nails, screws, and bolts, into al-Masri's guitar. He glanced around the busy restaurant and saw parents eating with their children, and hungry travelers enjoying a slice, and then detonated his lethal payload.

Fifteen were killed in the powerful blast that tore through the restaurant. Five members of the Schijveschuurder family—parents Mordechai, age forty-three, and Tzira, forty-one, along with half of the family's children: Ra'aya, fourteen, Avraham Yitzhak, four, and Hemda, two—were killed. One American, thirty-four-year-old Judith Greenbaum of Passaic, New Jersey, was also killed.[22] Another victim, Chana Nachenberg from New York, had a screw, one of the bomb's lethal pieces of shrapnel, lodged into her brain and remains in an irreversible coma at the time of this book's writing.

Tamimi was arrested by Israel and eventually sentenced to sixteen life sentences after pleading guilty to her involvement in the suicide bombing. She insists she had no regrets and stressed she would, given the opportunity, do it again. "It was a calculated act, performed with conviction and faith in Allah," Tamimi said in an interview posted on the Hamas website. "Jihad warriors are always ready to die as martyrs, to be arrested, or to succeed."

After these two bombings there was a consensus in Israel that the country was embroiled in a total war. Israel responded with largely symbolic actions. Police squads shut down a Palestinian office in East Jerusalem, and F-16 fighter-bombers attacked a Palestinian police station in Gaza, but the moves fell far short of popular opinion looking for Prime Minister Sharon to eviscerate the PA and its use as a safe haven for groups like Hamas and the PA.

There were strong words from Washington, D.C. U.S. President George W. Bush condemned the attacks but held back from allowing Israel to reenter the territories it had turned over to Arafat as part of the Oslo Peace Accords. The United States and Europe continued to press Sharon to show restraint.

The world changed one month later. For the first time in United States history, a catastrophic terrorist event—the largest and costliest in world history—had taken place on American soil. The September 11, 2001, attacks against the United States were a turning point in history. The United States could never again be ambivalent to one nation's struggle against fundamentalist terror. Israel no longer had friends in Washington, D.C.—it now had a full-fledged ally.

Hours after the Twin Towers fell, as the Pentagon burned, news cameramen filmed Palestinians reveling in the streets of Ramallah. Candy and treats were handed out at an intersection to celebrate the American terror attacks; women in black ululated, barely able to contain their joy. Arafat ordered his security forces to arrest cameramen filming the adulation; their videotapes were to be confiscated. As a gesture of his solidarity with the American people, Arafat gave blood. Weeks later, during his last visit to the opening of the United Nations General Assembly in New York City, Arafat was humiliated when President Bush refused to grant him an audience. Arafat left his Waldorf Astoria suite days earlier than planned. The United States never looked at him the same way again.

Prime Minister Sharon declared a day of national mourning to honor the victims of the September 11 attacks. Shortly after the dust settled in lower Manhattan and the magnitude in Jerusalem, Sharon convened an emergency meeting of his security staff. The State of Israel was determined to do what it could to help the United States in the war on terror.

And, with American support, the effort to bankrupt the terror armies that threatened Israel could now become a global effort.

CHAPTER SIX

Money Kills

By the time mothers around Israel were putting the final touches on the dishes that would adorn their festive Passover tables in March 2002, 361 Israelis had already been killed in the seventeen months of the intifada. More than seven hundred had been seriously wounded. March had been the bloodiest month of all. In the first three weeks of the month, Israel's cities had endured seven suicide bombings, including a particularly horrific attack in the Café Moment in Jerusalem that left eleven dead and scores more wounded; earlier in the month, a Palestinian sniper had shot and killed seven soldiers at a checkpoint in the Valley of Thieves between Ramallah and Nablus. By the time fathers around Israel motioned for the youngest child at the Seder table to ask the traditional four questions concerning why this night was different from all others, thirty Israelis would be dead. Another 150 were rushed to hospitals fighting for their lives.

At just after sunset that Passover night on March 27, a Hamas suicide bomber disguised as a woman walked into the Park Hotel in the city of Netanya, a coastal town halfway between Tel Aviv and Haifa, and detonated a powerful explosive device that had been meticulously hidden inside his female disguise. The bomber had managed to get past the hotel security guard and walked straight past the lobby toward the dining room, where hundreds of people had gathered to enjoy the Passover feast. The powerful device punched a fiery hole through the crowded hall; the blast chewed up everything and everyone in its path. The first responders were overwhelmed by the scale of the devastation.

The *New York Times* described the crime scene at the Park Hotel as a

bloodbath.[1] White tablecloths were soaked in red. The banquet hall floor
was littered with the dead and the dying. Thirty people were killed and
140 were wounded in the bombing. The Passover Massacre was the bloodiest attack of the second intifada and, for Israel, a point of no return. As
forensic detectives and Shin Bet agents scoured the remnants of the Park
Hotel dining room for clues to help identify the bomb builder and the cell
commanders that dispatched him on his homicidal mission, Prime Minister Sharon convened his national security cabinet.

The Passover Massacre was the intifada's 9/11 moment. The IDF had
been preparing for a large-scale operation back into the West Bank and
Gaza Strip for years, with $150 million allocated to prepare the military
for counterinsurgency operations in areas that Israel had just returned as
part of the Oslo Peace Accords.[2] Sharon immediately declared a state of
emergency and mobilized twenty thousand reservists. On March 29, IDF
Chief of Staff Lieutenant General Shaul Mofaz ordered the soldiers in.

The IDF assault against areas under the control of the Palestinian
Authority was known as Operation Defensive Shield. Supported by F-16
fighter bombers and attack helicopters, Israeli armor and infantry units
rolled into the West Bank cities of Jenin, Bethlehem, Nablus, Qalqilya,
and Ramallah. One of Operation Defensive Shield's primary objectives was to surround and isolate Arafat's Ramallah headquarters, the
Muqata. Merkava main battle tanks stormed into the center of Ramallah and quickly ringed the headquarters, laying siege to the fortress. Arafat claimed that he wished a martyr's death for himself,[3] but the Israelis
weren't about to let him off so easy. Israeli forces cordoned off most of the
Muqata and forced Arafat and his aides into a few rooms; the electricity
was cut for much of the time, and the Israelis saw to it that the toilets
didn't flush. U.S. State Department officials who visited Arafat described
the stench inside the headquarters as overwhelming. Arafat would remain
holed up in the Muqata for two more years, until he was rushed to France
for medical treatments in 2004 shortly before his death.

Less than one hundred meters south of Arafat's buttressed bunker was
the office of Fuad Shubaki, the PA president's trusted chief procurement

and finance officer. Israeli special operations officers raided Shubaki's office and uncovered a large cache of weapons, including Russian-made light machine guns and RPG antitank rockets—all forbidden under the Oslo Accords. Sophisticated suicide vests were also found in Shubaki's office that were destined for the al-Aqsa Martyrs Brigade, the Islamic-fueled terror faction that Arafat used as a rival to the other fundamentalist groups with spectacular suicide bombings.[4] Israeli forces also uncovered hundreds of thousands of counterfeit Israeli money in denominations of 50, 100, and 200 shekels; and $100,000 in counterfeit U.S. dollars along with the plates to print more.[5]

Shubaki had been fired, allegedly, by Arafat months earlier following intense American pressure for his role in an attempt to smuggle twenty million dollars' worth of Iranian arms into Gaza and the West Bank courtesy of the *Karine-A*, a Tongan-registered merchant ship that had sailed from Iran to the Sudan. Israeli naval commandos stormed the *Karine-A* in Operation Noah's Ark in January 2002 seizing weapons, the ship's Palestinian crew, and intelligence linking Shubaki and Arafat to the arms purchase. After being presented by Israel with the evidence of Arafat's involvement in the weapons smuggling effort, President George W. Bush decided to sever ties with the Palestinian leader and an unannounced policy of isolation by the Americans was put in place. The seizure of counterfeit currency, some of the bundles of cash that Arafat was using to wage the intifada, was one of the many intelligence by-product dividends of Operation Defensive Shield.

The Israeli military incursion into the West Bank following the Passover Massacre was launched to eradicate the Palestinian terrorist state that had been established as a safe haven for terror. Israeli forces battled hard-core Hamas and PIJ units, fighting street to street, alley to alley, house to house, and room to room. The heaviest fighting was in Jenin, where Hamas, the PIJ, and Fatah's al-Aqsa Martyrs Brigade used the population as human shields in close-quarter urban warfare. Much of the fighting was hand-to-hand. Israeli forces arrested hundreds of wanted terror suspects, uncovered scores of bomb-building labs and safe houses, and seized tons of weapons—some America supplied to the PA security apparatus—and explosives. Vast terror networks were crushed under the weight of armor forces, and D9 bulldozers were used to flatten buildings where terrorists were hiding.

The IDF assault was lightning fast but its achievements were temporary. The Israeli government had no plan on remaining inside the West Bank cities, and the IDF did not receive orders to take over the PA. Once the objectives of the operation were met, Israeli forces were poised to redeploy to lines established by Oslo. But the Shin Bet had no intention of abandoning the cities. Israel's intelligence services had been forced out of Area A under Oslo and forced to rely on intelligence shared by Arafat's services; the intelligence was sanitized, colored, and often spotty, as the Palestinian security chiefs were determined not to spy for the Israelis.[6] Israeli intelligence officers were not allowed in Area A. Handlers from the Shin Bet and A'man's Unit 504, the military intelligence force that ran human assets, could not meet with sources freely, severely hampering intelligence operations. The human contact between handler and asset was critical in the spy game. Operation Defensive Shield changed the intelligence equation back to Israel's favor. The files, computers, and cellular phones that IDF combat units seized provided a king's treasure of information from secret Hamas ties with Hezbollah agents to money transfers. For Dagan and his task force, the choice was operational—how could they attack the vast financial resources flowing in from around the world as well as the shekels, dollars, and dinars that financed what appeared to be the incessant bloodshed?

A misnomer persisted in the counterterrorism world—one perpetrated by those who never spent time on the front lines and in the trenches—that suicide bombers were a poor man's cruise missile. It was written that the bombing of a café or a bus constituted nothing more than storebought materials, perhaps only $150, especially since the terrorist commanders didn't have to invest in an escape plan for the attacker.[7] In fact, the suicide bomber was but the final link in a long supply chain of men, machines, and infrastructure that cost tens of thousands of dollars.

In the case of Hamas, there was an entire overt political operation behind the very secretive military wing. The political wing controlled the money and they alone controlled the military wing's expenditures. Running the political wing was expensive. Hamas officials earned salaries; their wives and children required medical care, food, shelter. The political chiefs needed cars and clothes. Even though these men bled with the people and the faith they swore to serve, there were monetary perks to being a member of the Hamas political apparatus. For every school, mosque, clinic, and apartment building Hamas financed, the political bureaucrats earned kickbacks from the cost of concrete poured and pipe laid. These men controlled hundreds of millions of dollars. Temptation and corruption were natural by-products of this reality. The top Hamas political leaders, individuals dedicated to serving Islam, became incredibly wealthy men.

Running the military wing was very expensive, as well. A group like Hamas and the PIJ ran on much more than mere faith. Terror was a lucrative skill set, and the most talented in the pool required top dollar: Commanders had to be paid and their families had to be sheltered and looked after. The military commanders controlled coffers that had to procure the talents of many men and yield spectacular results.

In order for a cell to be operational, a recruiter had to be hired and paid. The men who worked for the Recruitment Section were responsible for selecting and vetting new recruits and investigating a volunteer's background and motivation. The Training Section was responsible for teaching all operatives how to use military equipment and improvised explosives. The training syllabus also included the A to Z's of booby traps; assassinations and cold killing; and kidnapping techniques and hostage taking. The men who trained others had to earn salaries, as well. Money had to always be set aside with escrow cash to be paid to their families should the "soldiers" in the organization be captured or killed.

The suicide-bombing campaign was expensive and required a constant flow of cash. Safe houses had to be rented; cars had to be purchased. These buildings were either turned into weapons caches or bomb-building factors. Quartermasters were responsible for the acquisition of weapons, as well as the raw materials for bombs, such as nuts, bolts, nails, rat poison to dip the shrapnel into, and the acetone and hydrogen peroxide for the witches' brew of explosives.[8] Bomb-making engineers had to be hired to build the suicide vests and knapsacks crammed with homemade explosives and shrapnel. The military wing had to employ intelligence officers to figure out the best ways a bomber could negotiate the roadblocks and security gauntlets and make it to a point where he could be smuggled across the invisible barriers of the 1967 line. A guide had to be hired to drive a bomber from his or her home to the target in Israel. Invariably the guide was an Arab citizen of Israel because they possessed Israeli identity papers, and Israeli license plates, and they spoke Hebrew—given the risk, the guides could sometimes earn tens of thousands of shekels for each mission.

Hamas employed men to staff the Indoctrination and Ideological Guidance Section. These operatives were the ones who recruited the bombers and sold the line about the virtues of martyrdom and the rewards of the seventy-two virgins in paradise. The recruiter had to be slick and charismatic—part salesman and part travel agent shepherding a young soul to the afterlife—and had to travel to mosques and schools looking for that shining star who would strap the explosives to his body and not have second thoughts. Video recorders and men to produce professional propaganda accompanied each cell. The bomber's "living will" had to be produced and filmed; the film, which depicted the bomber standing in front of a Hamas flag, explaining to a camera why he or she had decided to become a "martyr in the Islamic war against the Jewish infidels," then had to be handed to press offices, CDs had to be printed, lavish music-scored videos had to be uploaded to pro-Hamas websites. Finally, when the intelligence on a target was assembled, a bomb built, and a bomber selected, a minder had to be summoned to sequester the bomber in the rented safe house and keep him from any contact with the outside world, lest he have second thoughts.[9] The process was complex and ongoing. Every element of it cost money.

In life, the suicide bomber was the least expensive element of the equation. But after the bomber was dead, Hamas had to pay for a lavish spread to celebrate the martyr's death—lambs had to be slaughtered and pastries purchased. The bomber's family would need to be taken care of financially, of course, for the rest of their lives. The balance sheet by which Hamas could analyze the cost benefit of a particular attack as part of this enormous investment was measured by the number of Israelis killed and maimed in a particular attack.

Major General Giora Eiland was a veteran airborne officer who had participated in the stunning Entebbe rescue, he was the head of the IDF Planning Branch, and he participated in many of the tense political negotiations during the peace process, often accompanying Foreign Minister Shimon Peres in his meetings with Arafat. Eiland understood the expensive infrastructure that groups like Hamas and the PIJ had been allowed to establish in the West Bank and Gaza under Arafat's protection and tacit support. "Each and every one of the suicide bombings cost upward of tens of thousands of dollars," he said. "It was a well-oiled machine that couldn't be stopped by military strikes alone. If you stopped that mechanism and dried up the money you stopped the machine."[10]

The man who ran the machinery responsible for the Passover Massacre was Abbas al-Sayyid. Al-Sayyid didn't look like a master terrorist. Chubby and bookish, the American-educated biomedical engineer had a soft-spoken demeanor and a salt-and-pepper coif that made him look more like a professor, or an artist, than one of the most dangerous terrorist field commanders in the West Bank. Al-Sayyid, however, was a senior commander in the Hamas political wing. In that capacity, he spoke at Hamas functions and politicked openly. But al-Sayyid was also the military commander for the Tulkarm area. He planned operations, received instructions from operatives in Lebanon and Syria, and was responsible for financing a great deal of bloodshed.[11] This duplicitous reality enabled al-Sayyid to maintain communications with Hamas offices in Lebanon and Syria through which money and instructions were funneled to the territories. According to reports, monies from overseas, believed to be more than $10,000 a month, were transferred into al-Sayyid's personal bank accounts; in order to avoid suspicion, he even opened bank accounts in the West Bank under fake American-sounding names.[12]

Abbas al-Sayyid had used that money to pay for murder. In December 2000 he acquired assault weapons, ammunition, and explosives, using funds that had been relayed to him from Syria. Those weapons were used to kill two Israelis in March 2001. In May 2001, al-Sayyid masterminded the suicide bombing of the Ha'Sharon Mall in Netanya, which left five dead and one hundred wounded.[13] Abbas al-Sayyid personally placed the explosives inside the clothing that the suicide bomber wore when he blew himself up inside the Park Hotel.

Israeli commandos caught up with al-Sayyid in May 2002. He was captured in a late-night raid in the West Bank. During his interrogation, he was incredibly forthcoming concerning the financing of his suicide bombing campaigns. In his interrogation, carried out at Kishon Prison in northern Israel on May 12, al-Sayyid explained that he had received the money for the weapons and material from a bank transfer into his personal Arab Bank account in a branch in Tulkarm. The money was sent from America and in dollars. A Hamas operative in Syria coordinated it. The money was ostensibly donated to finance political activity but had to use the money to acquire weapons for the Izzedine al-Qassam Brigade. The money came in monthly payments, each for $13,000. The last money received was in February 2002. Abbas al-Sayyid confessed that he was in touch with his benefactors through letters and SMS messages from his mobile phone. He contacted a Hamas operative, a forty-year-old resident of the Balata Refugee Camp in Nablus, to have the money placed into the Arab Bank account.[14]

The process was that simple. All a cell commander needed was a disposable mobile phone and SIM card, a list of contacts, and a bank account.

Harpoon met twice a month following Operation Defensive Shield. Israeli forces in the West Bank uncovered intelligence treasures that provided the Shin Bet, A'man, and the Mossad with in-depth insight into the architectural blueprints of the massive terrorist infrastructure that Hamas and many others had built under the auspices of the Palestinian Authority. The unit analyzed all the material pertaining to money. The sheer volume of intelligence uncovered by the Israeli military incursion was overwhelming. The Palestinian terrorist war against Israel was local. The money that financed it, though, was coming in from all over the world.

Iranian intelligence viewed the hundreds of millions of dollars it invested in Hamas and the PIJ as an inexpensive means by which to wage a proxy war against Israel. Telethons in the Kingdom of Saudi Arabia raised money on behalf of suicide bombers and their families; the money, raised by "the Saudi Committee for the Support of the Al Quds Intifada," was stored in a special bank account. In April 2002, less than twenty months after fifteen Saudi men* hijacked four aircraft and turned them into flying missiles on 9/11, Saudi monarch King Fahd sponsored a telethon that raised $110 million to support the intifada, with much of the money marked for the facilitation of terror and on behalf of the families of the suicide bombers.[15]

There were also collection plates—placed in mom-and-pop operations, basically—in Palestinian- and Arab-run businesses in communities worldwide that solicited donations of coins and trinkets. Under the guise of registered and well-established charities, men from the territories came to Palestinian and Muslim communities in the United States and around the world to address coffee klatches and postprayer meetings. These men were promoted openly in flyers and at prayer; audiences were promised to hear war stories from the trenches of the holy struggle against the Zionists. Dr. Musa Abu Marzook,** one of the heads of Hamas based in the United States, launched a financial empire raising money this way,

---

* The other four hijackers included two men from the United Arab Emirates, and one each from Egypt and Lebanon.

** Marzook was arrested in 1995 and deported in 1997; the U.S. government allowed him to keep much of the money ostensibly raised for the struggle in Palestine. He was one of the first billionaires to emerge in the Hamas hierarchy. Today, Marzook is widely viewed as the Hamas second-in-command.

eventually turning this apparatus into banks and lending institutions in the 1990s.[16] Others followed suit even after September 11, 2001, when such gatherings were placed under the microscope of law enforcement.

Much of the money raised was laundered through charities. The Holy Land Foundation, based in Richardson, Texas, was the largest. Originally called the Occupied Land Fund, the HLF was a major conduit of zakat to the West Bank and Gaza; much of the money ended up in the hands of the Hamas military wing. Both Dagan and Uri had traveled to the United States on numerous occasions in 1996 and 1997 to talk to the U.S. intelligence community in an effort to stop the Holy Land Foundation from operating duplicitously as a benign and benevolent charity. The arguments fell on deaf ears irrespective of the global component. "Parallel to our discussions with American elements," Uri recalled, "we have had long discussions with the relevant parties in the United Kingdom, France and Germany regarding Hamas money coming out of their countries."[17] Dagan and Uri enjoyed better success with the U.S. Department of Justice and the Department of Treasury, once they convinced key officials that the Holy Land Foundation, as well as similar organizations, aided and abetted Palestinian terror organizations. Actions such as Presidential Executive Order 12947 prohibited transactions with terrorists who threatened to disrupt the Middle East peace process. Shortly after 9/11, the Holy Land Foundation was designated a terrorist organization.

The money headed to the territories came from vast and diverse sources. There were, though, three primary means by which these funds were delivered: smuggling suitcases full of cash, or smuggling merchandise that could be sold; money changers utilizing their cash reserves and traditional Islamic forms of money transfers; and, of course, established banks. The smugglers and the money changers were a tactical challenge for Israel and Harpoon specifically. Smugglers could be stopped at the border crossings with Jordan; Israeli forces in southern Gaza were battling Hamas tunnels that secreted supplies, consumer goods, money, and even livestock into the Strip. But the banks, legitimate financial institutions responsible for the vast millions entering the terrorist coffers, presented a more complex challenge.

Banks had never been the target of a nation's intelligence and military forces before. In order to effectively stop funds flowing into terrorist coffers by cutting them off at their source, Harpoon would have to go global.

Efraim Halevy's term as the ninth *memuneh*, or director, of the Mossad came to an end in August 2002. The London-born Halevy had served the Mossad for nearly thirty-five years, during good years and bad. Urbane and witty, Halevy excelled as a liaison officer and as a diplomat, and he had endured criticism by many inside the organization for exactly those attributes—some joked that Halevy preferred talking to Arab leaders at cocktail parties rather than leading an operational force of spies. But the diplomatic skills paid great dividends. He had been particularly close with Jordan's King Hussein and was instrumental in forging the path for a treaty between the Jewish state and the Hashemite Kingdom.[18] In 1997, Halevy had been recalled as an ambassador in Europe to return home to personally negotiate the release of the Mossad hit team members who had been apprehended in Jordan after the failed attempt on the life of Khaled Meshal, the Hamas political leader living in Amman. Halevy was appointed the Mossad director shortly thereafter.

It had been a tumultuous four-year tenure for Halevy as Mossad director. The battle against Hezbollah escalated daily, ultimately culminating in Israel's unilateral withdrawal; al-Qaeda had emerged as a global force to be reckoned with throughout the Middle East, the Asian subcontinent, and the Horn of Africa. Peace talks with Arafat failed during Halevy's tenure, and the intifada erupted. Efraim Halevy was the Mossad director when the United States was attacked on September 11, 2001, and the global war on terror commenced. Halevy, a director in the classic le Carré mold, was forward thinking and analytical. In an address before NATO, Halevy understood the ramifications of the attacks against the United States, declaring that fateful day as the "formal and potent declaration of World War Three."[19]

Prime Minister Sharon was reported to have enjoyed a splendid working relationship with the sixty-eight-year-old Halevy. But the Mossad needed a new direction. By August, more than five hundred Israelis had been killed in the intifada and close to one thousand had been seriously wounded. The time for an analytical approach to Israel's intelligence wars had come to an end. Many inside the organization urged the prime minister to select a veteran Mossad commander to lead the agency during the dark days of the intifada. But Sharon wanted a man from the outside, someone with a fresh perspective and a dagger between his teeth, who could restore Israel's covert deterrence by initiating the complex and daring missions of danger and intrigue that the Mossad was famous for. There was only one man that Sharon considered. Meir Dagan enthusiastically accepted the challenge.

On September 10, 2002, Prime Minister Sharon announced that Meir Dagan would serve as the tenth director of Israel's Mossad. A celebratory ceremony was later held inside the prime minister's office. A plaque bearing the Mossad emblem was placed on a shelf for the benefit of the cameras. Sharon couldn't contain his pleasure at the ceremony. He looked like a proud father watching as his favorite son fulfilled a family destiny. Dagan wore a dark suit to the ceremony. He was full of energy and dynamic as ever as he took the hand of his prime minister vowing to lead Israel's secret warriors into battles. The glasses were raised for the camera, toasts given, and a hearty *l'chaim*, "to life," offered. Indeed, life at the Mossad would never be the same again.

The Dagan revolution was immediate. There were rapid resignations—by those who knew they wouldn't survive inside an organization run by Dagan, an outsider. "Many officers and analysts left, and many were shown the door," Rami Ben-Barak, the former head of special operations in the Mossad, remembered. "Dagan only wanted the type of men and women in the agency who shared his vision and could meet his expectations. They had to be the best of the best. Dagan had a very specific set of priorities that he was determined to instill in the Mossad."[20] Dagan didn't want mindless killers. He called such individuals psychopaths. He wanted men and women with purpose and talent.

Dagan believed that his work leading the Mossad was a sacred duty. His dedication went far beyond the State of Israel. "If a Jew was hurt or killed in a terrorist attack in Paris, Dagan wanted the men and women of the agency to feel responsible," Ben-Barak stated, "it was their mission to protect Jews all over the world."[21]

As the Mossad director, Dagan controlled an operational organization with numerous divisions and units: *Tevel* (World) was the branch that liaised with other intelligence services and controlled station chiefs based around the world; *Tzomet* (Node) was responsible for intelligence-gathering; *Kesaria* (Caesaria) was the agency's special operations branch and its near-legendary subunit *Kidon*[22] (Spear or Bayonet), according to published accounts, was a direct action force used for the most spectacular of operations;* *Neviot* (Springs) was responsible for gathering electronic intelligence; *Bitzur* was responsible for safeguarding Jewish interests worldwide and endangered Jewish communities; and several other smaller forces. Virtually every unit had their commanders replaced under Dagan. He completely rewired the organization and changed its command structure from top to bottom.

Under Meir Dagan's leadership the Mossad's primary mission was counterterrorism.[23] There was an immediate emphasis on proactive missions to bring a sense of deterrence back to the Mossad. Dagan wanted Israel's enemies to fear the Mossad once again. He was determined to bring the Mossad back to its glory days when daring, courage, and awe defined the agency's operations.

Some generals on the NSC were pleased to see Dagan promoted to the Mossad helm. They viewed his new post as a possible career opportunity

---

* According to published accounts, a *Kidon* team was behind the assassination of Fathi Shiqaqi in Malta.

for themselves. Once eager to abandon the notion of Harpoon, these generals now wanted to lead the task force that the prime minister embraced with such exuberance. Dagan would have none of it. Harpoon was his baby and it was going to remain under his guidance. He was more than capable of taking the reins over two separate entities. Uri remained to serve as Harpoon's deputy commander. Dagan made sure that most remained at their posts. Dagan felt confident going to war with the team he fielded.

CHAPTER SEVEN

Blood Money

I believe that banking institutions are more dangerous to our
liberties than standing armies.
—*Thomas Jefferson*

The banker, whom we'll call Adnan, didn't know how the Israelis got
hold of his special mobile phone number, the one that only his mis-
tress called him on. The voice on the other end spoke fluent Arabic with
a flawless Palestinian flair, but Adnan could guess that Hebrew was his
native tongue. The caller was polite, though insistent. The caller wanted
a sit-down meeting. No threats were made; quite the opposite, in fact.
The caller told Adnan that he had his best interests at heart. He was a
friend. To allay any concerns Adnan might have had that the person on
the other end of the call wanted to kidnap him, the caller suggested that
the meeting transpire in a public place, a restaurant; he'd feel safe there,
he was assured. The caller explained to Adnan that all precautions would
be made to ensure his security and anonymity in the meeting. The caller
gave him the date, time, and place of the sit-down. Adnan was told to
come hungry. The lunch specials were delicious.

Adnan ran a small, though successful, commercial bank. It was run out
of the West Bank but had interests throughout the Arab world. The bank
was by no means a financial powerhouse, but it was a mainstay in the Palestinian Authority and in some of the smaller towns, Area B, where Israel
maintained security control and the Palestinians exercised political and

law enforcement sovereignty. Adnan lived in a huge villa in Area A with a red clay roof and a garage large enough to accommodate a fleet of brand-spanking-new Mercedes-Benzes. His wife and children lived a privileged life; the older kids studied in universities abroad. A satellite dish brought television from around the world to the lavish home. The family vacationed in Europe and the United States.

Adnan was a good Muslim. He gave charity to the needy; he prayed five times a day. He was a good Palestinian, as well. He always gave assistance to the national liberation movements when asked to, and he always made sure Arafat's lieutenants were looked after with tribute. There were accounts in his bank that belonged to men wanted by the Israelis. The money that flowed into these accounts was significant but not staggering. Adnan was certain that the Israelis wanted to talk to him about those funds. Adnan did business with Israeli banks, after all, and even at the height of the intifada he crossed back and forth between the PA and Israeli lines without much fuss. He knew he had to make the meeting.

The caller, the man who summoned Adnan, was named Shai U.* He was, by trade, a master at mental manipulation. His nickname was "the Illusionist." All good spies were masters of men and the circuitry that controlled their brains and impulses. Shai had spent the better part of twenty years working for the Shin Bet, getting inside the minds and under the skins of difficult and special human targets. Unassuming and lanky, Shai was an experienced field hand who had spent more nights on stakeouts behind terrorist lines, his hand clutching his Beretta semiautomatic pistol, than he could remember. He was brilliant in recruiting and running highly valued assets, using rapport, reassurance, and a razor-sharp use of fear, to talk a terror suspect into revealing all that he knew. Shai had been described as "charming and enchanting."

Shai joined Harpoon as a head of operations. Dagan had heard of his reputation and, when expanding his financial counterterrorist force, sought men who thought like him and would act like him. Yet what Shai

---

* Shai U. is a pseudonym.

added to Harpoon was significant. He brought a fresh and gritty approach to the espionage and diplomatic missions Dagan and his emissaries were planning. Although Shai was very different from Uri in style, temperament, and backgrounds, the two men became partners and, ultimately, close friends. They were known as the U2s, or Heckle and Jeckle. Both men would be dining with Adnan at lunch.

Uri and Shai plotted their meeting with a manipulative forethought that would have made George Smiley proud. They selected a restaurant that had outdoor seating; the sit-down was planned at high noon when the sun was its most unmerciful. Uri was jovial and friendly, but his barrel-sized chest and large forearms could appear menacing. He planned to sit closest to Adnan. Uri brought several binders crammed with papers. The papers were filled with research for his doctorate, but Adnan didn't have to know. The two Israelis arrived first. For security the Shin Bet had followed the Palestinian as soon as he crossed over Israel to ensure he came alone and was not coming with company. Adnan arrived on time, but the Israelis could tell he was nervous. He parked his brand-new Mercedes as if he was taking his driver's test, making sure that he was in the center of the spot. Adnan wore a jacket and tie. He looked nervously around to make sure he wasn't being followed.

Uri and Shai made it a point to sit Adnan so that the sun was in his eyes. The Israelis spoke in Arabic in a friendly tone, yet they let it be understood that they were clearly in charge. Both men spoke about family, and how the lunch meeting was to benefit Adnan's wife and children. There were some bad men with violent intentions who had money going through Adnan's bank, Uri and Shai explained, and this arrangement was fraught with danger and risk. Danger was bad for a man who lived so well, Adnan was told. It threatened his family's wealth and security. When Uri spoke, Shai stared directly into Adnan's eyes with laser-like focus. When Shai took over, specifically when he brought up the names of Hamas and PIJ commanders who received wire transfers through the bank, Uri searched his binders as if he was looking at classified files. Adnan perspired. When the sweat stained his button-down shirt, Shai asked the waitress to bring a pitcher of the restaurant's signature lemonade with mint leaves. "Our friend is hot," Uri told the young woman. "Make it extra cold." The Israelis slowly drank coffee.

Uri and Shai played good cop–good cop—they told Adnan how much they wanted to help him and to make sure his business was clean and above the terror nonsense. He asked if he could go to the bathroom; the lemonade had rushed through his system quickly. The Israelis wouldn't let him go until his bladder nearly burst.

The banker returned from the men's room looking pale. His hands shook. He stammered like a skipping LP record. Adnan was so nervous, in fact, that he grabbed a kiwi from the bowl of fruit on the table and began to eat it like an apple, skin and all. The worst that Hamas could do was kill him. The Israelis could slowly but surely unravel his fiefdom built on gold and dollars. The man understood that he had little choice but to work with the Israelis. Uri and Shai walked away with the information they were after.

The intelligence gleaned from the banker about the terrorist accounts in his bank was very useful for Harpoon. But larger Palestinian banks operated inside the West Bank and the Gaza Strip, as well as indigenous Islamic banks that served the community. There were also banks, head-quartered throughout the Arab world, that maintained vibrant branches in the West Bank and Gaza. Of all the banks, the Amman-based Arab Bank was the largest and, for Israel's war on terror, the most problematic.

The Arab Bank was established in 1930 in British-mandate Palestine and was the first private-sector bank in the Arab World. The Arab Bank's founder was Abdul Hameed Shoman, who was born in 1890 in Beit Hanina, at the time a village halfway between Jerusalem and Ramallah. Shoman immigrated to the United States in 1911, making his fortune in New York City in textiles. A fervent Arab nationalist, Shoman returned to the Middle East to open his bank—launched with 15,000 Palestinian pounds—and headquartered it in Jerusalem, then under British control.

The bank ceased operations in Jerusalem, Haifa, and Jaffa following

Israel's victory and achieving independence in 1948. Shoman made sure that account holders who had their savings in those branches were reimbursed, a promise that endeared him in the eyes of Palestinians, and many throughout the Arab world. Even in times of political violence and revolution, the financial institution boasted that it never defaulted on a single payment to any of its customers.[1] The Arab Bank moved its headquarters to the Jordanian capital, following Israeli independence; the bank flourished in Jordan. It expanded markets and revenues as an oil boom hit the region. The construction projects that the bank oversaw were Herculean in scale; the financing that the bank offered enabled many projects—from the Persian Gulf to the sands of North Africa—to emerge from blueprint to sky-rise glitter in a way that only an endless flow of petro-profits could produce.

Shoman was a religious man, and he injected Islam into many of his business dealings. The Arab Bank's world headquarters, on Prince Shaker Street overlooking Queen Noor Street, was designed to look like the Kaba in Mecca—a black glass cube situated on a base of desert-colored stone. Shoman remained a presence in the operations of the bank until his death in 1974. His body was laid to rest at al-Aqsa Mosque in Jerusalem.

The day-to-day running of the bank was then left in the hands of Shoman's eldest son, Abdul Majid Shoman. Born in 1911, Abdul Majid first met his father at the age of fourteen in New York, and joined the bank in 1936.[2] Like his father, the younger Shoman was a Palestinian nationalist who, at one time, maintained the Palestine National Fund. Abdul Majid was also a banker, and he used the Oslo Accords to bolster his institution's business in the West Bank and Gaza. Abdul Majid Shoman was Arafat's personal banker and handled all of the PA president's investments and holdings. Arafat reciprocated by enabling Shoman's bank to operate freely in the West Bank and Gaza: The Arab Bank opened twenty-two branches in fifteen Palestinian cities, eager to be part of the boom that was expected in peace and guaranteed to become the largest financial power in the PA. The economic explosion promised by the peace process never came, though; quite to the contrary, the bank floated loans to Arafat that helped pay the PA salaries. The loans, of unspecified amounts, were a small part of the Arab Bank's global empire: The bank created "to serve the Arabs of Palestine and their national welfare" in the 1930s ultimately fielded 278 branches in twenty-seven countries across the world with combined assets valued over $35 billion.[3]

Shoman made a point to visit Palestinians hurt in the intifada who were transported to hospitals in Amman for treatment. In addition, Arab Bank employees were subjected to a tax on their salaries called the "Support the al-Aqsa Intifada fee." The money amounted to 5 percent of every paycheck and was sent back to the PA, or Hamas, as well as foundations to support the intifada.[4] The funds were substantial. But the greatest amount of money that the institution handled for the intifada came from outside sources.

The Arab Bank was the bank of choice for many who were fighting Israel—especially for governments eager to finance the intifada. The "Saudi Committee for the Support of the Al Quds Intifada" used the institution's accounts as pipelines to funnel large sums of monies, through charities and known terrorists in the West Bank and the Gaza Strip, who were associated with Hamas, the PIJ, Islamic Jihad, and other groups responsible for the violence. Beginning in December 2000, and continuing for years into the violence, some two hundred thousand transactions resulted in more than $90 million, sent to a multitude of Arab Bank accounts. The monies, the bank would later contend, were destined for the unemployed and the infirm; the donations were supposed to help Palestinians harmed by Israeli security forces.[5]

But in fact the funds provided pensions, insurance payouts, and support to the families of suicide bombers, operatives killed in clashes with Israeli forces, and those serving sentences in Israeli maximum security prisons.[6] They were a type of death-and-dismemberment fund. The family of Sa'id Houtari, the sixteen-year-old suicide bomber of the Dolphinarium Discothèque bombing, and the family of Izzedine al-Masri, the hippie-disguised suicide bomber who eviscerated the Sbarro Pizzeria in Jerusalem, received cash payouts through Arab Bank accounts.[7]

*   *   *

Both the Shin Bet and military intelligence had developed a unique expertise in unraveling the human makeup of a particular terror organization, from the top political leaders down to cell commanders and the knuckle-dragging muscle they employed. Arabic-speaking analysts laboriously followed flow charts linking men to other men who were linked to masterminds. Family ties were examined, as were cellular phone logs and even school and mosque connections. Dagan, when he sat in on the biweekly Harpoon meetings that included the delegates from the Shin Bet, the IDF, and even the Israel Prison Service, directed that forensic analysis and detailed charts be drawn up connecting the commanders of the various terrorist organizations with their sources of income.

Dagan wanted to try new ideas, including fine-tuning Israeli efforts to mirror the antiracketeering efforts that the United States Department of Justice had so successfully used against organized crime connecting illegal enterprises to proceeds. Dagan had visited the FBI and other U.S. federal law enforcement agencies during his tenure as head of the Prime Minister's Counterterrorism Bureau and enjoyed hearing stories about how organized crime and other nefarious enterprises were taken down as a result of financial improprieties. "It was all about follow the money," Uri recalled. "In fighting terrorism, the Arab Bank was like a solar system— every solar system we discovered led to new stars, new planets, and new universes. The money was at the root of everything."[8]

Analysts and forensic accountants, together with some of the best investigators in Israeli intelligence service, created an organizational chart of the most dangerous men in Hamas, the monies they held, and the attacks those funds financed. The Arab Bank turned out to be the common denominator. By the fall of 2002, accounts in the institution's branches had been tied to a dozen suicide bombings and other terrorist attacks, including the Dolphinarium Discothèque, the Sbarro pizzeria, and the Park Hotel in Netanya.

One of these belonged to a man named Ibrahim Hamed. Born in 1965, Hamed was a relative of Hamas leader Khaled Meshal and the Hamas

Ramallah commander.[9] He had been on Israel's most-wanted list since 1998. Arrogant and cocky, Hamed refused to be photographed and had been responsible for organizing multiple suicide bombings during the intifada, including the Café Moment bombing and the suicide bombing of a billiard hall in the city of Rishon Le'Tzion that left fifteen dead. Hamed had masterminded a grandiose attempt to incinerate the Pi Glilot fuel depot north of heavily populated Tel Aviv, in a weapon-of-mass-destruction attempt that could have left hundreds, if not more, dead. In the summer of 2002 one of Hamed's cells, a group of petty thieves from the East Jerusalem neighborhood of Silwan known as the Gang of Death, offered to bomb the Hebrew University. Hamed's cell had recently received a gift from the Palestinian Authority—the arbitrary release of Abdullah Barghouti, Hamas's top bomb builder. Barghouti had been held by the PA, on the demand of American and Israeli authorities, over his role in the Sbarro restaurant bombing. Angry at Israelis, however, Arafat decided to release Barghouti back to his work as explosives mastermind. Hamed's cell received Barghouti's bomb and withdrew funds from his Arab Bank account to carry out an attack against Jerusalem's Hebrew University.*

At just after 1:00 PM on the afternoon of July 31, 2002, a powerful explosion punched through the crowded student cafeteria in the Frank Sinatra Building of Jerusalem's Hebrew University. The device, a powerful bundle of homemade explosives wrapped in nails and screws, was hidden in a bag and placed on a table to be detonated by remote control. Most of the students grabbing a quick lunch were from overseas, enrolled in Hebrew-language classes before the start of the fall semester, and were not aware of the "if you see something, say something" campaign that the Israel National Police had run on television, on radio, and on billboards and

---

* It took Israel four long years to apprehend Hamed following the arrests of the Gang of Death. He was captured by the Ya'ma'm, the Israel Border Guard's special operations counter-terrorist unit, while holed up in a safe house in the al-Balu'a section of Ramallah. He was ultimately tried and convicted of the deaths of seventy-eight Israelis; he was sentenced to forty-five life sentences.

on placards in buses for years. The explosion turned the cafeteria inside out—the fiery blast and puncturing shrapnel were followed by suffocating black acrid smoke. "The force of the blast blew windows and glass facades to bits and tore panels from the ceiling. The stench of smoke and burned flesh wafted through the air," a witness recalled.[10] Israeli bomb squad officers walked among the wreckage.

The bombing attack killed nine people and wounded one hundred. Five American citizens were among the dead: Marla Bennett, twenty-four, a vivacious young woman from San Diego who had fallen in love with the State of Israel; Benjamin Blutstein, a twenty-five-year-old hip-hop DJ who was studying to be a teacher; and David Gritz, twenty-five, who was studying philosophy. In addition, the bomb also murdered two Hebrew University employees: Janis Coulter, thirty-six, from Massachusetts; and Dina Carter, thirty-eight, from North Carolina. Carter's father had to identify his daughter by her fingerprints. Eighty-five people were wounded in the bombing.

The attack, yet another on a growing list of bloody strikes against Israeli civilians, convinced Meir Dagan that decisive action was necessary against the Arab Bank.

Meir Dagan had always hoped to use a velvet glove rather than a granite fist to deal with the Shoman family—even before he was appointed Mossad director. The Shoman family bank was a pillar of the Jordanian economy, and Jordan was in many ways a strategic and regional ally of Israel. There was day-to-day urgency needed to do whatever could be done to stop the bombings. But Israel had long-term strategic interests with Jordan that transcended the day-to-day. It was sometimes difficult for Harpoon to balance these divergent interests.

The direct diplomatic effort between Harpoon and the Arab Bank began with simple one-on-one meetings in 2003 and 2004. Uri and Shai were dispatched to meet with Arab Bank executives in the West Bank and Gaza, much in the same way that Uri and Shai met with Adnan the Banker. The sit-downs were cordial, yet serious. They were all carried out in Arabic. The Israelis explained to the men they met that the situation was intolerable and that a bank that did business freely in the PA—and with Israeli banks—in all sorts of routine and innocuous transactions could not continue to do business with terrorists responsible for so much bloodshed. Some of the bank managers were sympathetic, but, as they explained, powerless to do anything; after all, the head office dictated bank policy. Other bank managers did not take kindly to any attempts at coercion by the Israelis. The Harpoon emissaries received what amounted to a "Fuck you" from the indignant bank officials.

A similar response came from Salam Fayyad, the Palestinian Authority's Finance Minister. Fayyad, who was educated at the American University in Beirut and had earned a PhD in economics from the University of Texas at Austin, had previously worked as the regional manager for the Arab Bank in the West Bank and Gaza.[11] Fayyad knew everything about Arafat's finances; he certainly knew about the Hamas accounts that ran through his bank.

The Hebrew University bombing was, in many, ways, a turning point for Harpoon and its campaign against the Arab Bank. President George W. Bush condemned the deaths with visceral rage, declaring, "There are clearly killers who hate the thought of peace, and, therefore, are willing to take their hatred to all kinds of places."[12] Most important, though, the mass murder of Americans in terrorist attacks enabled a new tactic in the war against terror money: fighting terrorism financing through the U.S. legal system. The September 11, 2001, attacks created new legal provisions to fight terrorism, including the USA PATRIOT Act of 2001, which expanded the federal government's ability to monitor the financial activities of criminals under the Foreign Intelligence Surveillance Act of 1978. The new legislation was designed to prevent banks from being used to launder and dispense monies to known terrorist entities.[13] Terrorists were not allowed to bank with institutions that did business with and in the United States.

An operation, nicknamed Show Me the Money, focused on bank account information and the transfer of funds from Lebanon, Syria, and Iran to the West Bank and the Gaza Strip. The data that was gathered was analyzed by specialists who were able to connect the dots that linked dollar transfers made into various Arab Bank accounts that paid for the murders of the terror victims. The money had been wired into the Arab Bank from the Islamic Republic of Iran. But beyond the moral complicity of helping to facilitate the murder of Americans and Israelis, the Arab Bank was in direct violation of the American laws by maintaining accounts in the names of eleven globally designated terrorists and terror organizations.* These included Hamas founder Sheikh Ahmed Yassin, Hamas spokesman Osama Hamdan, the Holy Land Foundation, the al Aqsa Foundation in Germany, the al-Salah Islamic Society, and Interpal in Great Britain.[14]

Of all the Harpoon leadership, Uri racked up the most frequent-flier miles. In the early days, when it operated under the Counterterrorism Bureau and then the NSC, Uri was the chosen for one-on-one networking with the Americans. He was dispatched on numerous occasions to Washington to meet with U.S. officials to close down the pipeline of hundreds of thousands of dollars that flowed monthly from the Holy Land Foundation in Texas to the West Bank and Gaza for Hamas military activity. The transatlantic flights increased following the passage of the Financial Anti-Terrorism Act. The Presidential Executive Order had greatly expanded the Treasury Department's ability to target terrorist money—it froze the U.S. financial assets of known terrorists and prohibited transactions with organizations, individuals, corporations, NGOS, and banks that were in association with terrorist groups. Shortly after the order was issued, Under Secretary of Treasury for Enforcement Jimmy Gurulé began to block suspected terrorist money.[15] But in bilateral meetings, talks about the Arab Bank topped their agenda.

Dagan had two objectives in mind when he targeted the Arab Bank. First and foremost was the hope that he could convince the bank managers and its board of directors to cease and desist enabling internationally recognized terror organizations from maintaining accounts.

---

* The Arab Bank maintained the accounts of seemingly benevolent organizations that operated in the West Bank and Gaza that were, in fact, mere fronts for the Hamas military wing and that were all outlawed by Israel.

A second objective was to make the movement of money more expensive. If bank transfers—indeed, bank access—was removed from the terror arsenal, money would have to flow in through other means—smuggling, money changers, and crime. These methods of moving large amounts of money from Point A to Point B were effective but they were expensive; money changers would, of course, charge a steeper premium to move a million dollars if they knew that the client had no other options available to them. Risk came at a premium, Dagan knew. Transferring money solely by these means was not foolproof. There were seizures by corrupt border guards in Jordan and Egypt; some of the seizures were by the Arab intelligence services acting on tips from Israel. Egyptian border guards noticed increased smuggling attempts along the frontier with Gaza in 2002 after Israel closed the accounts of some Hamas commanders.[16]

Sometimes Israeli troops seized large bundles of cash coming across the borders. Physically carrying the cash across the border was risky business. Dagan wanted the million-dollar donation earmarked for Hamas from a wealthy Saudi sheikh to lose much of its value as it crossed borders and war zones earmarked for the terrorists. Diluting the money that flowed into the terrorist coffers meant less violence.

Harpoon's failure to get the Arab Bank to stop its tacit support for Hamas and the other Palestinian terrorist groups forced Dagan to think of other options. In discussing these possibilities, Dagan quoted the old Turkish proverb: "If the mountain won't come to Mohammed, then Mohammed must go to the mountain."[17]

CHAPTER EIGHT

Operation Green Lantern

Go where the money is . . . and go there often.
—*attributed to Willie Sutton*

The goal of the Palestinian terrorists perpetrating the intifada violence was to coerce Israel to capitulate to the demands that Palestinian Authority President Arafat couldn't achieve at the negotiation table. As the brutal bombings and shootings continued, Israel became an armed camp. Every school, every cinema, every bar and café had guards posted at their entrances. Frequently, they were the first victims of the suicide attacks. Tourism collapsed, leaving thousands of tour guides and hotel workers unemployed. Families began to avoid taking buses. Once-crowded shopping malls were empty, and diners in restaurants kept a nervous eye on the doorway. Israelis, who were once addicted to listening to the hourly news updates on radio, now dreaded tuning into the Voice of Israel, fearing what they would hear. Television broadcasts were frequently interrupted with live reports from the scene of the latest attack.

The year 2003 was a bloody year in Israel. There were twenty-three suicide bombings in the twelve months of intifada violence; 145 Israelis died in the bloodshed, and more than five hundred were critically injured. Some of the attacks were absolutely horrific. It started off on January 5 with twenty-three people killed and another 120 wounded in a double suicide bombing near the old Central Bus Station in Tel Aviv. The attack was carried out by two terrorists from the al-Aqsa Martyrs Brigade, a faction of Yasir Arafat's Fatah group that was responsible for many of the bombings. The suicide bombing of a bus in Jerusalem on August 19 resulted in twenty-three dead and more than one hundred wounded. One of the worst attacks was the Islamic Jihad suicide bombing of the Maxim restaurant in Haifa, which killed twenty-two people and wounded nearly one hundred; the bomber, a female lawyer from Jenin, looked into the eye of a small child sitting across from her before she detonated her lethal payload.[1]

The battles between Israeli counterterrorist forces and the Palestinian terrorist infrastructure escalated. The IDF targeted senior terrorist leaders. Israeli intelligence maintained a determined vigil monitoring phone calls and movements, and still the bombers managed to slip through. The loss of life was numbing to Meir Dagan. He spent sleepless nights grappling with the conviction that another front had to be opened.

The Arab Bank remained the hub behind much of the bloodshed, linking the attacks to their commanders and interlocutors overseas. But no matter how much pressure was applied against the financial powerhouse, the bank continued to do business as usual. Saudi money, donations from Muslims living abroad, money disguised as charity, all flowed into the bank and into the Palestinian areas. Dagan tried to keep the pressure on. In Harpoon meetings, Dagan and Uri L. pressed the Shin Bet and A'man representatives for any information that enhanced their understanding as to how the bank facilitated the suicide bombing campaign. On Dagan's orders, anyone who touched the blood money was targeted—including those who enabled the transfer of funds from overseas. Europe was very problematic for Dagan. Europe hadn't been struck hard by terrorism like the United States on 9/11 and its commitment to the war on terror, in Jerusalem's eyes, was spotty.

As the Mossad director, Dagan valued Israel's strong relationships with the European intelligence services. As a Jew, and one shaped by the Holocaust, Dagan viewed European interest in Israel's security with great skepticism. He grew frustrated by Europe's lack of collective concern in doing something meaningful to stop the funds flowing into the territories. His personal efforts with the European Union were a failure. "Dagan and I met many dozens of times with senior officials from the European Union, as well as in European capitals, to try our best and convince these leaders to shut down the Hamas charitable foundations on the continent," Uri recalled.[2]

The niceties of European diplomacy infuriated Dagan and Uri. The two men were used to dressing casually, even in meetings with the prime minister. But to fit in inside the civilized confines of the European Union's seat of power, the Israelis now were required to wear dark suits; they positively hated wearing jackets and ties. Still, the Israelis went, carrying attaché cases full of sanitized intelligence that implicated charities situated on the continent, funneling money from the Iranian Islamic Revolutionary Guard and Hezbollah through branches of banks that ultimately ended up in the hands of Hamas and PIJ cell commanders.

Their efforts met with little success. "Not only did the European Union do nothing to stem the flow of money flowing into Hamas from the continent, but they also said that the issue was ours to deal with and had nothing to do with them. Moreover, in the niceties of European diplomacy that we should cease and desist in our efforts to investigate money transfers and the continent's banking system, as we would then be in violation of bank privacy laws."[3] Dagan and Uri were flabbergasted.

Dagan, incensed by European inaction and the flow of terrorist money, began to finally cultivate the seed of a dramatic idea that had been ruminating in his mind for a while.

The traditional thinking of Israeli counterterrorist operations was to attack up: Compromise a cell, use the information gleaned from physical evidence such as a phone or notes, combine it with interrogation sessions, and then press upward and forward to target the command structure—the bomb builders, the operational planners, and, of course, the financiers. Dagan wanted to change the paradigm. He wanted to strike at the top of the food chain. What Dagan was thinking required action that was raucously effective; he sought a game-changing move. He didn't care about political repercussions. He wanted results.

As 2003 came to a close, Dagan convened a meeting of his Harpoon roundtable. The representatives from the various agencies and units sat around the conference table and reviewed the agenda over pitchers of coffee. The Arab Bank was one of the primary agenda items. As Dagan and the assembled men and women around him discussed intelligence reports and the raw data, Dagan smiled and paused. "Why not just take over the bank and the terror-related accounts," he asked, "just as had been done with Ghazi Qassam Issa A'juli."[4]

A'juli had appeared on Harpoon's radar months earlier. He was one of the most prominent money changers in Ramallah and maintained vast revenues and cash assets. He moved around like a head of state, protected by heavily armed security men, but few would have been foolish enough to rob him—A'juli was connected to both Hamas and Fatah. He was a money facilitator who played a key role in financing the suicide bombing attacks perpetrated against Israel's cities.[5] A'juli was a smart businessman and didn't trust his cash reserves solely in the floor safes he had dug under his residences throughout the West Bank, and he didn't trust Arab financial institutions. His money was spread throughout Israeli banks, in branches in Tel Aviv and Jerusalem. And that was where Dagan's force struck first. Harpoon at first froze and then confiscated his bank accounts in Israel—the Israeli Attorney General's Office liaison to Harpoon made sure that the endeavor was legal. And then the Shin Bet and the special operations units took over.

Late one chilly winter's night, the Shin Bet and Israeli commandos stormed A'juli's office in Ramallah. The forces seized A'juli's computers and his coded list of clients, including what monies were handled, who deposited them, and where the payouts had to be made and how. The raiding party also seized cash—hundreds of thousands of dollars, shekels, British sterling, and Jordanian dinars.

Some of the officers, including representatives from the Mossad and Shin Bet, now thought that Dagan was joking when he spoke of mounting an operation against the Arab Bank that would mimic the one carried out against A'juli. They chuckled uncomfortably, hoping not to offend the Mossad director. But Dagan was dead serious. A successful operation in Ramallah against one of the region's most powerful money changers cemented the notion in Dagan's head that Israel's intelligence services and military could target the terrorist money sitting inside the banks. One of the primary West Bank money pipelines to Hamas had been shut off. Dagan wanted to replicate the A'juli model with the Arab Bank.

There was precedent for the proposed operation. In 2001, in a small raid, the Shin Bet and the IDF raided a bank in al-Eizariya, a village east of Jerusalem, after intelligence had linked an account with 37,000 new Israeli shekels in it to a terror chieftain and specific terror attacks.[6] Israeli forces entered the bank and seized the account with the supervision of the branch manager and other witnesses so that there could be no accusations that Israeli forces helped themselves to cash or anything else. The raid in al-Eizariya yielded a paper trail of accounts, addresses, and phone numbers. It was a whole different concern, though, to go after a bank the size of the Arab Bank.

There was political risk in targeting a bank, but the Amman-based Arab Bank posed unique sensitivities. Israel did not want to harm its relationship with Jordan, one of the two Arab nations that had diplomatic relations and a peace treaty with the Jewish State. King Abdullah II, the Jordanian monarch and a former commando officer, was one of the few world leaders who understood the tactical necessities of bold steps in the fight against terror. But the Arab Bank was a financial pillar in the Hashemite Kingdom and a key to economic stability in the country, and stability—while a terrorist war raged against Israel and the United States led by an international coalition to topple Saddam Hussein in Iraq—was critical. More than 60 percent of the Jordanian population was Palestinian or of Palestinian descent and now hundreds of thousands of refugees were pouring into the country from Iraq. A stable Jordan was critical for Israeli security. The Americans, too, Dagan knew, would weigh in against any unilateral Israeli operation against a bank that was so intrinsically linked to the day-to-day lives of the Palestinian population. President Bush had always made it clear that Israel's war should be against the terror factions and not against the

Palestinian people, and doing anything that could topple the Palestinian economy would evoke the ire of the American president, even one who was so outspokenly pro-Israel as George W. Bush.

Dagan could have sent Uri to Washington, D.C., to plead Israel's case and measure the American administration's feelings about an operation against the Arab Bank. But Dagan decided against it. There wasn't time to shake hands and beg for permission. Iran, Harpoon would learn, made a serious effort to wield influence over the Hamas and PIJ cells planning and perpetrating the bombing campaign by flooding the West Bank with money. The Iranian cash, most of which came into the PA via the Arab Bank, was in a series of accounts that were centered in the bank's branch in Ramallah; other accounts were in branches of the Cairo Amman Bank, a forty-four-year-old financial institution based in Amman with twenty-one branches throughout the West Bank.

As many arguments as there were advising against a strike on the Arab Bank, the most compelling argument supporting an operation was the fact that the bloodshed continued without letup.

The New Year brought even more terror attacks. On January 29, 2004, once again a member of the al-Aqsa Martyrs Brigade, a twenty-four-year-old Palestinian policeman from Bethlehem named Ali Yusef Ja'ara, boarded the No. 19 bus in Jerusalem. Ja'ara wore civilian clothes and carried a bag weighed down by a powerful combination of high explosives and metal shards collected from a construction site. Ja'ara paid his fare and then moved toward the rear of the crowded bus.

The bus ferried passengers between the two main Hadassah Hospital campuses, one in Jerusalem's city center and one on Mount Scopus. Shortly after 9:00 AM, as the bus reached a crowded intersection near the prime minister's residence, Ja'ara triggered his device. The seven kilograms of explosives he carried chewed through the bus, blowing out the windows and punching a gaping hole through the side of the vehicle. The force of the blast ripped the roof open like a can of sardines; the ensuing inferno incinerated victims and plastic seats.

The suicide bombing killed eleven and left more than fifty seriously wounded. One of them was Canadian-born therapist Scott Goldberg, who had opted not to take his regular bus to work. That morning, for reason unknown, he took the No. 19 en route to his clinic, where he treated at-risk kids. He never made it. He left behind a wife and seven children, aged two to sixteen.

A few weeks later, on February 22, another al-Aqsa Martyrs Brigade suicide bomber blew himself up on a bus in Jerusalem. This time eight people were killed and sixty wounded.

Although Dagan no longer cared about the repercussions of going after the Arab Bank, the Israeli Attorney General Menachem Mazuz did. Naturally reticent and new to the job, Mazuz wanted to make sure that Israel was in full compliance with the law. A member of Mazuz's staff was assigned to Harpoon, but Dagan and Uri had decided to meet with Mazuz directly and present him with the compelling legal argument, showing the attorney general the sensitive intelligence that prompted them to propose so controversial an operation.

Dagan and Uri were a convincing team. Mazuz gave them the green light they sought. Once the planned strike received the legal thumbs-up, Dagan took his idea to Defense Minister Shaul Mofaz, who also endorsed it. The final word, however, belonged to Prime Minister Sharon. There was a blind trust between Dagan and Sharon, and the Mossad director knew deep down inside that the operation would be authorized. Sharon, like Dagan, cared little for political fallout when the question of action or inaction involved Israeli lives.

Brigadier General Danny Arditi, the head of the Counterterrorism Bureau, was quickly summoned. Arditi was a veteran of Sayeret Mat'kal and had participated in the legendary commando raid to free Israeli and Jewish hostages on a hijacked French airliner in Entebbe in July 1976. He had served as the coordinator for Israeli special operations and understood the value of lightning raids in rewriting the counterterrorist narrative. The commanders of Israel's most secretive units as well as Shin Bet and IDF operations officers were summoned to work out the details. The operation was codenamed "Green Lantern."[7]

The army cooks at the Binyamin Territorial Brigade, the IDF formation responsible for security operations around the Ramallah area, were up well before dawn on the morning of February 25, 2004. In addition to the normal breakfast rush they were asked to feed close to a hundred counterterrorist commandos, soldiers, and Border Guard paramilitary policemen who would muster at the base for an operation later that morning. The soldiers filed into the dining hall quietly, weapons slung across their shoulders, and grabbed available seats for a quick fill of eggs and cheese and the obligatory Israeli chopped vegetable salad that completed every military breakfast. The soldiers and police officers bantered with one another and laughed; most of the jokes centered on the horrible coffee. The soldiers checked their watches and hurried up to finish what was on their plates. The briefings were at 0700.

Every mission, regardless of size, was always preceded by lengthy and often exhaustive briefings by divisional commanders, the brigade staff, unit commanders, and team leaders. These men, the generals and colonels, used PowerPoint presentations, topographical maps, aerial photographs, and blackboards with different-colored chalk scribbles to address each and every aspect of the morning's counterterrorist operation. The intelligence heads, the men who ran spies and those who analyzed the data, were always present. They were, after all, the brains behind the firepower. The operations began with them, and they were always present to connect the dots for the men who would be bursting through doors and taking hostile fire. Israel's counterterrorism strategy was predicated with intelligence work—from small-scale operations involving a case agent and a human source, meeting in a safe house, to large-scale operations involving a hundred commandos.

At 0940 a small armada of vehicles and armored personnel carriers departed the brigade's headquarters for three targets in Ramallah. Members from the Border Guards' undercover unit, known as the Ya'mas, had already been positioned inside Ramallah, deployed at strategic locations throughout the city to assist the task force; the undercover operatives, disguised as Palestinians, were used to operating deep behind enemy lines. The Green Lantern convoy headed north at full speed toward the Palestinian capital, and then the vehicles split into several different contingents. One force headed toward the Central Bank of the Palestinian Authority. Another rushed toward the city's main branch of the Cairo Amman Bank. The largest contingent raced toward the main Arab Bank branch in Ramallah, as well as four other smaller branches in the area. Drones flew overhead, providing the intelligence chiefs and the divisional commander with a bird's-eye view of real-time intelligence; the small yet invaluable unmanned aerial vehicles were, for the most part, piloted by nineteen-year-old female conscripts. Israel Air Force attack helicopters flew cover overhead.

At precisely 1000 the commandos raced out of their vehicles, rushing to the main doors of the targeted banks.[8] They breached the fortified doors and secured the teller stations and the rear offices, making sure no armed men were present. Dagan wanted the banks to be raided during business hours to deliver the message that Israel could and would reach into the lives and the pockets of the Palestinians involved in paying for the blood across the Green Line, the demarcation frontier from the pre–1967 War borders. There was a message to be sent in displaying the military might. But the assaulting teams were under strict orders to treat the customers and employees inside with the greatest respect. Arabic-speaking specialists explained to the bank managers the nature of the operation.

Infantrymen and Border Guard policemen protected the outer perimeter, keeping Palestinian Authority security personnel far from the operation. But the soldiers and policemen were met by a steady barrage of rocks and Molotov cocktails thrown from young Palestinian men who had gathered to respond to the Israeli incursion. Arabic-speaking Israeli police officers pleaded with the crowds to disperse, explaining that the bank operation had nothing to do with law-abiding residents, but violence ensued. The Israeli soldiers fired tear gas and rubber bullets to keep the protesters away. Several of the Palestinians were wounded, as were some of the Israeli soldiers. Ramallah was Area A under Oslo, and even after Operation Defensive Shield, Israeli forces were not supposed to operate inside the city.

Shin Bet agents and analysts from A'man and the Israel National Police entered the targeted banks carrying boxes and large white canvas bags, as did, according to one eyewitness, several men who looked as if they were accountants and bank officers.[9] The spies wore black-cloth balaclavas to shield their identities from prying eyes and freelance photographers. The intelligence agents had the names and numbers of 390 accounts that funneled monies from around the world into charities that were connected to the military wings of Hamas, as well as straight into the planning and procurement coffers of the PIJ and Fatah. The accounts included those that had been used to funnel money from known terrorist factions like Hezbollah; accounts directly linked to known terrorist groups; accounts held by terrorists already incarcerated by the State of Israel that had been used to finance operations; and accounts belonging to organizations, such as charities, that had been declared illegal by the State of Israel and still directed funds into these accounts from banks around the world.[10]

"There were additional raids against bank branches in Jenin and Tulkarm," Lavi S. remembered. "In some of the operations, we didn't want to go in and burst through the main doors. We wanted the search of the accounts and the bank computers in an orderly and courteous manner." As the COGAT representative to the Harpoon task force, Lavi operated in the Palestinian cities, and he knew the bank managers personally. He had their cell phone numbers; he knew where they lived. When Israeli forces were outside the banks, Lavi called the bank officers at home and asked them to come in and open the main door and to watch and witness what the investigators were doing.[11]

Computers were grabbed and files downloaded. Operation Green Lantern resulted in the confiscation of more than 40 million shekels of money destined for terror cells in the West Bank.[12] Every dollar bill and shekel note seized was photographed, videotaped, and cataloged. The Israelis wanted to make sure that there could be no accusations against any of the soldiers that money had been stolen.

There were several arrests, as well, including the director of computer systems for the bank. Most of the bank customers and employees were released after their identities could be established; the managers and their technical assistants were held for a few hours longer.[13] "The first thought that struck me was that it was an armed robbery," Emil Barham, a manager at one of the banks targeted by Israeli forces operating on the Harpoon directive, told Canada's *Globe and Mail* newspaper, "then we realized it really was an armed robbery."[14]

According to one Border Guard special operations commander at the scene, "The raid was a discovery of enormous reward. It was like discovering a new element or oil. It opened up possibilities to expand our efforts to stop the money."[15]

Israeli forces were in Ramallah all day. The files had to be cataloged and boxed and then taken to the regional Shin Bet headquarters, where Arabic-speaking specialists and police economic-crime analysts could review the paperwork and computer files for evidence that could be used to roll up terror networks and be used in the subsequent criminal prosecutions.

The soldiers and policemen were all debriefed at length by their commanders upon their return to base, before being dispatched to the dining hall. The cooks greeted the returning soldiers and policemen with a late dinner, though most of the soldiers simply wanted to go grab some sleep. The Shin Bet case officers, and members of the Harpoon team, however, didn't want to leave the evidence. They stayed at headquarters all night. The captured material was that good.

The U.S. State Department weighed in on Operation Green Lantern before the commandos even had a chance to eat their meals. Richard Boucher, the veteran spokesman who had served under several secretaries of state, stated, "The Israeli action threatens to destroy the Palestinian banking system. We prefer that Israel work with the legal Palestinian authorities to stop the flow of money to terror groups."[16] The response from Foggy Bottom, however, was muted compared to what Israel received from the White House. President Bush was furious. "He was livid with what we did in Green Lantern, absolutely livid." Uri recalled hearing that Bush lectured Prime Minister Sharon that seizing money was the kind of thing that Third World dictators did. "The U.S. president said that what we did reminded him of the 'Wild West.'"[17]

Daniel C. Kurtzer, the American ambassador to Israel, demanded a full explanation—Harpoon, and the NSC, scrambled to assemble their case. An Israeli contingent met Ambassador Kurtzer and several other U.S. embassy staffers—political and economic officers—off post from the U.S. embassy, at an undisclosed location in Tel Aviv. Brigadier General Arditi and Uri led the Israeli contingent; they were joined by an operative, who was responsible for counterterrorist cooperation with the United States, and an officer who was responsible for international counterterrorist cooperation.[18] Kurtzer knew all the players in the room quite well; the interaction was routine. But the ambassador's mood was dour and he reiterated President Bush's anger.

Arditi explained that the operation came at great political concern for stability in the PA and that American and, indeed, international concerns were taken into consideration. But Arditi stressed that there was a pressing immediacy for the Israeli action. Hezbollah, he explained, was benefiting from the emerging sense of chaos in the Palestinian territories and had managed to exploit gaps in operational coverage between the IDF and security services in the West Bank and Gaza. Arditi explained to Kurtzer that Hezbollah was able to inject support for the terror factions through three main channels: smuggling funds, drugs, and weapons across the Lebanese border; the recruitment of Israeli-Arab citizens to serve as spies and couriers who are approached during the Hajj, the pilgrimage to Mecca, or when traveling or studying abroad; and through funds deposited into the Arab Bank. Uri and Arditi stressed to Ambassador Kurtzer that not only were Hezbollah, Hamas, and the PIJ using the Arab Bank, but so was al-Qaeda and forces loyal to Saddam Hussein.

But Kurtzer, speaking on behalf of the president he served, was adamant that as far as the White House was concerned, the raid on the Arab Bank branches in particular crossed a line in the sand. The ambassador lambasted the optics of driving tanks and armored vehicles straight up to a bank entrance and simply to steal bags of cash. Kurtzer emphasized that these John Dillinger tactics should not be used again.

The Israelis explained that their intelligence officials could prove that every penny, pence, and dinar seized from Operation Green Lantern was directly related to terror. Arditi and Uri also argued that PA Finance Minister Salam Fayyad's inaction presented Israel with little choice but to act militarily. The Israelis weren't like Jesse James or Bonnie and Clyde, Kurtzer was reassured; the Israeli Ministry of Defense pledged that the funds confiscated from the three targeted banks would be channeled back to the PA finance minister for the benefit of humanitarian aid and welfare for the Palestinians.[19]

The Palestinians, publicly, at least, didn't want to hear anything about the money that Israel pledged to return. Operation Green Lantern caught the Palestinian Authority completely by surprise. Negotiators who worked with the Israelis and even the Palestinian security services that maintained communications with their counterparts in Israel, especially with the Shin Bet and COGAT, were dumbfounded by the aggressive Israeli move.

Ahmed Qureia, the Palestinian prime minister, called the Israeli operation a very dangerous violation of the norms even between the two parties. "To go to the banks, to take photos of all the documents, to take the employees out, the customers of the bank, to kick them out and to take the bank. It's like Mafia. It's a kind of Mafia war," Qureia said.[20]

There was another, and more pressing, concern that the Palestinian politicians only hinted at. Saeb Erekat, the Palestinian minister for negotiations who was a mainstay on news networks around the world as a surrogate for Arafat, expressed his concern that the action could cause Palestinians to fear the stability and safety of the banking system and to pull all their cash out of the banks. "This is destructive to the Palestinian economy, and people are really worried," he said.[21] The Palestinians were fearful that Israel was set to unravel the very threads of the Palestinian economy. Green Lantern came days after the Palestinian security services had just confirmed that Iranian money, some sent as Hezbollah wire transfers, had paid for—lock, stock, and barrel—the last two suicide bus bombings in Jerusalem that killed nineteen and wounded close to one hundred.[22] The Palestinians were worried that the Israelis would target the very fabric of their lives just as the suicide bombers had targeted the very pillars of day-to-day life in Israel. The fear on the Palestinian street was that the Israelis would exact a price for the violence and that the price wouldn't come in the form of land or symbols of nationalism, but rather from the wallets of the average Palestinian.

The fear on the streets made Meir Dagan and his Harpoon inner circle happy. He wanted there to be a price paid for the innocent Israelis killed and the families forever destroyed by the violence. Harpoon's very mandate made it abundantly clear that any person or nation that provided anything of value to a terrorist or terrorist organization would be deemed to be providing them with material support. Money was recognized as an essential component of terrorism—the same as training, safe houses, weapons, and explosives. Money was the oxygen of the terrorist groups, and without it they could not carry out their recruitment, training, or deadly operations.

Dagan wanted the terrorists to look for money instead of targets. He wanted them poor and feckless. Dagan didn't give a damn about the international outcry; he knew that American outrage would dissipate.* And

---

* Ironically, Harpoon's position and the merits of Operation Green Lantern were exonerated in the United States Supreme Court landmark 2010 decision, *Holder v. Humanitarian Law Project*. In that decision, the court held that money was fungible and that it was not necessary for law enforcement agencies or private plaintiffs to track the actual dollars, rubles, rials, euros, nor pounds being supplied to the terrorists or attribute them to an actual use or attack. In the eyes of the Supreme Court, providing any services, even wiring funds from account to account on behalf of designated terrorist groups, would make banks and financial institutions liable for criminal and civil penalties.

Dagan certainly didn't lose a moment of sleep about the negative press. He was convinced the intelligence gleaned from the operation would be so good that it would outweigh all concerns.

It took weeks for forensic accountants to decipher all the intelligence gleaned from Operation Green Lantern. Each account seized was analyzed and every transaction studied. Some troublesome realities were revealed from the boxes and boxes of paperwork, and that involved the Western Union Company. All of the Arab Bank branches that were addressed in "Green Lantern" enabled the wiring of money to and from the West Bank from any place in the world. Western Union, founded in 1866 as a telegram company, was based in Colorado. Targeting this major corporation presented Harpoon with a significant quandary. Millions of dollars that had come into the hands of Hamas commanders came through this established American institution.

But Green Lantern revealed something more valuable. Sitting inside the boxes and bags of evidence were paper trails that shattered the notion that institutions, like the Arab Bank, weren't responsible for the funds they maintained for known terrorists. The smoking guns, as far as Israel was concerned, involved funds transferred through innocuous accounts to the families of suicide bombers. There were examples that stood out in Dagan's mind: the Arab Bank branch in Tulkarm transferred grants to families of PIJ suicide bombers through third parties; the family of a suicide bomber who wounded thirty-four people in the March 2003 attack at the Café London in Netanya who received 15,000 Jordanian dinars for his death and the subsequent Israeli punitive operation that destroyed their home; and rounds of payments that were transferred to the Saudi Committee for Aid to the al-Aqsa Martyr Families through the Arab Bank, which averaged 20,000 Saudi rials.[23]

Had he been a prosecutor, Dagan knew, the material seized in Green Lantern would have been enough to sway a judge and jury. When faced with such evidence and its own internal logs and files, the Arab Bank couldn't plausibly deny that it had facilitated the transfer of monies into accounts used to finance acts of murder—in some cases the monies transferred to the West Bank and Gaza originated from the official accounts belonging to Hamas and the PIJ. In other cases, money sent from Damascus, Beirut, Tehran, and Jeddah were transferred into Arab Bank accounts in the West Bank and Gaza that were maintained by men who were known—to the Israelis and to the PA—as members of a terrorist group.

The information seized in Green Lantern was ammunition. Dagan and the Harpoon team simply had to figure out how to use it.

CHAPTER NINE

The Letter of the Law

Intelligence that isn't used is simply being wasted.
—*Meir Dagan*

M eir Dagan expected that the Americans would be irritated by the Israeli action, though he could not understand the extent of the outrage. Sometimes the Americans were baffling to the Israelis; Dagan was certain the Israelis baffled the Americans, as well. But President Bush's sincere outrage over an Israeli military operation that didn't result in any casualties was a litmus test to the limitations of America's resolve. Israel realized that it had restrictions in what moves it made, especially going after banks and Arab economies. Some in Israel said that Americans simply lacked the creativity to be successful at combating terror. "What do Americans know about counterterrorism?" the commander of a special operations unit operating along Israel's border with Gaza once scolded a group of visiting U.S. police chiefs during the intifada. "You don't have to live with this day in and day out."[1]

The lackluster international interest in targeting the money puzzled the Israelis to no end. Early on, for example, Harpoon had discovered that Hezbollah in Lebanon had set up an operation to counterfeit United States currency. Harpoon officials met with law enforcement agencies around the world to inform them of the threat of international security posed by a terrorist outfit that had the means to successfully counterfeit a major global currency. As a Harpoon member recalled, "We were passed from agency to agency and no one cared. We said we are talking about fake U.S. dollars, the super bill, being printed up by the dangerous Hezbollah terrorists, but people didn't seem to care. One American law enforcement agency asked us how much money Hezbollah was printing, and we responded $50 million. 'That's all?' was their response. It was like it didn't matter. But we told them, 'This is money for terrorism. Do you know what terrorists can do with $50 million?'"[2]

Meir Dagan sat in his chair and smiled as he reviewed the classified reports detailing what was learned from Green Lantern. As director of Mossad, he had a schedule that ran from dawn to dusk, but he always had time for Harpoon business. He reviewed the information seized with great interest; Dagan discussed the findings from Uri and his counterparts in the Shin Bet and A'man. The trove of data showed a highly detailed trail of money from point of origin to detonation on an Israeli bus and inside a crowded café. From Harpoon's perspective, the evidence linking money that traveled through the Arab Bank and the salaries and pensions of dead or convicted terrorists was irrefutable. The files were cataloged and stored in subfolders inside other subfolders, inside a folder on a government server. And that was where they stayed. And that infuriated Dagan to no end.

Dagan believed that intelligence that wasn't used somehow was wasted material. "It was collected for a reason," he once told a Harpoon representative during a meeting of the roundtable, "so it was up to the spies to use it."[3] Many Israeli intelligence officials were horrified when Dagan dispatched Uri and Shai around the world to friendly nations to share files, albeit watered-down versions. Letting outsiders glimpse Israeli intelligence files was considered sacrilegious to these veterans. They believed that maintaining absolute secrecy about the information in their possession was critical to Israel's security. The stalwarts argued that Israeli intelligence's means and methods for gathering information were compromised the more people saw it. Dagan would have none of it. Still, the information failed to spark the interest of the allied nations involved in the war on terror. Dagan was dumbfounded and frustrated. In fact, he was continuously thinking of novel approaches to use the Green Lantern bounty in the most innovative ways—ways that the Americans would understand and, begrudgingly, admire.

There was a new battlefield in the war against terrorist finances that was gaining traction and grabbing headlines that didn't involve spies or soldiers. In fact, it involved lawyers. When Dagan and Uri sat down together in the director's office to exchange ideas and talk about operational matters, the conversations could last for hours. The two men fed off one another, like scientists in a lab on the verge of a monumental breakthrough, and together they conceived plans and complex missions that were daring and quite imaginable. The two men also talked about academic matters that touched on Middle Eastern issues. Sometimes, the two men spoke about the limits of Israeli power. Green Lantern highlighted the reach of Israeli might, as well as its constraints.

In one of the meetings when Dagan and Uri spoke shop, the director discussed an idea that was taking place in the war on terror about going after the banks in a new type of battlefield where lawyers, rather than commandos, would do the fighting. What if the victims of terror sued the banks for damages? Some lawyers in Israel and the United States had already filed suits against the PLO and other terror groups, as well as the outlaw regimes that sponsored them. The financial institutions that allowed this money to flow could be next. The media attention of such a legal onslaught would be humiliating and damaging to the banks' owners. Suing for damages could even result in the banks' collapse, denying Hamas, the PLO, and the PIJ with their financial lifeline.

There was no recourse in Israel for such a litigious idea. The State of Israel did not have the legal power or jurisdiction to bring the Arab Bank—or the other financial institutions used by the terrorists—to court. The International Court in the Hague, the Netherlands, wasn't an option, either. Public opinion wasn't very pro-Israel, and the world body didn't have enforceable laws on the books—or the political will to compel them—to make banks in the Arab world cease and desist the use of their financial institutions to fund the bloodshed. Its jurisdiction was extremely limited as well. The answer was in the United States and, more specifically, in the 1992 Anti-Terrorism Act.

The law,[4] sponsored originally by Senator Chuck Grassley, a Republican from Iowa and later by Representative Edward Feighan, a Democrat from Ohio's nineteenth congressional district,[5] came as a response to a growing scourge of terrorist attacks that had targeted American citizens and American properties around the world, including the bombings of two United States embassies in Beirut, Lebanon, in 1983 and 1984; the hijacking of a foreign cruise liner, the MS *Achille Lauro*, by the PLO and the gruesome murder of an elderly New Yorker, Leon Klinghoffer, in his wheelchair; the kidnapping of American citizens in Lebanon; the 1986 hijacking of Pan Am Flight 73 in Karachi, Pakistan; and the December 1988 bombing of Pan Am 103 over Lockerbie, Scotland. The law was to provide a new criminal and civil cause of action in federal law for international terrorism that allowed extraterritorial jurisdiction over terrorist acts abroad against United States nationals. The execution of Klinghoffer and America's legal impotence to respond because it lacked jurisdiction outside the United States' borders had outraged congressional leaders.

But a subsection in the act interested Harpoon the most. Subsection 2333(a) covered civil remedy provisions, namely:

> Any national of the United States injured in his or her person, property, or business by reason of an act of international terrorism, or his or her estate, survivors, or heirs, may sue therefore in any appropriate district court of the United States and shall recover threefold the damages he or she sustains and the cost of the suit, including attorney's fees.

Lawsuits seeking remedy under the 1992 Anti-Terrorism Act were decided in U.S. federal court, usually in New York or Washington, D.C. The Israeli agents liked to fight their battles on friendly ground. They also knew that the notion of "threefold the damages" could possibly be fatal to an institution that facilitated the deaths and horrific injuries of so many.

"A ruling in a U.S. courtroom," an agent from Harpoon recalled, relaying the sentiment, "could be more lethal than a squadron of Israel Air Force F-16 fighter bombers."[6] In the years following the September 11, 2001, attacks, the number of lawsuits filed under the U.S. Anti-Terrorism Act and similar laws have more than tripled compared to the fifty cases the decade before.[7]

Certain criteria had to be met in order to initiate third-party legal action, however. There had to be victims of Palestinian terror who were killed or wounded in attacks that could be linked directly to the banks. The victims had to be American citizens, of course. They had to be interested in suing in court and reliving the death of a loved one, or their own harrowing encounter with suicidal terror. And, of course, the plan needed lawyers, preferably Israeli attorneys, with enough knowledge of terrorism and the American legal system to successfully sue.

There was one attorney who had already started some work in this realm, going after state sponsors of terror and bringing suits against the terror organizations in the Israeli and American courts. She and her colleagues had won large judgments and posted liens on terror money. Dagan wanted to better understand what was happening in lawsuits being filed against Israel's enemies and suggested Uri make a call.

Nitsana Darshan-Leitner didn't hear the phone ringing one summer morning in 2004. Construction crews were using dynamite and heavy earth-moving equipment to rip apart the 471 Road that connected Highway 40 to Highway 4, and residents of Kiryat Ono, a quiet Tel Aviv suburb of quaint homes and lush rows of eucalyptus trees, who hadn't escaped the inconvenience were forced to shut their windows to keep the suffocating dust out.

Nitsana maintained an office in a two-story house in Kiryat Ono that could accommodate her growing practice dedicated to assisting the victims of terrorism and placing the spotlight on the nations—Syria, the Islamic Republic of Iran, and North Korea—that openly supported the Palestinian terrorist factions killing Israeli civilians. The daughter of an

Iranian-born school teacher and a dressmaker, Nitsana became interested in legal remedies to the terrorism issue while completing her legal studies at Bar-Ilan University, and attended the trials of Palestinians charged with terrorism offenses in military courts in the West Bank to not only observe the procedures but to learn more about the victims.

Her first action, mounted in 1994 while she was still in university, was to petition the Israeli Supreme Court to deny Muhammad Zaidan entry into the newly formed PA through Israel's borders. Zaidan was, in fact, Mahmoud Abu Abbas, the commander of the Palestine Liberation Front and the man who ordered the seizure of the cruise ship MS *Achille Lauro* in 1985 and the murder of Jewish-American Leon Klinghoffer. Nitsana and some classmates brought the suit but they selected her to present the case before the magistrates, she would later tell the Israeli daily *Ma'ariv*, hoping that the judges, old-timers without much tolerance for antics in their courtrooms, wouldn't yell at a young woman and hit her with a fine for court costs.[8]

Nitsana envisioned using the courtroom as an alternative weapon to the battlefield in the fight against terrorism. Crowded and uncomfortable, Nitsana's law offices looked more like a frat house than a legal nerve center. It hardly seemed like the setting for a group of lawyers that an arm of Israeli intelligence would turn to. The white walls were decorated with framed portraits of courtroom scenes and legal images. A cigar-store Indian figure rested near a doorway; an antique Victrola sat on a shelf. Rock posters were hung in the staff office, and a carpet of papers and files, in both English and Hebrew, were strewn about the floor. Interns from the United States slept in the office. Attorney Roy Kochavi virtually chained himself to his desk, working on cases against the Palestinian Authority and the PLO around the clock.

The men and women who had worked COGAT before and after the intifada knew who the lawyers were. Nitsana was a frequent spectator in the Israeli courtrooms and often petitioned the military authorities for copies of case files. She had started her activism with an array of terrorism cases, including those filed in U.S. federal court, on behalf of Americans killed or wounded in terrorist attacks seeking damages as well as to shine the spotlight on the state sponsors. As she tried desperately to sustain her practice doing criminal, real estate, and collections work, the terror victim litigation began to absorb much of her time.

When Nitsana finally heard the phone ringing amid the earth movers and the blasts of dynamite detonations, she wondered if the person on the other end was a possible client or maybe even a bill collector. Instead, it was a baritone voice who spoke in a curt cadence laced with authority. The voice belonged to a man in charge, someone from the security services, which was used to issuing orders. She recognized the voice. "The man on the other end of the call asked me to come see him at an office near Tel Aviv, to meet with some government officials," Nitsana recalled. "I was told not to discuss the appointment with anyone. I was ordered not to record the meeting, or the address, in my diary. Come to an official meeting, the invitation went, but remember the meeting doesn't exist." This was not the first time she had met with agents from the intelligence branches. Periodically over the past few years, she and her associates had been called to casual meetings with Harpoon representatives at different locales to discuss her legal work against the terrorist organizations and rogue regimes. The updates seemed to Nitsana to be a curiosity for them. This time, however, the caller sounded more cryptic, more serious. The call was official.

There was always a risk, of course, in involving outsiders. And, both Dagan and Uri knew, the interests of an attorney, even one with a greater social agenda, might not necessarily coincide with the intelligence branches' agenda or even the long-term strategic outlook of the State of Israel. "We had known about Nitsana and we wanted to speak with someone who understood terrorism and the law," Uri remembered. "And of all the attorneys out there who did this sort of thing, we felt comfortable working with someone imaginative whose long-term philosophy was similar to our own."[9]

Several intelligence officials were also present at the meeting Nitsana attended. They chose to remain anonymous. The discussions lacked the usual familiarity that Israelis used in meetings with one another, even inside the security establishment. Nitsana was asked to explain the murky world of lawsuits. The spies were on a fishing expedition, curious students trying to absorb as much as they could at one meeting in a secretive location in Tel Aviv. How did the U.S. courts work? How would the families of the victims be involved? What type of expert witnesses would be needed in courtroom testimony? Would anyone from the intelligence community—indeed, from Harpoon itself—need to testify in open court? Dagan's grand vision wasn't one that was new to the Israelis, but it was one that would be, in most parts, outside their realm of control. The last thing that Dagan wanted was for Harpoon to become the center of attention in a courtroom where the press, outside the security protocols of the State of Israel, could print methods of intelligence gathering. Still, the Harpoon representatives were intrigued.

The first meeting inevitably resulted in a second sit-down. Less formal gatherings soon followed, always with Dagan's representatives. The initial tension around the appointments lessened. Nitsana was asked to meet the men in cafés and restaurants. The spies always came early to the meetings, and they always came in pairs; out of habit, they tended to prefer back tables so that a wall was to their backs. The conversations were also held in low voices, so that nearby tables or waitresses couldn't eavesdrop. No one ever ordered any food—only coffee or soft drinks. The intelligence branches were never known to spend lavishly. The men were always glancing past Nitsana's shoulders, hoping that prying eyes were not focused on them.

At first, the intelligence specialists scoffed at a judicial battlefield option. One of the men, a hulking Shin Bet official who had obviously made his career in the field fighting terrorists in the most dangerous precincts of the West Bank, thought that the whole idea was pure bullshit. When, in one of the meetings with Nitsana, they discussed how Iran moved money through Lebanese banks for Hezbollah and other groups, the Shin Bet agent leaped up from the other side of the table and yelled, "So what are you going to do, ruin Hezbollah's FICO score?"

But that was exactly what Meir Dagan hoped the lawyers would do. He wanted to wreak havoc inside the terrorists' financial world. Dagan advised Uri to empower the legal option. There were other attorneys in Israel and the United States who were also looking into the possibility of lawsuits, but Dagan believed the effort needed to be focused and sharp, like a dagger, and not a free-for-all of litigious bodies fighting an ineffective fight and possibly fighting with one another.

In late 2002 as the bloody intifada violence continued, the Israeli lawyers were determined to respond to the challenge and focus their energies solely on cases that helped the terror victims to fight back. As more and more bombs exploded, more and more families were calling the law office asking to be represented in lawsuits. The government was also pressing how important the cases were and encouraging the lawyers to file more of them. But the families could not afford to pay the costs involved with the litigation. Somehow a better structure had to be created so that all these additional cases could be filed and resourced.

Nitsana, along with attorney Mordechai Haller, a brilliant young legal strategist, and her husband, Aviel, who she met at Bar-Ilan University Law School, assisted in organizing a framework to help the terror victims in their legal struggle. They modeled it on a U.S. organization, the Southern Poverty Law Center, and its use of legal remedies in the fight against racism. The Southern Poverty Law Center, created in 1971 in Montgomery, Alabama, was a nonprofit legal organization that targeted racial intolerance and specifically racist groups such as the Ku Klux Klan and neo-Nazi movements in the United States with great success. Their Israeli version of this project would be called Shurat HaDin, Hebrew for the "letter of the law." Shurat HaDin's main goal would be to support litigation against those who perpetrated terrorism targeting Israel and the world Jewish community. A committed legal front would be opened in the battle. The first tactical discussions between Harpoon and Shurat HaDin were generally with Uri and Shai. The two men had become a tandem inside the ranks of Harpoon. The pair was entrusted by Dagan to use their unique skill sets to accomplish whatever tasks needed to be done. They were appointed to be

Shurat HaDin's liaison. Forensic accountants and in-house legal advisors, some completely fluent with the intelligence gleaned from Green Lantern, were also included in the mix. The accountants and lawyers didn't introduce themselves at the meetings. They were nameless experts who looked so benign that it would be impossible to ever mistake them for talents working for Israel's famed espionage service. Other individuals, more of the anonymous intelligence specialists, were brought around for introductions so that they could one day be summoned to serve as expert witnesses.

Harpoon never instructed the newly launched law center to sue any specific financial target. Shurat HaDin wasn't working on behalf of any government agency. That would have been inappropriate. But there were always suggestions, though; useful hints that were offered. "Harpoon never directed us," Nitsana recalled, "but rather they explained situations and threats and dangers that Israel and the Jewish community were facing and there was a challenge to be creative in thinking up solutions or tactics. We were able to draw our own conclusions."

For the lawsuits to work, Dagan knew, Uri and Shai would have to work in coordination with Shurat HaDin on the facts and details, some of which would provide irrefutable evidence linking targets to specific attacks. Security officers in the Shin Bet and A'man waged a furious campaign to stop Dagan from releasing information to those who were not "eyes only" worthy. But he wielded the same persuasive sledgehammer used when he commanded the undercover unit in Gaza and wanted things done his way. "There was no point in challenging him," Uri remembered. "He was always right."[10]

The first cases that were brought were pursuant to a special exemption to the Foreign Sovereign Immunities Act, which allowed terror-sponsoring regimes, such as Iran, Syria, Sudan, Libya, Iraq, North Korea, Algeria, and Cuba, to be sued in American federal courts for liability in attacks perpetrated by the terrorist groups they supported. Each time that Hamas or the PIJ carried out a terrorist attack and killed an American citizen, a lawsuit would be filed by the attorneys against Iran and Syria, which provided material support to the Islamic terrorist groups. The support could be weapons, training, safe haven, and especially financial backing. The plaintiffs argued that the outlaw regimes were vicariously liable for the extremist violence they supported. Most of these suits were filed in the district courts in Washington, D.C.

Next were the cases against the terror organization themselves along with the entities that supported them. Civil actions against Hamas, the PIJ, the PLO, and the Palestinian Authority were commenced in the district courts in New York and in Jerusalem. The suits being brought were filed under the Anti-Terrorism Act and Israeli tort law. International terrorism experts, former intelligence officials, and retired military officers were hired to prove legal liability. Medical doctors, psychiatrists, accountants, economists, and videographers were retained to establish the emotional and physical damages as well as the economic losses inflicted upon the victims and their families. Translators specializing in Arabic, Persian, and Hebrew were employed to decipher the foreign-language documents and materials, and allow the lawyers and judges to understand them and utilize them as evidence in court. Depositions were held both in Israel and across the United States. Some were held in Europe as well. Many lawyers traveled back and forth between the Middle East and the United States, sometimes several times a month.

One of the earliest cases that was brought was on behalf of Aaron Ellis. Ellis belonged to a community known as the "Black Hebrews." They were followers of Benjamin Carter, a former Chicago bus driver who went by the name Ben Ami Ben-Israel after he immigrated to Israel from the United States in 1970 with a short stopover in Liberia. Declaring themselves to be the true Israelite people, the forty-eight families arrived on tourist visas and then refused to leave, insisting that under Israel's "law of return" they, like all other Hebrews, had a right to citizenship. The group moved to the then most-neglected region of the country, the Southern Negev Desert, and set up camp in the city of Dimona. The Israeli government, sensitive to public opinion in the United States, decided not to create an international spectacle by deporting the African American families. Aaron Ellis was the first child born to the community in the Negev.

Blessed with musical talent, he pursued a career in singing, often being employed at Israeli weddings and celebrations all across the country. On the evening of January 17, 2002, he was onstage with his band in the Armon David Hall in the town of Hadera, performing before 180 guests, mostly recent arrivals from the former Soviet Union, at a Bat Mitzvah celebration.

Unknown to the revelers at the hall, a Palestinian from the al-Aqsa Martyrs Brigade, Abed Hassouna, had infiltrated into Israel that night. Armed with an automatic weapon, he opened fire on guests leaving the celebration and then killed the guard at the door of the hall. Once inside, he began to spray the crowd with gunfire. As the chaos erupted, Aaron Ellis attempted to shield another performer by pushing her to the ground and covering her with his own body. He was hit several times and bled to death on the floor. By his actions he managed to save the life of his band mate. Five others were killed in the attack and thirty-five were wounded.

As the intifada violence continued, and more and more lives were lost, the victims and families began to seek out the Israeli lawyers, asking that they represent them in legal actions. In short order the young attorneys were overwhelmed with all the cases being brought to them. Their meager resources and work space were proving way too inadequate. Shurat HaDin moved into a new office in Ramat Gan, just across the highway from Tel Aviv. The Victrola was gone, as were the rock posters and files on the floor. Additional staff was hired.

In July 2004, Gary Osen, an attorney from New Jersey, took the lead and filed the first civil action under the Anti-Terrorism Act against the Arab Bank in Brooklyn, New York. The plaintiffs, victims of the intifada violence, alleged that the bank had aided and abetted terrorism by providing financial services to the terrorist organizations in the West Bank and Gaza. They accused the bank of administering and transferring the funds that were being solicited and paid out as a rewards program to the terrorists and the families of the suicide bombers. It was claimed this intentional provision of payments to the terrorist induced the violence and encouraged additional suicide attacks. The Arab Bank had recklessly provided its services for the terrorist rewards program while maintaining an office in Manhattan. The federal courts had jurisdiction over the case and the bank could not escape. The case created quite a stir in U.S. litigation circles. Nitsana and her colleagues served as cocounsel with Osen in a number of the civil actions filed against the Arab Bank in New York.

In the aftermath of this first, well-publicized proceeding against a banking institution for terrorism, many law firms across the United States sprang into action and filed their own proceedings against the Arab Bank, copying the legal theory and allegations. The litigation firms understood that unlike the actions being brought against the state sponsors and the terror groups or even the Palestinian Authority, financial institutions had very deep pockets, and judgments against the banks could be easily enforced. Overnight these high-risk cases were now attracting the attention of the cowboy trial lawyers looking for the next broncos to break in.

The Israelis suddenly saw a gold rush of big American litigators, some with even bigger egos, flying into Israel and requesting urgent meetings with them. They were members of the personal injury and mass torts bar; they believed terror-victim litigation against financial institutions was going to become the next big trend in law, and they were determined not to miss out. The publicity from the early cases and the large judgment awards had gotten their attention and set off a frenzy of American law firms that wanted in on the action. Many lawyers fearful of being in the Jewish state at the time of intifada violence hired private security guards and armed drivers to accompany them around.

"It was really surreal. We spent days in hotel lobbies meeting with these asbestos, tobacco, plane crash, and silicone breast implant lawyers, dressed to the nines, pleading with us in their strange accents and southern drawls to work with them on terrorism cases," Nitsana recalled. "They started to take ads out in the papers soliciting victims to join their suits. The ads seemed very crude to us; it was like out of some John Grisham novel." Regardless of the motivation of the lawyers or the lawsuits, the fact remained that more and more cases started to get filed against the terrorists, the state sponsors, and the banks on behalf of the victims. A new area of international legal practice had been established.

Meir Dagan and the Harpoon leadership looked at this development with great delight.

CHAPTER TEN

The Higher Cost of Murder

Israelis divide the year by the Jewish holidays. The New Year signals in the onset of autumn and an end to the oppressive summer heat. Hanukah is the festival of lights, and the winter holiday illuminates homes across the country with a joyous sense of miracles. Passover—or Pesach, as it's known in Hebrew—is the holiday of freedom. Passover commemorates the story of the Exodus, and liberation from slavery in Egypt. The holiday ushers in the arrival of spring when hopes blossom throughout the country. The trees are lush and the flowers bloom during this festive season. It is a time of the year when the optimism is infectious.

Passover is a peak season for tourism to Israel and tourism *in* Israel. Jews from all over the Diaspora rush to the country to spend the precious few days with family and friends, while Israelis, off from work and school, visit the country's landmarks in massive numbers. Airlines and hotels raise prices to profit off the demand; traffic around the country is gridlocked. Tourism to Israel suffered a mighty blow during the intifada—only 718,000 foreign tourists visited in 2002, the bloodiest year of the violence, reflecting a sharp decline from the 2.7 million travelers who flocked to the nation's hotels and eateries in 2000.[1] Industries like tour guides and bus companies, as well as many hotels, had all but shut down as the suicide bombings escalated. The tourists, though, began to return. In 2006 they returned in strong numbers. The suicide bombings had become less frequent in the two previous years.

The tourists even returned to the gritty side streets around the old central bus station in Tel Aviv, in the Neve Sha'anan neighborhood. The area had deteriorated over time, and the neighborhood had become a slum, home to scores of Romanian, Bulgarian, African, and Filipino workers who flocked to Israel as replacements for Palestinian day laborers barred from entering the country because of the intifada. The area was high-crime, and littered with bars and brothels, as well as fast food holes-in-the-wall.

The Rosh Ha'Ir Shawarma restaurant on Salomon Street was always packed with hungry customers who were looking for a bargain meal. On January 19, 2006, the restaurant sustained serious damage when it was the target of a suicide bomber. The bomber, sent to Tel Aviv by the PIJ's Jerusalem Brigade, was inside the restaurant's restroom preparing his suicide vest when a malfunction caused it to detonate prematurely, muffling the force of the explosion. Still, thirty people were wounded in the blast.

Three months later the PIJ tried again. It was Passover. At 1:30 on the warm and brilliantly sunny afternoon of April 17, 2006, a suicide bomber attempted to enter the Rosh Ha'Ir Shawarma restaurant. A fair-skinned twenty-one-year-old from a small village near the West Bank town of Jenin, he zigzagged his way through the holiday chaos between the foreign workers and shoppers. A security guard, who had just been hired following the earlier attack, was positioned outside the establishment and challenged the young man. When he searched the young man's bag, a thunderous explosion punched through the restaurant and the surrounding street. Storefront windows disappeared into a million razor-sharp shards.

The guard, Benjamin Haputa, a forty-seven-year-old bachelor, was the first one to be killed. When he had taken the job, his sister asked him if he wasn't concerned for his safety. Haputa replied: "Wherever it's written I'll die, that's when I'll die. What is the chance that a terrorist will come twice to the same place to carry out an attack?"

The dead and the dying were eviscerated by the force of the blast and the shrapnel it spewed in all directions. By the time CNN was ready to go to air with a live report, nine people were already dead. Two more, Lior Anidzar, a twenty-six-year-old resident of Tel Aviv, and sixteen-year-old American Daniel Wultz of Weston, Florida, would die weeks later.[2]

*   *   *

The bombing of the Rosh Ha'Ir eatery in Tel Aviv was the deadliest Palestinian terrorist attack since the April 31, 2004, double suicide bombing of two buses in the southern city of Beersheba, in which sixteen were killed and more than one hundred were seriously wounded. It was the last catastrophic suicide attack of the intifada. In 2002, the year that Harpoon fell under the Mossad's order of battle, the Palestinian terrorist groups carried out forty-seven suicide bombings against civilians inside Israel, resulting in almost five hundred killed and thousands wounded. There were seventeen suicide bombings in 2004—sixty-four Israelis were killed in these attacks and several hundred more were seriously wounded.* By 2005, Palestinian terrorists launched nine attacks that killed thirty Israelis.

The war wasn't over, of course. The terrorist groups were still intent on dealing lethal blows to Israel's population centers whenever they could. But that window of opportunity had diminished over time. The Shin Bet and A'man had undermined the Palestinian terror leadership with a relentless intelligence-gathering effort involving human assets and signals intelligence. Entire networks had been destroyed by the Israeli intelligence surge. The special operations units that hunted terrorists for a living had more targets than they could go after as a result of the incoming intelligence. The most capable Palestinian lieutenants and operational commanders were dead or incarcerated; the next generation was too scared to rear their heads out in the open. The Shin Bet had a term for decapitating the terrorist leadership: It was known as "cutting the grass."

It had become harder for the suicide bombers to get into Israel. The government built a formidable security barrier stretching for much of the length of the West Bank. Palestinians struggled to smuggle suicide bombers across the once-invisible frontier. The separation barrier, which in some stretches was a sixty-foot-high concrete wall, mainly consisted of multi-tiered rows of fences, pyramid-shaped stacks of barbed-wire concertina,

---

* An additional thirty-four Israelis were killed on October 7, 2004, when a suicide bomber blew himself up at a resort in Egypt's Sinai Desert, targeting Israeli holiday travelers.

anti-intrusion technology, as well as adjacent patrol roads; watchtowers, manned by Israeli soldiers, dotted the barrier.

Just as important, the terror commanders no longer had free access to the endless flow of money from overseas. Meir Dagan and his Harpoon team had redefined the cost of terror. Fewer dollars and dinars were getting through the gauntlet. Financial institutions that had earned a hefty percentage point off of every wire transfer and martyr payment were now under great scrutiny. Transactions meant to be invisible were now public. Lawsuits had been filed. Bank managers and boards of directors in the Middle East were careful to exercise fiduciary responsibility over who their banks did business with, eager to avoid the spotlight of a federal courthouse in lower Manhattan or covert measures from Israeli intelligence.

Israel's security services had, at Harpoon's lead, focused on the men carrying cash with the same zeal that they did pursuing the suicide bombers who carried their explosive payloads into Israel's cities. The couriers, the smugglers, and the money changers found themselves under enormous pressure from police and the IDF.

That year, the disputed prime minister of the Palestinian Authority in Gaza, Ismail Haniyeh, visited Iran and was given a $40 million advance on the $250 million pledged by the Islamic Republic, in donations for Hamas. Haniyah was unable to utilize the banking system to wire the funds home, because financial institutions now refused to operate in terror zones like Gaza. The banks' fear of lawsuits outweighed their interest in the fees they could earn by transferring funds for the terror groups and rogue regimes. Haniyeh was forced to load the cash into twenty-five suitcases. After flying from Tehran to Sudan, the Hamas leader loaded the bags onto a leased truck and drove with an entourage of heavily armed security men across the desert into Egypt and then through Sinai to the Gaza border.

At the checkpoint, Haniyeh was stopped by the IDF. Tipped off about his hidden treasure, Israeli forces refused to allow him to enter with the funds that they knew would be utilized for terror. Ismail Haniyeh, however, would not agree to enter the Hamas enclave without his suitcases.

A standoff at the checkpoint ensued. Haniyeh demanded to be admitted with his luggage, insisting that he had diplomatic immunity. Israel refused to budge, stating that the Hamas leader could enter Gaza but the bags had to stay behind. The armed Hamas men grew impatient and wildly began to fire their weapons, shooting up the border crossing facility. Egyptian security forces fired back. At least fifteen Hamas members were injured in the fray.

Alerted to the escalating standoff on the Gaza border, the Arab League, and its twenty-two-nation membership, stepped in to assist Haniyeh. They offered to ferry the funds to a bank in Cairo and deposit them in a designated account in their name. The Hamas leader would proceed to Gaza and the Arab League would find a way to get the Iranian donations to Haniyeh in due course. Haniyeh and his colleagues reluctantly stuffed some of the money into their pockets and crossed into Gaza, while the remaining $35 million was deposited in the Cairo Amman Bank.[3]

Harpoon understood that the Arab League could interfere with their plan to keep the funds out of Gaza at all costs and decided to enlist some help of their own. A quick phone call was made to Nitsana Darshan-Leitner to see if there was a legal means to obstruct the money from getting to Hamas. There was.

Shortly before, Nitsana and her colleagues had won a judgment against Hamas in a federal court case on behalf of terror victims; damages were in the amount of $116 million. The civil action involved a young couple who had been ambushed and killed by Hamas gunfire near Beit Shemesh, a suburb of Jerusalem, in 1996. They were returning from a wedding with their infant child when the shooting took place. The parents were killed on the spot; the baby, below the line of fire in his car seat, was saved.

The family of Yaron and Efrat Unger were represented in the proceeding by attorneys Mordechai Haller, David Strachman, and Robert Tolchin, as well as by Nitsana. Legal proceedings were brought against the Arab League in Washington, D.C., where the group maintained an office. The suit demanded that the Arab League pay the Ungers the $35 million being held in its account in Cairo in partial satisfaction of the unpaid

$116 million judgment. Counsel for the Arab League filed a motion to dismiss the proceeding, arguing that the funds were not owned by Hamas but still belonged to Iran. The proof they pointed to was the fact that the money had never crossed the border into Gaza.

Yet, despite their public protestations, the Arab League secretly informed Ismail Haniyeh that upon the advice of their legal counsel they were restrained from moving the money from the bank account. The Hamas funds were tangled up in the American legal proceeding and they could not be moved. They would remain in Cairo for many years to come.

The terrorist leadership paid a price for the Harpoon-led vigilance. The cost of doing business increased significantly. "Bringing in suitcases full of cash from Lebanon or Gaza, or smuggling it across the Allenby Bridge inside cargo or inside someone involved greater risk, and risk cost money on the street," a COGAT officer assigned to Harpoon remembered. "Bringing in $100,000 into the West Bank now cost $200,000. Bringing in money through the Gaza Strip was incredibly difficult, and expensive. Many Palestinians suspected that the Egyptians didn't confiscate money they captured; they stole it. Egyptian Border Patrolmen and intelligence officers made a fortune off the bundles of cash destined for Gaza that had to take its circuitous route through Sinai."[4]

On February 14, 2005, a high-level U.S. Department of the Treasury delegation traveled to Israel for top-secret meetings with the heads of the National Security Council and representatives from Harpoon.[5] The American delegation was led by Stuart A. Levey, the Department of the Treasury's first Under Secretary for Terrorism and Financial Intelligence. A native of Akron, Ohio, Levey was a Harvard Law School graduate who had worked at the Department of Justice before moving over to Treasury. He was appointed to his position in 2004 by President George W. Bush and tasked with creating a U.S. counterterrorism response to 9/11 and unraveling the intricate web of terrorist financing that had enabled al-Qaeda to present a clear and present danger to the United States and the world. Levey's office, known by the acronym of TFI, was President

Bush's point man in the money side of the global war on terror; Levey's responsibilities also included dealing with the dollars and dictators from rogue states like Syria, North Korea, Libya, and, of course, Iran.

From their first meeting together, Meir Dagan and Levey hit it off. The Mossad director recognized in the American a kindred spirit and a man of action. Below Levey's runner's physique and calm outward appearance was an iron determination and tough-as-nails resolve. The Treasury official was constantly trying to push the envelope in the financial war. The Harpoon guys all thought highly of him, as well. Levey was joined by other Department of Treasury deputies, as well as Internal Revenue special agents, and members of the U.S. Secret Service.

Brigadier General Danny Arditi led the Israeli team. Most of the Israeli representatives were from the IDF and A'man. Uri L. and Shai U. represented Harpoon. The Americans didn't know that Dagan's unit was called Harpoon—they referred to Uri and Shai as belonging to the "Counterterrorism Financing Bureau."[6] The meeting was held in Ramat HaSharon, an affluent suburb north of Tel Aviv.

The Americans and the Israelis reviewed recent events on the ground in the West Bank and the Gaza Strip. Pressure from the United States convinced the Saudis to stem the flow of unregulated NGO funding to the territories. The end of Saudi money was a dire blow to Hamas, but still funds came in. Hamas, the principals discussed, still received a $3 million stipend annually from the Iranians; additional funds still came in from wealthy oil sheiks in Kuwait, Qatar, and the United Arab Emirates.

Most of the discussions centered on Iran and Hezbollah. The Israelis wanted to coordinate efforts with the Americans to target the Islamic Republic and their Party of God proxy in Lebanon. They discussed stopping the banks in Lebanon that facilitated the laundering of Hezbollah money. Shai U. shared some intelligence that the Israelis had gathered: The Arab Bank, involved in a make-or-break lawsuit in lower Manhattan for its role in helping fund Palestinian terror, was now openly dealing with Hezbollah.[7]

Both sides tried to figure out a coordinated strategy—the Americans with political moves and the Israelis through COGAT—to siphon money destined for Hamas away from the terrorist group and into the coffers of Palestinian social service agencies and legitimate charities.

Later that year, Prime Minister Sharon surprised most Israelis—and much of the world—and announced that Israel was abandoning the Gaza Strip. The unilateral withdrawal from Gaza, in the late summer of 2005, was one of the final acts in office for Prime Minister Ariel Sharon and one of the most controversial. Sharon had known what a headache Gaza was and how impossible it would be for the IDF to seize the narrow, densely populated sliver of land again without unacceptable casualties in combat that would certainly be close-quarter. Sharon had kicked around the idea of Israel just pulling stakes and departing the Strip on its own terms for two years. By September 2005 the "disengagement" had been completed: A total of twenty-one settlements, some there since the 1967 War, were evacuated despite fierce emotional and riotous protests; eight thousand settlers were relocated to other towns throughout Israel. Israeli forces controlled all access points in and out of the Gaza Strip. A mighty Israeli presence remained along the frontiers; the Palestinian Authority was given control over day-to-day government in the Strip except for the borders, the airspace, and the territorial waters. Israeli forces still continued the campaign of preventing the smuggling of arms and money in the hundreds of tunnels that had been built underneath the Philadelphi route along the Strip's southern border.

The disengagement from Gaza sent a fissure into the heart of right-wing Israeli politics. In November 2005 Sharon split from the Likud Party to launch a new centrist-of-right party called Kadima, or "Forward"; his arch political rival, Benjamin Netanyahu, assumed the helm of the Likud Party. New elections were expected. Then, in January 2006, Prime Minister Sharon suffered a debilitating stroke, placing him in an irreversible coma. Ehud Olmert, his deputy and the former mayor of Jerusalem, was slated to assume the premiership.

Olmert was sworn in as the Israeli Prime Minister on April 17, 2006—hours after the lethal suicide bombing of the Rosh Ha'Ir Shawarma restaurant. "We had hoped to celebrate the Israeli democracy today in a different atmosphere," Olmert said in response to the horrific blast scene, "and now we are again forced to cope with murderous terror."[8]

Olmert would have been well within his rights to ask Meir Dagan for his resignation. Dagan, and Shin Bet Director Yuval Diskin, served at the pleasure of the prime minister. But Olmert wasn't a soldier, nor was he a steadfast ideologue. He was a politician and, as mayor of Jerusalem, he had learned pragmatism in the toughest city to govern in the world. Olmert appreciated his shortcomings. He realized that with the intifada running out of steam, there would be new threats facing the State of Israel and that he'd need the best and brightest—and the most audacious—by his side. Even though Dagan had lost his prime benefactor and cheerleader when Sharon fell ill, Olmert was a great fan of the Mossad director. What was more, the new prime minister championed Harpoon and the campaign against terror money. "Olmert liked us," a Harpoon veteran remembered, "not only did he like what we were doing but he constantly maintained contact with us to see what he could be doing to help us."[9]

A lawyer by training and practice, Olmert took a vivid interest in the legal warfare on both a professional and personal level. He enjoyed pumping the agents about the details of the litigation, the motions that were filed, and the defense's response, as well as the blow-by-blow of the court rulings. Nitsana observed how Olmert was always asking to be updated about what was happening as the pioneer civil suits against the rogue regimes, the terror groups, and the financial institutions were being prosecuted. "He was captivated and amused by what creative private lawyers could do to wreak havoc against the terrorists and their funding networks," she said. Every time we met with the Harpoon guys, they always told us 'Olmert loves these lawsuits, he's always laughing about them, he always wants to hear about every little detail and maneuver.'"

Even with Sharon gone, Dagan and his team weren't going anywhere. Olmert wanted his intelligence chief to continue what he had started with Harpoon. The financial campaign against Hamas, while still ongoing, had been a success. Everyone knew that Hezbollah was the next target.

PART II

THE PARTY OF GOD AND THE DEVIL'S PORTFOLIO

CHAPTER ELEVEN

The Party of God

Pity the nation divided into fragments, each fragment
deeming itself a nation.
—*Kahlil Gibran, "The Garden of the Prophet"*

Meir Dagan sat in his office on the morning of July 12, 2006, immersed in his morning's routine. Wednesdays were busy at Mossad HQ, and Dagan often began his day at 7:00 AM. Like his predecessors, Dagan wore a button-down shirt and a blazer to work, Israeli business casual. The spymasters needed to wear a tie only on occasions of ceremony, or when visiting their counterparts overseas.

Dagan's office was large and spacious, an impressive room befitting a man whose legend and responsibilities were larger than life. The room was adorned with memorabilia from Dagan's days in uniform—wooden plaques and unit banners from his time in Gaza. There were photos all over, quite a few of Dagan and Sharon and other friends and contemporaries in the intelligence world. There were also paintings, colorful oils, of Middle Eastern vistas and sheikhs adorned in colorful robes. Dagan was an amateur painter, and the Arab world was his favorite subject. The photo of his grandfather, moments before being killed by the Nazis, was the centerpiece of the office. "Dagan felt that it was his responsibility, the Mossad's responsibility, to protect Israelis and Jews anywhere in the world. It didn't matter where or how, the lives of Jews weighed on his conscience," Rami Ben-Barak, head of Mossad special operations under Dagan, recalled, "and he let everyone he met know it."[1] Dagan used to brief agents in his office before they were sent overseas on difficult assignments and talk about the photograph.

Dagan's desk was large and antique, and made of wood. The desk was full of framed photos of Bina, his wife of thirty-four years, and photos of their three kids. Many of the photos were from the jeep trips that the family took on weekends. Meir Dagan worked from sunrise and often came home at midnight, five days a week. Weekends were always reserved for hiking or jeep trips in the desert or the Israeli countryside.

Dagan always kept a cup of piping-hot tea within arm's length. The tea was always served in a glass, the way a Russian general would drink his tea. A slice of freshly cut lemon was always in the glass. He never drank coffee. Dagan had one vice—his pipe. An ashtray was buried somewhere amid the mountains of papers and folders. The smell of sweet tobacco wafted over Israel's most sensitive secrets, files marked *Sodi Be'Yoter*, or "Top Secret." Books were piled on Dagan's desk and lined shelves; books sat on the floor, too, and on chairs not being used. Although he was in charge with Israel's most secretive intelligence force, Dagan always surrounded himself with books, mostly historical or biographical. There was also a bank of telephones, some with straight connections to the prime minister's office. The phones, like other items on Dagan's desk, were all stained by the pipe smoke.

Chairs were always prepositioned for visitors. Dagan liked it when he had visitors in his office, especially men like Uri, who shared his sarcastic sense of humor. Bina Dagan recalls that Meir loved to tell off-color jokes when in the company of his friends.[2]

Dagan's security detail was always outside his office. Sarah,* his secretary, was the true gatekeeper, however. She was an iron lady. She, more than others, could see the weight of responsibility carved into Dagan's face on those nights when men and women were risking their lives in

---

* Sarah is a pseudonym.

dangerous precincts far from Israel's shores. The burden of commanding Israel's spies was, at times, overwhelming, and it involved long hours of discussion and planning. Tension, it seemed, was a permanent guest in Dagan's office. Sarah always made sure that the director adhered to his frenetic schedule. She, too, arrived at work at dawn and she stayed until he called it a day. Even when the director stayed at his desk well into the night, sometimes after midnight, Sarah kept her boss's hours.[3]

The television monitors inside Dagan's office were always tuned to CNN and one of the European news networks. Sky News was always popular in Mossad headquarters—more popular, at least, than the BBC, whose news tended to have an anti-Israeli bias.

The news that morning was of particular interest to Dagan. The leaders of the G-8* nations were set to meet in Russia, in the opulence of Constantine Palace, located in Strelna on the Gulf of Finland. The palace had been a favorite of the czars, and now the backdrop of gold and splendor would be used by the world's most powerful elite to discuss the pressing issues of the day. One of the primary topics was the Islamic Republic of Iran and its pursuit of a nuclear weapons capability. Israeli prime ministers had pressed several American presidents to push all the diplomatic—and economic—buttons at their disposal to stymie Iran's effort. Meir Dagan had spoken to several CIA directors and conveyed a similar request. Now the subject had come up for an international consensus. He watched the news coverage, hoping for something that was releasable prior to the conference beginning.

Mostly, though, the Mossad director watched the news that morning to hear if there were any Arab media reports from the Gaza Strip. On June 25, 2006, a Hamas squad tunneled its way under the rows of concertina wire separating the Gaza Strip from Israel and emerged on the Israeli side of the fence. The squad attacked a tank with grenade and small-arms fire, then abducted a soldier, Corporal Gilad Shalit, dragging him back into

---

* The G-8 included the leaders of the United States, Canada, Great Britain, France, Germany, Japan, Italy, and Russia. The European Union was also represented at the summit.

the abyss of the Gaza Strip. Dagan pressed all the resources at his disposal to assemble some sort of actionable intelligence that would give the IDF the option to prepare a reasonable sort of rescue bid for Shalit, and sometimes the news offered interesting tidbits. Without pinpoint intelligence, it was unlikely that Israel would mount a rescue operation into the Gaza Strip. Covert negotiations were underway to try and figure out how Israel could get its young soldier back. Hamas knew that the State of Israel would pay a hefty price for Shalit's return. Even though Israel had, as one of the pillars of its counterterrorism doctrine, a vow never to negotiate with terrorists, the Jewish state routinely agreed to horrifically lopsided trades to get its troops—both alive and dead—back in exchange for hundreds, sometimes thousands, of terrorists released from prison.

Dagan watched the news. He read the reports. Hamas was what was known in Hebrew as a *Kotz Ba'tachat*: it was "a thorn in the ass," and it wasn't going away. There were other, more dire threats that would occupy Dagan and especially Harpoon.

Shortly after 9:00 AM on the morning of July 12, 2006, Dagan was in his office reviewing papers. He glanced at the network coverage and took a sip of tea. He held his pipe. And then the phones in his office began to ring. Sarah rushed in with a concerned, angry, look on her face; deputies and military liaisons also rushed in. Prime Minister Ehud Olmert's office was on the phone.

Hezbollah, the Lebanese Shiite Party of God and the Islamic Republic of Iran's proxy along Israel's northern border, had launched close to one hundred fire-and-forget rockets at Israeli military positions near the border village of Zar'it, as well as on several small farming communities near the frontier with Lebanon. The barrage was nothing more than a destructive diversion. A Hezbollah direct-action team, dressed in IDF uniforms and fluent in Hebrew, crossed the frontier into Israel and attacked a patrol of two IDF vehicles with improvised explosive devices (IEDs), and anti-tank missile and small arms fire. Three IDF soldiers were killed in the attack and two injured. Two reservists—Sergeant Ehud Goldwasser and Sergeant Eldad Regev—were hurt in the fusillade and then carried back into Lebanon. Five more soldiers were killed in the Israeli attempt to rescue the two wounded soldiers.

Full-scale combat erupted hours later as large-scale Israeli forces entered Lebanon to look for the two kidnapped soldiers. Hezbollah rockets rained down on northern Israel, wreaking havoc upon the northern towns and cities; the border had been relatively quiet for nearly six years. The Second Lebanon War had begun.

The summer of 2006 marked the twenty-fourth year that the Shiites of Lebanon were at war with the State of Israel. The Shiites, the largest of the three primary religious groups that made up the Lebanese patchwork of rival faiths and tribes, were also the poorest and most politically disenfranchised. A large percentage of Lebanon's Shiites lived as farmers, as their parents and their grandparents had done for centuries. The Shiite population centers were in the fertile lands of the south, between the Mediterranean and the mountains, and in the eastern areas near the Syrian frontier in the Beka'a Valley. A large Shiite population also lived in the impoverished neighborhoods in south Beirut. The Shiites had suffered under Ottoman rule; their lot improved slightly at the end of the First World War under French rule. The Lebanese constitution drafted in 1943 mandated that the president of the country be a Christian, the prime minister be a Sunni, and the speaker of the parliament be a Shiite. The lopsided power share was designed to keep the peace.

Lebanon's delicate balance of power, one secured by tribal chits and vengeance, endured four seismic shifts. The first was in 1948 when some one hundred thousand Palestinian refugees fled the fighting around Israel's independence and headed north. Most were settled in refugee camps near the coastal cities of Tyre and Sidon, and in the slums of Beirut. The Palestinian arrivals were largely Sunnis. They came in 1971 when, following the Jordanian Civil War, the Palestinian terror factions set up their global headquarters in Beirut and a new front against Israel opened up in southern Lebanon; groups ranging from Arafat's Fatah to the North Korean–supported Democratic Front for the Liberation of Palestine used the camps of southern Lebanon as launching pads for horrifically bloody attacks against northern Israel. Each attack warranted Israeli retaliation. The Shiites were often caught in the crossfire and often subjected to harsh treatment at the hands of the armed Palestinian gangs who imposed a lawless state in the countryside of Lebanon's south.[4] Farmers often had to surrender a portion of their crops, of their earnings, to local Palestinian commanders.[5] South Lebanon slowly morphed into what became known as "Fatah Land."

Lebanon's bloody civil war was the third blow to the mosaic of coexistence that had miraculously endured a weak central government compromised of heavily armed factions beholden to one of the region's more powerful nations. The civil war redefined the Middle East's definition of carnage: More than fifty thousand civilians were killed in the bloodletting. Most of the fighting pitted the Sunni factions, especially the Palestinians, against the Israeli-backed Christian militias. The Shiites were not active combatants in the civil war, though the power vacuum in Beirut coincided with a new sense of Shiite pride and devout religious faith. Religious universities in Iraq, such as those in Najaf, fueled a new breed of clerics whose sermons were aflame with honor and a demand for political and social justice. Sayyid Musa al-Sadr was the spiritual leader of Lebanon's Shiites. He vanished, never to be seen again, during a trip to Libya in August 1978. Iran's new Islamic revolutionaries—and the emissaries they sent—sensed an opportunity to extend their influence, and their extremist ideological insurrection soon filled the void.

The Shiites and the State of Israel were, at first, beneficiaries of the ancient Middle Eastern axiom that "the enemy of my enemy is my ally." Israel had supported a Christian militia in southern Lebanon that attracted many Shiite volunteers. This was a type of proxy force that acted as a stoppage against the increasingly aggressive PLO. When the IDF entered Lebanon on June 6, 1982, to launch Operation Peace for Galilee and rid the country of the twenty thousand armed Palestinian fighters that had become its de facto rulers, the Shiite villagers of southern Lebanon greeted the advancing Israeli soldiers as liberators. Israeli soldiers were

A money changer in the Old City of Jerusalem, circa 1974. Such unofficial but traditional means of money transfers remain common inside the Palestinian areas.
(Moshe Milner, Israel Government Press Office/ Photo Archives)

Captain Meir Dagan (left), the commander of the Sayeret Rimon undercover commandos, masquerading as a Palestinian fisherman, during operations with his unit off the Gaza coast, 1971.
(Courtesy Bina Dagan)

A photo taken during a lull in his reconnaissance unit's operations in Gaza, Meir Dagan poses with his pistol.
(Courtesy Bina Dagan)

With a military rabbi officiating, Meir Dagan marries his wife, Bina. After four years of dating, the future Mrs. Dagan gave Meir a nuptial ultimatum that prompted him to race to a market in Gaza and purchase his wedding suit.
(Courtesy Bina Dagan)

Colonel Meir Dagan, commander of the 188th Barak Armored Brigade, smiles at his command post at the outskirts of Beirut, July 1982. The bitter fighting and carnage in Lebanon would forever change him and his outlook on war.
(Courtesy Bina Dagan)

Sitting in his wheelchair, Sheikh Ahmed Yassin, the founder of Hamas, is flanked by two IDF military policemen at his 1990 trial for the murder and kidnapping of Israeli servicemen and civilians.
(SVEN NACKSTRAD/AFP/ Getty Images)

The tourists from the Windy City: Mohammed al-Hamid Khalil Salah, and Mohammed Jarad, the two Palestinian-Americans from Chicago arrested by the Shin Bet for bringing suitcases full of cash to Hamas from the United States in early 1993.
(Ya'acov Sa'ar/Israel Government Press Office/Photo Archives)

Israeli Prime Minister Yitzhak Rabin and PLO leader Yasir Arafat shake hands on the White House lawn on September 13, 1993, ushering in new hopes for peace in the Middle East that would rapidly deteriorate into vicious terrorist bloodshed.
(Avi Ohayon/Israel Government Press Office/Photo Archives)

FBI wanted poster for Ramadan Abdallah Shalah, former professor at the University of Southern Florida at Tampa and head of the Palestinian Islamic Jihad.

(FBI)

Rescue workers and first responders sift through the eviscerated remnants of the No. 18 bus in downtown Jerusalem, hit by a Hamas suicide bomber on March 3, 1996, killing 19 people. A week earlier, a Hamas suicide bomber blew himself up on the same exact bus route in an attack that killed 26 people and wounded scores more.

(Photo by David Rubinger/The LIFE Images Collection/Getty Images)

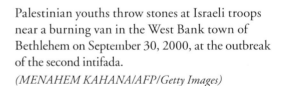

Palestinian youths throw stones at Israeli troops near a burning van in the West Bank town of Bethlehem on September 30, 2000, at the outbreak of the second intifada.

(MENAHEM KAHANA/AFP/Getty Images)

The bombed-out remnants of the Sbarro pizzeria on the corner of King George Street and the Jaffa Road in Jerusalem, decimated by a Hamas suicide bomber on August 9, 2001. Fifteen people were killed in the attack and close to 100 wounded. The money that funded the attack had been funneled through banking institutions in the West Bank.

(Avi Ohayon/Israel Government Press Office/Photo Archives)

The FBI wanted poster for Ahlam Tamimi, an accomplice to the Sbarro pizzeria suicide bombing attack, seeking her arrest for the killing of American citizens. Tamimi was captured by Israeli forces but freed in the Gilad Shalit prisoner exchange with Hamas in 2011, then exiled to Jordan. The U.S. Department of Justice filed criminal charges against Tamimi in 2013 for conspiring to use a weapon of mass destruction against American nationals outside the continental United States.
(FBI)

Counterfeit Israeli shekels found by Israeli forces inside Yasir Arafat's Ramallah headquarters on March 30, 2002.
(IDF)

Prime Minister Ariel Sharon (right) toasts Meir Dagan with a *Le'Hayim*, "To Life," as he appoints his old friend to head the Mossad on October 30, 2002 —it was a job that Dagan had wanted his entire life.
(Sa'ar Ya'acov/Israel Government Press Office Photo Archives)

The photo of Meir Dagan's grandfather, moments before being murdered by the Nazis, was one of the most important fixtures inside Dagan's office at Mossad HQ. Agents about to embark on dangerous assignments overseas were briefed on the image's symbolic importance to the intelligence agency and its mission in protecting Israelis—and Jews—around the world.
(Courtesy Bina Dagan)

Operation Green Lantern: An Israeli Border Guard counterterrorist operator stands in front of the Cairo Amman Bank in the West Bank city of Ramallah on February 25, 2004. Israeli forces raided banks in Ramallah and other West Bank cities to locate and seize money and accounts used by Hamas and other terrorist factions. *(ABBAS MOMANI/AFP/Getty Images)*

The "U2s," Shai U. (left) and Uri L. (right) pose with Nitsana Darshan-Leitner at a Shurat HaDin conference in Jerusalem. *(Aviel Leitner)*

U.S. President George W. Bush and Israeli Prime Minister Ehud Olmert embrace Meir Dagan (center) during a top-level meeting in Washington, D.C. Dagan helped to foster an alliance with the CIA in the global war on terror, as well as with other facets of the U.S. government. President Bush was a big admirer of Dagan's courage and imaginative dare. *(Courtesy Bina Dagan)*

Hezbollah chief Sheikh Hassan Nasrallah appears at a rally with armed guards. Under Nasrallah's ruthless leadership, Hezbollah became the most powerful military force in Lebanon and helped to turn the southern portion of the country into a de facto Israeli border with Iran. *(Yannis KONTOS/SYGMA via Getty Images)*

Israeli warplanes pound the tarmac at Beirut International Airport during the opening days of the Second Lebanon War. Israel was determined to isolate Hezbollah inside the country and to dismantle the state-within-a-state that the Party of God had built.
(JOSEPH BARRAK/AFP/Getty Images)

Salah Ezzedine, the self-made small-town boy who became a millionaire a hundred times over, is seen here waving at the cameras during a philanthropic event in southern Lebanon. Ezzedine would later be called the "Lebanese Madoff" after defrauding countless Shiites throughout Lebanon, including virtually all of the Hezbollah hierarchy.
(AFP)

IDF soldiers cross the Israel–Lebanon border on August 15, 2006, at the end of the Second Lebanon War.
(GALI TIBBON/AFP/Getty Images)

Palestinian terrorists prepare to fire Qassam rockets into Israel from a concealed location on the outskirts of the Gaza Strip, December 20, 2008.
(AP Photo/ASHRAF AMRA)

An image grab taken from a video released by Dubai police on February 24, 2010, allegedly shows two suspects sought in the January 2010 murder of Hamas commander Mahmoud al-Mabhouh at Dubai International Airport.
(AFP PHOTO/DUBAI POLICE)

Muslim Brotherhood and Hamas movement poster plastered on a wall in the Gaza Strip on January 29, 2010, mourning Mahmoud al-Mabhouh, allegedly killed by Israeli intelligence in Dubai.
(MOHAMMED ABED/AFP/ Getty Images)

During a press conference on February 15, 2010, Dubai police chief Dhafi Khalfan holds up identity pictures of 11 suspects, all with European passports belonging to the alleged hit team that killed Hamas commander Mahmoud al-Mabhouh on January 20, 2010.
(AFP PHOTO/DUBAI POLICE)

Firefighters clear the wreckage of the car that carried Hamas finance chief Mohammed el-Ghoul and several million dollars, after it was hit by an Israeli airstrike in Gaza.
(Naaman Omar—Anadolu Agency)

Courtroom sketch of lead trial attorney Kent Yalowitz giving his closing arguments on February 20, 2015, in the case of *Sokolow vs. Palestine Liberation Organization* in federal court in lower Manhattan.

(Courtesy Elizabeth Williams)

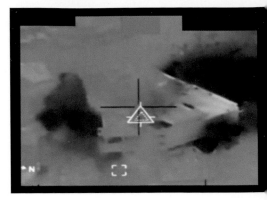

Coalition aircraft strike an ISIS financial center and cash warehouse in Mosul, Iraq, on January 13, 2016.

(U.S. Department of Defense)

Nitsana Darshan-Leitner and Kent Yalowitz address the media in the wake of the landmark jury verdict in the case of *Sokolow vs. Palestine Liberation Organization* outside the federal courthouse in New York.

(Aviel Leitner)

The authors with Meir Dagan, Tel Aviv, September 2015.

(Aviel Leitner)

blanketed with rice and sweets thrown by the appreciative Shiite villagers. The affection and gratitude were short-lived, however. On November 11, 1982, a Shiite suicide bomber drove a Peugeot crammed with explosives through the Israeli military headquarters complex in the Lebanese port city of Tyre. The blast killed seventy-five soldiers, Border Guard policemen, and Shin Bet agents.

For the next eighteen years, Israeli forces in Lebanon found themselves at war against fanatic suicidal Shiite militias. Hezbollah, Arabic for "the Party of God," became the most powerful and prominent. Handsomely subsidized by the Islamic Republic of Iran and a global network of smugglers, drug merchants, and other criminal pursuits, Hezbollah was able to match Israeli forces on the battlefield and develop into one of the most powerful of all the Arab armies. Israeli forces, like many counterinsurgency forces, operated in southern Lebanon out of a series of outposts and fortifications that became easy targets for Hezbollah IEDs and attacks. Casualties mounted. Many inside Israel viewed the continued and costly Israeli presence in southern Lebanon as pointless.

In May 2000 Prime Minister Ehud Barak ordered the IDF to unilaterally withdraw from the quagmire. Hezbollah was determined to have the last word. In October 2000, Hezbollah kidnapped three Israeli soldiers patrolling the fence along the border with Lebanon; there were subsequent accusations that United Nations peacekeepers assisted the terrorists in the operation.[6] The bodies of the three soldiers were returned four years later in an exchange of live Party of God prisoners for the three coffins. Many in Israel now referred to the north as "our Iranian border."

As Israel fought the intifada against Palestinians in the West Bank and Gaza, Hezbollah prepared for its own war against Israel—one that it intended to fight on the Israeli side of the fence. Hezbollah's army consisted of suicide squads armed with explosive vests and small arms; there were missile batteries, some firing advanced Iranian-supplied rockets, that were capable of hitting the major population centers of northern and central Israel. Hezbollah's missiles and rockets were hidden inside densely populated areas, in the hope that Israeli retaliation would result in heavy

Lebanese casualties that could be presented to the international community as war crimes against civilians. Sheikh Hassan Nasrallah, Hezbollah's Beirut-born and Iraqi-educated leader, was a savvy tactician who did not mind sacrificing his own people for the political and battlefield advantage. This was a direct page out of the ideological teachings of his Shiite hero, Iran's Ayatollah Ruhollah Khomeini. In the eyes of world opinion, in trying to mobilize the Arab street, Nasrallah knew that the images of women and children killed by the Israel Air Force would play well on the carnivorous Arab news networks seen twenty-four hours a day.

Israel responded to the Hezbollah rockets with air and artillery strikes, just as Nasrallah predicted. Israel then imposed an air and naval blockade on Lebanon.[7] The IAF cratered the runways at Beirut–Rafic Hariri International Airport to prevent arms from being flown in and Hezbollah commanders from fleeing. Bridges and tunnels throughout southern Lebanon were also struck in an effort to close off escape routes for the team that abducted the two Israeli reservists. There were fears that Hezbollah would try to fly the two captured Israeli soldiers out of the country.

Prime Minister Olmert convened an emergency meeting for his security cabinet shortly after the war's eruption. Unlike many of the other prime ministers before him, Olmert knew little about war; he worked as a military journalist during his mandatory IDF service. Olmert was a professional politician. His platform was status quo, possibly peace, and not a new war in Lebanon. Olmert's defense minister, Amir Peretz, had reached the rank of captain in the military, but he was a labor organizer and union chief. In an infamous photograph, widely circulated during his tenure, Peretz was snapped looking out across a battlefield with the protective caps still on the field glasses. Olmert and Peretz, as the pair at the helm of Israel's war machine, did little to instill confidence in the nation. Moreover, IDF Chief of Staff Lieutenant General Dan Halutz had come from the air force and had very little ground combat experience. The IDF had spent the last six years fighting suicide bombers and was caught off guard by the audacity and ferocity of the Hezbollah attack.

Olmert's security cabinet, the ministers and the generals wearing a rainbow of different berets tucked under their epaulettes who sat around the conference table, knew that dislodging Hezbollah from Lebanon's south would be a difficult task—even for a military as mighty as the IDF. There were no lightning victories foreseen, no waving the Star of David atop a hill in southern Lebanon that would signal an end to hostilities. Hezbollah vowed to fight to the death, and the IDF would have to remove the Party of God fighters from their heavily fortified villages and caves; the Iranians wouldn't stand for anything less.

There was no singular target, no head of the snake, that the might of the Israel Air Force could strike that would decisively render Hezbollah rudderless and ineffective. Local commanders were battle experienced and disciplined. Some had undergone advanced commander courses in Syria and Iran. The organization was rigidly constructed with a hierarchy of structure, with both military and political wings dedicated to power and might. Still, Sheikh Nasrallah conveniently went into hiding hours before the kidnapping operation, reportedly bivouacked in an underground bunker dug deep under a building in south Beirut that had been prepared for the eventuality.

There were no illusions—either in Israel or in the west—that the Hezbollah strike was anything but a war by proxy green-lit by the Islamic Republic of Iran. The kidnap operation was seen as an attempt by Tehran to deflect attention at the G-8 Summit away from talks about Iranian nuclear aspirations. Prime Minister Olmert knew that in eradicating Hezbollah from southern Lebanon, Israel wasn't alone. Publicly, U.S. President George W. Bush supported the Israeli military response. "Israel has the right to defend herself," the president stated as he prepared to fly from Germany to Russia for the G-8. "There are a group of terrorists who want to stop the advance of peace. The soldiers need to be returned."[8]

All over Israel, men between the ages of twenty and early forties closed their businesses and grabbed worn-out olive uniforms from cellars and closets. They said tearful good-byes to their wives and children and headed toward assembly points throughout the country for transports heading north so that they could join their units. The IDF was a citizens' army dependent on its reserve divisions. The conscripts were already fighting and dying in Lebanon. Israeli forces met stiff resistance inside Lebanon. Rockets, sometimes in barrages of hundreds at a time, continued to fall all over Israel's north. As Israel contemplated a strategy and a response, tens of thousands of Israeli families headed to their bomb shelters where one night under fire would soon turn into a destructive and agonizing month under siege. Over the course of the next few days more than one million Israelis, one-seventh of the nation's population, had to stay near or in bomb shelters or security rooms. Nearly a quarter of a million men, women, and children, had to be evacuated away from the northern population centers.[9]

Many of Hezbollah's rockets, especially those that came in from Iran and as far afield as North Korea, were assembled in Syria, in a village called al-Hameh, located in a valley northwest of the capital of Damascus. Under the cover of darkness, the assembled Katyusha rockets were loaded onto trucks bearing no markings and nothing distinguishable from the ground or air. The trucks traveled only at night. The convoys moved slowly and cautiously, across the Beirut-Damascus Highway into Lebanon and then through the Beka'a Valley toward Hezbollah-controlled lines. Before dawn's first light, Hezbollah operatives unloaded the trucks and stored the rockets in a network of residential buildings all across the Shiite towns and villages of the south.

The Bedouin village of Arab al-Aramsa was situated just inside the Israeli side of the northern border with Lebanon. Because of its close proximity to the Lebanese frontier, it was subjected to endless warning sirens during the summer war that had erupted between Hezbollah and Israel. Each time Hezbollah terrorists fired one of their rockets toward Israel the alarms would begin to blare, and everyone in the village would scramble. While most of the missiles flew far overhead, some impacted nearby. Not everybody ran to the shelters once the red alert sounded, however. Many could not believe that Hezbollah would deliberately aim their weapons against their Arab brothers and sisters. The Jumaa family was extra cautious. They had built a special security room in their house—as Israeli law now required in all new construction—to protect them from the fall of the missiles coming from the Hezbollah positions a mere mile or two away.

On the evening of August 5, 2006, the family ran to their security room when the alarm sounded. They crowded into the small reinforced bunker. Fadia, the sixty-year-old family matriarch, was at home with her two daughters: Sultana, thirty-one, and Samira, thirty-three. They waited the full ten minutes, as is required, until they felt the danger had passed and it was safe to emerge from the shelter. They were careful not to take any chances, especially when the family's patriarch, Harush, was not home. It was a Saturday, a day off in Israel, so the three women stepped out to sit on their balcony to get some fresh air after the nerve-racking ordeal of squeezing together in that small, cramped room.

The moment the women sat down, however, another missile was fired from Lebanon. This time no alert was sounded. The rocket exploded right on the balcony of their modest home and killed the three of them on the spot.

Word spread quickly throughout the small village that the Jumaa family home had been hit by a Hezbollah missile. Harush, who was visiting a friend nearby, heard the rocket's impact, as well, and rushed to his house fearful of what he would find. He frantically dug through the rubble for an hour that seemed endless, hysterically yelling the names of his wife and daughters. "Where are you, Samira? Where are you, Sultana?" Harush screamed, his voice caked with indescribable grief and horror.

Sultana's fiancé, a neighbor, rushed over as well. When he saw the damage inflicted to the home, he was paralyzed by anguish. Tears rolled down his cheeks as his lips quivered in sorrow. "Sultana visited me just this morning and told me how much she loved you," a neighbor told the young man. The words seemed to make everything even worse. The rocket from al-Hameh had destroyed a family's world completely. Hezbollah's war was far more than a conflict for the political pleasure of the Party of God's patrons in Iran. Nasrallah's campaign was an all-out total war, one specifically targeting civilians, and it was killing men, women, and children, of all faiths.

There was fierce debate inside Israel as to its endgame in Lebanon. Some politicians and generals feared that Nasrallah was laying a trap for Israel, hoping to lure the IDF into another bloody quagmire, and warned that the Israeli response should be tempered. Others viewed the Hezbollah provocation and an opportunity to once and for all eradicate the Party of God, or at least dismantle its military infrastructure for a generation. Israeli generals and politicians concurred on one thing: that Israel would have a limited time to carry out its mission before American political backing came to an end and international pressure, already demanding a cease-fire, obstructed their hand.

Of all the men who made the decision as to how Israel could and would prosecute its war against Hezbollah, Meir Dagan was one man who understood just how dangerous and completely volatile the Lebanese battlefield was. Dagan knew the country as a military commander who led columns of tanks inside the country and as the man who ran agents inside Lebanon—both during his time as liaison commander during the 1990s and now as Mossad director. Dagan wanted to spearhead Israel's response with Harpoon tactics in the conventional fight against the Shiite militants. During heated conversations—sometimes yelling matches—inside Olmert's security cabinet, Dagan demanded that the IAF bomb Lebanon's banks. Dagan called for the specific targeting of financial institutions that were used by Iran and Hezbollah.

Israel had never bombed an Arab bank from the air: not in the 1948 War of Independence, not in 1956, and not even in 1967 when Israel's air force destroyed targets as far away as the Iraqi desert and the Egyptian Nile Delta. Even in the 1973 War, when Defense Minister Moshe Dayan—who, fearing that the unstoppable charge of Syrian tanks atop the Golan would lead to Israel's destruction, suggested that Israel display its nuclear weapons potential[10]—didn't target financial institutions in the

Arab capitals. Israeli ground forces never targeted Arab banks with artillery barrages or tank fire.

The generals, including Chief of Staff Halutz, would have none of Dagan's argument. The aircraft were needed for tactical targets in support of IDF ground operations and the effort to eradicate the Hezbollah missiles; hundreds of sorties were flown to destroy medium-range Fajr rocket launching sites throughout the south of the country, as well as long-range Zelzal-2 missiles that could hit Israel's heavily populated areas in the central part of the country. Hitting the banks was considered superfluous, too wasteful. More than one hundred Hezbollah rockets hit Israel's towns and cities every day.

Prime Minister Olmert had to personally approve any IAF sortie on a Lebanese bank. Olmert was reluctant to give Chief of Staff Halutz the green light to redirect the aircraft on nonessential strikes, especially since President Bush warned Israel not to focus on targets that could "weaken the government in Lebanon."[11]

Dagan despised decisions with far-reaching national security implications based solely on political pandering. The argument was made that the American president was one of the last people who could or should lecture Israel on how it responded to a terrorist declaration of war. The American president, after all, wasn't hunkered down inside a bomb shelter in the basement of a Haifa apartment building. Lebanese institutions that funded the Hezbollah war machine were legitimate military targets. But Dagan's argument was precisely that in order to turn Hezbollah into a pariah that the Christians and Sunnis of Lebanon could rally against, as well as Shiites who did not want the Iranian brand of Shia Islam crammed down their throats, impacting the Lebanese economy was a strategic objective that the State of Israel had to achieve. "Targeting the money," a Harpoon operative remembered Dagan arguing, "would cripple Hezbollah's ability to wage war, and it would also send a message to the Lebanese that the fate of their economy depended on reining in the Party of God."[12]

Dagan refused to take no for an answer. He was emboldened by the intelligence that the war was already pressing Hezbollah's cash reserves;

the fighting, and the destruction, had cost Nasrallah more than he originally calculated. "Hezbollah's frontline soldiers had to be paid, and ADP
didn't have the contract with the Party of God," a Harpoon operative
said. "These men were paid in cash. The landlords whose buildings were
hit by Israeli air raids and shelling had to be paid in cash. The families of
the fallen needed cold, hard cash to pay for the funerals. Hezbollah was a
pure cash and carry enterprise."[13]

Dagan persisted vociferously, refusing to let up. He pressed the generals to support his line of thinking and lobbied the ones who disagreed.
Ultimately, Dagan convinced everyone. As was often the case in matters
of Israeli national security, Dagan managed to be incredibly persuasive.

On July 25, two weeks into the war, IAF fighter bombers from bases
"somewhere" in central and northern Israel were prepped for sorties classified for missions of the highest national importance with 500-lb. and
1,000-lb. bombs. Harpoon, along with the various air force and squadron
intelligence commands, identified the targets: a list of banks that financed
Hezbollah's war. The targets included a dozen offices of Beit al-Mal, Hezbollah's unofficial treasury office; the offices, some occupying considerable real estate, were located in six cities including Beirut. The IAF also
bombed branches of Al Baraka and Fransabank throughout Beirut and
Lebanon's largest cities, as well as the Middle East Africa Bank, a key conduit in Hezbollah's pipeline of money.

Dagan was not satisfied with merely bombing the bank buildings and
incinerating the money. He wanted to send a big message; he wanted to
make it personal. At his insistence, the IAF also bombed the home of
one of Lebanon's most prominent banking families.[14] The bank manager lived on the type of palatial compound one would expect for a man
who handled hundreds of millions of dollars for Lebanon's most heavily armed clients in the terror and narcotics trades. The residence, large
enough to house an army, had servant quarters and a garage where a fleet
of Mercedes-Benzes and Range Rovers were polished around the clock.
Part of the intelligence that Harpoon gathered—and that was gathered for

Harpoon—prior to the operation was to find a time of the day when the house would be empty. Dagan didn't want the IAF to kill the banker—just to obliterate everything that was near and dear to him. The pilots were told to be precise and obliterate the house and property. Dagan was determined to send a message: Handle Hezbollah's money and the IAF would handle you.

In some of the sorties mounted against the banks, IAF F-16 and F-15 pilots were ordered to damage, but not destroy, the banks. Sometimes a warning was given so that those inside would have time to clear out, in order to minimize Lebanese casualties. Dagan wanted to wreak havoc and destruction on the bundles of cash that fueled the war against Israel. The Lebanese took great stock in the security of their money inside the country's banks. Men like Dagan knew that the Lebanese would be devastated to see their money obliterated in clouds of black smoke and fire. They knew that even Shiites who supported Hezbollah would demand an end to the fighting once they saw their financial institutions destroyed.

The IAF strikes were incredibly effective. Brand-new banks were rendered to smoldering heaps of rubble. Most important, close to $100 million in currency was incinerated in the Israeli raids; bank computing centers, as well as remote backup facilities and data centers, were also targeted.

The IDF went to great lengths to publicize its focus on the Lebanese—and Hezbollah—economies. "The message is for all the Lebanese banks," Brigadier General Danny Arditi, the prime minister's counterterrorism advisor, commented to NBC in an exclusive interview. "Assistance to Hezbollah is direct assistance to terrorist organizations. We know that they are looking for money. They are very desperate to have some cash and they don't have it."[15]

Israel's counterattack, fought inside the villages-turned-into-fortresses by Hezbollah fighters and IEDs, progressed slowly. Territory that took hours to conquer in 1982 now took days and weeks. Some battles, like the 1st Golani Infantry Brigade's 51st Battalion fight for the village of Bint

Jbail, personified the courage and resolve of the Israeli soldier, but were costly in the number of dead and wounded. But for two weeks, the IAF continued its aerial offensive on Hezbollah missile batteries, fortifications, and financial institutions.

The banks that the IAF targeted all denied involvement in financing Hezbollah's operations. A spokesman for Al Baraka said that "We have no relation to any organization like Hezbollah." A spokesman for Fransabank said, "We have no relationship with Hezbollah or any other political party anywhere. We don't have any relation and we refuse to have one." The denials were cookie-cutter and untrue. Tellingly, Hezbollah's own television station, al-Manar, aired a telethon for the terrorist group a week before the banks were bombed, urging people to donate for the war against Israel. Donors were prompted to call a Beirut number and to send funds into a Middle East Africa Bank account. An NBC News producer, posing as someone overseas who wanted to help the Party of God cause, phoned a Hezbollah operative, and they were told to wire funds into an account of the Banque Libano-Française; the caller was warned not to say that the funds were heading for the resistance because otherwise the transaction would be red-flagged.

What concerned Dagan and the Harpoon staff—as well as key directors of the U.S. Department of the Treasury's counterterrorism division— were the relationships that the targeted Lebanese banks maintained with their corresponding banks in the United States. The Banque Libano-Française had a relationship with two prominent U.S. banks—Citibank and the Bank of New York; the Middle East Africa Bank had a relationship with Wachovia. Hezbollah has been designated by the U.S. government as a foreign terrorist organization since 1995. It was a charter member of the Treasury's list. As such, it was illegal for U.S. businesses and financial institutions to do business with designated terrorist organizations; any payment going through such an entity toward Hezbollah would have been flagged, frozen, and reported to the Department of the Treasury. Matters were made more difficult for the transfer of terror funds following 9/11 and the establishment of the PATRIOT Act.

Two weeks after the IAF's targeting of the banks, Hezbollah sued for a cease-fire. They had run out of cash.

The 2006 Second Lebanon War lasted for thirty-four days. The conflict ended in what some military observers regarded as a stubborn stalemate. The Israeli public's shock wore off and quickly turned to anger and frustration. An Israeli government commission would look into the unpreparedness and sluggish command that allowed Hezbollah to surprise the IDF so decisively. There were other shortcomings, such as IDF reservist units that were ill-equipped and fallout shelters that had been stripped bare of their basic elements; some Arab communities in Israel's north that were also hit by Hezbollah rockets had no air raid shelters at all.

During the thirty-four-day war, 114 Israeli servicemen were killed;[16] hundreds more were injured. Forty-four Israeli civilians were also killed in the Hezbollah bombardments. More than one thousand were wounded by the shrapnel and destruction. The Israeli combat fatalities did not, as of yet, include the two reservists kidnapped at the launch of the war and whose fate was still unknown.* With the end of the Second Lebanon War, Israelis were growing tired of the relentless stream of terrorist attacks directed at them from all quarters. During the six years of what seemed to be an endless barrage of suicide bombings inside Israel's cities, the focus of Israel's military, law enforcement, and intelligence services was to end the

---

* For two years, the State of Israel engaged Hezbollah, through intermediaries such as the German Federal Intelligence Service, the Bundesnachrichtendienst, to secure the release of the two abducted soldiers. The negotiations were carried out under the premise that both captives were still alive. Hezbollah demanded that Israel release Samir Kuntar, a Druze, who had led a terrorist raid against the northern Israeli city of Nahariya in 1979 and murdered four, including a young father and his daughter, in cold blood before being apprehended. Israel vowed never to release Kuntar, but Nasrallah seemed to know how to manipulate the raw nerve endings of the Israeli psyche. The Israelis eventually agreed to release the aged Kuntar, but when the exchange of prisoners took place, the IDF received two coffins instead of the two alive soldiers. Hezbollah greeted Kuntar as a returning hero. The long arm of Israeli justice never forgot about Kuntar, however. He was finally killed in an explosion of a building in Syria in December 2015.

bloodshed of the Palestinian intifada. Israeli forces waged a determined and relentless fight in the West Bank and Gaza, and once again Israel's cities were spared the horror and the grief of buses and cafés being blown up. But the 2006 Second Lebanon War was a stark reminder to Israel's generals, commissioners, and spymasters that there would be no respite from the threat and the incessant conflict.

It is believed that more than one thousand Lebanese civilians living in the villages from which Hezbollah garrisoned its fighters, stored its weapons, and launched its missiles were killed in the war. Hezbollah had used an entire population as hapless human shields.

According to some IDF estimates, the IDF killed more than seven hundred Hezbollah fighters.[17] Hezbollah, as was its custom, swore that no more than two hundred of its frontline combatants were killed.

But Hezbollah was in many ways very different from the homegrown Palestinian terrorists of Hamas, the PLO, and the PIJ that Israel was now familiar with. The organization posed an immediate and existential threat against the State of Israel. Hezbollah was an authentic army, complete with antitank brigades and more short-, medium-, and long-range surface-to-surface missiles that could hit much of Israel. It had global capabilities—twice in the 1990s Hezbollah bombed Israeli and Jewish targets in Buenos Aires, Argentina. Hezbollah was financed by Iran and by an international network of criminal consortiums, dealing in everything from cocaine and heroin to stolen cars and, in the United States, the sale of tax-free cigarettes.

Vanquishing Hezbollah on the battlefields of southern Lebanon had proven difficult—especially as the Israeli military took extraordinary precautions to minimize civilian casualties. But Hezbollah had various weaknesses and failings that were of great interest to the men and women of Harpoon. Hezbollah had one primary Achilles' heel, and that was money. The organization was built around Shiite empowerment, but its leaders—in the Iranian Islamic Revolutionary Guard and in the slums of Beirut—were absolutely corrupt and obsessed with greed.

Dagan had, as a commando and as a spymaster, spent most of his career exploiting people's weaknesses and vulnerabilities. Hezbollah had thrown down the gauntlet against Israel. It was time for a suitable Israeli response. Dagan was eager to lead Israel's charge to once and for all dilute the organization's ability to wage war and to bankrupt the Party of God in ways that would diminish its capabilities and resolve for years to come.

CHAPTER TWELVE

Greed

Reality leaves a lot to the imagination.
—*John Lennon*

errorist wars have been fought for a myriad of reasons. Some terrorist groups fought for national liberation. Some fought for political ideology: communism, Maoism, neo-Nazism. Other terrorist armies mustered for ideologies on the left and the right. Some terrorist armies, the ones that have become the most potent in recent years, fight for religious salvation and conquest. Terrorist wars are fought differently in different locations and by men and women of endless beliefs and strange languages. But the one element that unites all of them is cost: the cost of executing attacks against governments and civilians and the cost that governments spend to defend against the carnage.

Uzi Arad is a former Mossad officer and advisor to several Israeli prime ministers and a founding director of the Institute for Policy and Strategy at the Interdisciplinary Center Herzliya. During a discussion of the short-term and long-term ramifications of the terrorism wars, he was once asked about the cost that bloodshed exacted on governments and societies. Forever the professor, Arad asked, "Has anyone ever thought to quantify the ramifications of one terrorist attack, like a 9/11? One series of hijackings that could have been prevented resulted in massive government spending at airports around the world. Has anyone ever measured the cost for the creation of something like the American TSA? Has there ever been a forensic accounting of cost of the salaries, the technological tools, and everything else that was implemented to prevent future aircraft hijackings or bombings? The amount must be astronomical and, when weighed against the risk, would cause many people to scratch their heads and think."[1]

There was, though, a way for the State of Israel to quantify the destruction it absorbed during the Hezbollah-initiated Second Lebanon War. There were the dead and the wounded, of course. There were the basic financial costs as well. Economists have estimated direct war damage at $3.5 billion, including losses in Gross Domestic Product; the Israeli Ministry of Tourism calculated a 37 percent drop-off in summer travel, during the peak season. Businesses closed because of the Israeli reservists who were called up and had to take leave from their civilian jobs. A quarter of the businesses in northern Israel faced the possibility of bankruptcy because of losing revenue for more than a month. The Israeli Chamber of Commerce said their lost revenues totaled about $1.4 billion. More than two thousand homes and apartment buildings were destroyed; nine thousand were damaged by the rocket and missile barrages. More than three thousand acres of forest were set ablaze by the incoming missiles setting fires to the dry bush.[2] In an area of the world where each tree is treated as a precious national treasure, this was no small matter.

The 2006 War was also costly to Lebanon, of course. The estimated casualties were 1,400 dead and thousands more wounded. Nearly a million were displaced, and the impact on the Lebanese economy was estimated at $2.8 billion in destruction, and nearly the same amount in lost income.[3] But Hezbollah soon fixed its cash flow problems. The Iranian government made sure that Hezbollah's coffers were overflowing with the profits of the oil industry. Hezbollah's commanders were presented with generous bonuses for their courage in launching the war, as well as for their steadfast directing of the forces in the field. The residents of south Beirut, and the villagers of the south, whose homes were destroyed by Israeli air strikes, soon had new homes built or rebuilt—all with the generosity of the Party of God. The new homes were fitted with the finest marble floors and the most lavish new appliances. New, imported German sedans were rushed from the port of Beirut straight to those who were deemed to merit receiving new vehicles as compensation.

Hassan Nasrallah publicly pledged that every home damaged or destroyed in the 2006 fighting would be rebuilt or repaired by 2010. The Hezbollah reconstruction program was called the Wa'ad, or "promise."[4] There was no official calculation of the costs involved, but estimates were at well over a billion dollars. Hezbollah's benevolence bought it support that it badly needed following the rubble and misery the war left behind. The money also temporarily silenced many of the accusations by Lebanese politicians and parties against the terrorist group that condemned it for recklessly sparking off the conflict with the Israelis and unilaterally bringing such destruction down on the country. The vow to spend the money guaranteed Nasrallah some temporary loyalty.

Even though Hezbollah's war against Israel achieved little and the suffering and loss of life were all unnecessary, the yellow-and-green flags of the Shiite Party of God flew proudly from the areas that bore the brunt of the combat. "The terrorist groups were like a blue chip stock, or the next and most innovative product from a start-up gone public offered on the Dow Jones," a former military intelligence officer summoned to work with Harpoon explained. "When the market was good and the dividends and the cash flowed, everyone loved it, but when the terrorist actions resulted in losses, large losses, landscape-altering losses, everyone turns on them and turns on them fast."[5]

Dagan wanted to short the Hezbollah stock. He wanted to undermine the net value of the Hezbollah corporate brand and do it in a way that would have long-term implications. The Mossad director wanted to teach Hezbollah's leadership a lesson, and make Party of God's most faithful supporters remove those yellow-and-green flags from the windowsills of the newly rebuilt homes.

The Mossad had, in its employ, men and women who were among the world's finest in turning a devious imagination into an operational plan. Harpoon also had Uri L. Dagan and his assistant discussed options, and they read the headlines in the *New York Times* and the *Wall Street Journal*. It was 2007. A financial crisis was enveloping the United States, and there were all sorts of stories coming out of Wall Street talking about hucksters and swindlers.

Like many Harpoon operations, the one that was gaining force inside Dagan's head began as an idea and then the fodder for discussion with Uri in the director's office over a cup of tea and the draw of his pipe. Both Dagan and Uri smiled at one another when the two openly exchanged the possibilities of the operation. The best way to get back at someone who had lots of money, Dagan realized, was to make him lose a chunk of it. The ideas coming in were brilliant and thought provoking. Israel's spymasters were known to be imaginative geniuses in the most devious sort of ways. That imagination, according to a veteran Israeli special operations and intelligence officer, was the force multiplier that allowed Israel to survive while surrounded and outnumbered.[6]

The target was Hezbollah.

It was just after New Year's Day 2007, and Salah Ezzedine was living what could be called a Horatio Alger tale penned amid the bombed-out chaos of the Lebanese landscape. The forty-six-year-old Ezzedine came from Maaroub, a small south Lebanese village some thirteen miles north of the Israeli frontier where the most a youngster could aspire to become was a farmer, a herder, or someone involved in the underground economy of smuggling or worse. Some of Ezzedine's contemporaries traveled overseas in search of their fortunes; there were large Shiite communities in South America and in the United States. Others headed for the slums of south Beirut for work. Some of the men joined the ranks of Hezbollah and were commanders of men in the field in the war against Israel. For many young men in the south, just making it to their forty-sixth birthday would have been achievement enough. Some of the boys Ezzedine had grown up with were buried in the village martyrs' cemetery.

Ezzedine was a stocky figure with a square face accentuated by an anvil-shaped jaw. He had a full head of hair that had, here and there, specks of silver gray. The hair was always immaculately shaped, as if he had it styled every morning at a barbershop; his moustache was close-cropped, and he always walked around with a couple days' worth of stubble that was neatly sculptured. Ezzedine wore a uniform of a button-down shirt, usually white or light blue with a subtle design, and a blazer: The fashion statement was wealthy and carefree but not overdone—a testament to his humble upbringing. A gold pinky ring on his left hand reminded him of the success he had achieved.

Salah Ezzedine's home is worthy of a Rockefeller, or a drug cartel king-pin. The grounds were protected by a wall of chiseled sandstones and steel. An electronic gate of black steel was controlled by a security guard from inside a command post that was bigger than many homes in the nearby village. The drive from the gate to the main house went uphill and took several minutes. Ezzedine's house was built to look like a Roman palace. There were fountains and enough green grass to accommodate an army of soccer players. Armed guards patrolled the grounds. Many of the guests at the lavish banquets he frequently hosted felt as if they were at the presidential palace rather than at a private citizen's home so near to the Israeli frontier. At night, guests nibbled on olives and sipped mint-infused lemonade while looking at the bright lights coming from the Israeli side of the border.

The people who knew him and did business with him referred to Salah Ezzedine as Sheikh Salah, a reverence reserved for people who were older and had earned the measure of respect that experience and accomplishments had bestowed upon them. Few were wiser. Ezzedine had made an unholy fortune in real estate and other industries. His investments produced a steady and seemingly endless revenue stream. Everything he touched seemed to turn to gold.

The vernacular of Lebanon's south demanded that someone who achieved great success praised Allah for their fortune in life. Ezzedine was a very religious man. His piety was subtle yet absolute. But beyond his Shiite faith, Ezzedine was an unconditional supporter of Hezbollah. By American standards, Ezzedine would be called a buff—someone who was fascinated by the men in arms, the weapons they carried, and the battles they fought. Ezzedine was close friends with many of Hezbollah's top leaders, including Sheikh Nasrallah. Many of Ezzedine's businesses were Hezbollah-centric. He ran a travel agency that coordinated pilgrimages to Mecca and the holy Shiite sites in Iraq and Iran for Hezbollah commanders and their families. The religious trips were renowned for their luxury and opulence. "Ezzedine's style was everything had to be the newest, the best," a resident of Maaroub stated. "For transportation, he'd have a brand-new bus, with zero mileage."[7]

Ezzedine also owned a children's publishing house that produced books for Hezbollah-run schools throughout the country; the Party of God indoctrinated future warriors and widows at a young age, and Ezzedine's schoolbooks were colorful products of propaganda. The publishing house, as well as a popular radio station that Ezzedine owned, were named after Hadi Nasrallah, the eldest son of Hezbollah's general secretary.[8] Hadi Nasrallah was killed in September 1997 fighting Israeli forces; his body, held by the Israelis, was eventually returned years later in a prisoner exchange that included the negotiated return of the corpses of those combatants killed in action. Following Hadi's death, Nasrallah said, "Israel should not feel satisfaction at my son's death, for he died on the battlefield, facing the conquerors as he wished, with a gun in his hand."[9]

Naming his business endeavors in the memory of Hadi scored Ezzedine an instant form of acceptance as a semiofficial member of the armed wing of the organization. He became personal friends to many of Hezbollah's top religious, political, and military chiefs. Before embarking on a venture, the businessman often sought the blessing of Hezbollah's spiritual leader, Sheikh Hassan Fadlallah.

Ezzedine was also close to the notorious Imad Mughniyeh, the military and special operations commander of all Hezbollah terrorist activities inside Lebanon and around the world.[10] Mughniyeh had engineered the term *suicide bombings* into the international terrorist lexicon and was responsible for blowing up two American embassies in Beirut, the U.S. Marines and French paratroopers in Beirut, and a slew of kidnappings and freelance murders. Mughniyeh was also behind the two suicide vehicle bombings perpetrated by Hezbollah in Argentina—one that destroyed the Israeli embassy in 1992 and the other that destroyed a Jewish cultural center; more than one hundred total people were killed in those attacks. Mughniyeh was behind much of Hezbollah's war against Israeli forces in southern Lebanon from 1985 to 2000. In fact, he was also the moving force behind the abduction of the two Israeli reservists that precipitated the Second Lebanon War. For his crimes against the United States, Israel, France, Argentina, and a dozen other countries around the world, Imad Mughniyeh was one of the most hunted terrorists in the world.* His very identity was a Hezbollah state secret of the highest order. If Salah Ezzedine was allowed to know where Mughniyeh was, then it certainly meant that the businessman had achieved the status of an inside player.

Ezzedine's psychological need to be accepted by the terrorist group's leadership compelled him to make generous charitable donations to the organization in official ceremonies and events that were covered by Hezbollah's media apparatus around the country. He received countless awards from the Hezbollah-affiliated charities he supported and the military units he embraced. Everyone wanted to be Ezzedine's friend, and if you were a Hezbollah official above a certain rank and influence, Ezzedine made the effort to be yours.

The money that Hezbollah paid to the residents of south Beirut and south Lebanon following the 2006 Second Lebanon War was called "clean money" by the locals.[11] The money was clean because it was brand-new.

---

* Imad Mughniyeh was killed in Damascus, Syria, on February 12, 2008, when a powerful explosive device was detonated inside the headrest of his Mitsubishi Pajero. The international media attributed Mughniyeh's assassination to a joint CIA-Mossad operation. Both the United States and the State of Israel neither confirmed nor denied any involvement in Mughniyeh's death. Neither expressed any remorse, either; many veteran CIA and Mossad officials were quite clear in interviews to the press that the world was a much better place with Mughniyeh dead.

The money, fresh off flights from Tehran to Damascus or Beirut, came in enormous plastic-wrapped bundles in containers that held hundreds of thousands of dollars. Heavily armed Hezbollah teams guarded the transfer of cash. The money flowed generously, too generously. Some of the money, in turn, was given to Ezzedine to invest and to hold for safekeeping.

Ezzedine traveled to the Persian Gulf following the war in search of investment opportunities for his Hezbollah comrades. The Gulf could be a magical place for a wealthy Lebanese investor who grew up dirt-poor in a village that hadn't changed much in hundreds of years. From Kuwait City to Doha, from Manama to Abu Dhabi, the opulence was mesmerizing. The sand was clean and endless. The robes worn by the sheikhs were pristine and snow white, the uniform of men who never had to work a day in their lives. Everything was polished to an exuberant shine. What wasn't gold-plated was made to look like gold. Plush carpeting, often ruby red, made every hotel lobby or private home appear to be a palace.

Dubai was by far the most bedazzling of the cities. The city, the emirate, was built on a geyser of financial wheeling and dealing. Billion-dollar real estate deals were consummated with a handshake and a glass full of sweet mint tea. Other deals were concluded over filet mignon at one of the many Michelin-rated restaurants in the city; some negotiations and celebrations were conducted at the clubs where Russian women entertained the locals with their generous charms.

Dubai had replaced Beirut in its glory days as the Middle East's ground zero for bankers, investors, scammers, and spies. Everyone was eager but wary once they landed at DXB, the three-letter airport code for Dubai. The contacts that Ezzedine met with, promising a portfolio of opportunities, were all referred to by friends of a friend. Some introductions were made by SMS. Text messages were king, and any millionaire worth his dinars carried several cellular phones—one in the blazer pocket, one in the trouser pocket, and one, the newest, always held in hand. Nokia was the brand of choice.

Dubai was a city of spies, riches, and despicable souls—intelligence professionals, heiresses, and shady arms merchants were everywhere in search of a deal. DXB was accessible from anywhere and everywhere. The men from Langley, Virginia, could fly to Dubai in business-class comfort on direct flights from Dulles International Airport. It took six hours and fifty minutes to fly from London to Dubai; it was only five hours from Moscow's Domodedovo International Airport; and it was a mere two hours and ten minutes from IKA, Imam Khomeini International Airport in Tehran, to the emirate city. Flying via Amman or Istanbul, it took half a day to get to Dubai from Israel's Ben-Gurion International Airport. The travel time was much shorter on one of the many private jets that could be chartered between the two countries.

Israel and the United Arab Emirates did not maintain formal diplomatic relations. Israeli nationals were not permitted in Dubai; Israeli newlyweds did not honeymoon in one of the suites of the Burj Al Arab Jumeirah, the most luxurious hotel in the world. But Israeli military officers, security specialists, and intelligence agents were common visitors to the lavish city.[12] Safeguarding the various emirates was big business, and Israelis with military-laced CVs were found anywhere in the world—even the Arab world—where there was money to be made. The Swiss-owned Asia Global Technologies, a company run by Israeli Mati Kochavi, was reported to have had extensive security contracts in the Persian Gulf emirates, including the safeguarding of key oil and other infrastructure locations. Kochavi ran another company called Logic, headquartered north of Tel Aviv near the Mediterranean coast. According to reports Logic hired Boeing 737s, painted all white, and flew engineers and technicians, many from Israel's intelligence services, from Ben-Gurion International Airport, via Cyprus or Jordan, ultimately ending up in Abu Dhabi. The men were sequestered. They ate and slept together inside fortified compounds, doing everything in their power to conceal their Israeli identities.[13] Other Israeli companies trained the local governments in counterterrorism and hostage rescue; some provided advanced security technology to the local intelligence services.[14]

It's been reported that some Israeli companies, staffed by former high-ranking military and security service officers, pitched their special field and technological talents to the Kingdom of Saudi Arabia to manage overcrowding in Mecca. Some of the Israeli companies work on force protection, safeguarding infrastructure.[15] Shmuel Bar, a former Israeli intelligence officer, was approached by Saudi officials because he developed a program that finds terrorist threats on social media.[16]

Former generals and spymasters were encouraged by the State of Israel—primarily by the Ministry of Defense—to do business in the Arab world. They were just reminded how unsafe it was.

But still Israelis, according to one American defense executive who travels to the Gulf regularly, were everywhere. Even former Mossad director Shabtai Shavit worked the area, though he and his firm did not disclose any details.[17] Dubai was a city where, given the right documents and connections, it was easy to hide one's nationality or true ambition.

It is not known exactly who Ezzedine met in Dubai and in his other sojourns to the Gulf,[18] but he trusted the men whom he met. Greed had a funny way of making someone with cash grow accepting of strangers with wads of cash and generous tastes in the city's finest eateries. These men from the Gulf had offices in high-rise buildings, complete with pretty secretaries. They drove cars that were expensive, but not too expensive. They were young and energetic, but respectful and religious. In Dubai there was no animosity between Sunni and Shiite Muslims—only a shared interest in profitable coexistence. Ezzedine was impressed with some of the men he met during the trip. Moreover, he liked the idea and the opportunity of branching out east. He trusted them enough to invest millions of dollars in a proposed fund that they had launched. The men who managed the fund convinced Ezzedine that it was a sure thing, and they promised hefty and immediate dividends—the earnings, they suggested, could be as high as 40 or 50 percent.

Ezzedine never bothered to launch a thorough investigation into the men he met in Dubai before doing business with them. Suspicion was a Lebanese trait, but the promise of money and the subsequent wire transfers from the Gulf overrode any worry. He never wondered if the men he had met were from Doha or from Tel Aviv. Ezzedine simply couldn't believe his eyes when the returns on his investment came in. The quick turnaround on his capital investment was above and beyond what was promised—a universe beyond what he could have ever expected. His partners in the Gulf vowed bigger and better things to come. More investments from the Lebanese businessman soon followed. The money swiftly flowed back in and then some. Millions of dollars were flowing in and the money showed no sign of drying up.

Salah Haj Ezzedine, the good Shiite Muslim and the good friend of Hezbollah, wanted to share this new investment fund with his friends inside the organization. In early 2007 he founded al-Mustathmir, described as a financial institution that focused on money management.[19] At first, Ezzedine offered senior commanders access to al-Mustathmir. He promised returns, both short- and long-term, ranging from 40 to 50 percent. The lines of men eager to invest in his funds stretched outside his office in the south Beirut suburb of Dahieh. It is believed that Sheikh Hassan Nasrallah invested hundreds of millions of dollars of his own wealth with Ezzedine, most of it funds coming straight from Hezbollah's coffers.

Few ever bothered to ask Ezzedine where he invested the money. Those who did heard explanations that were as varied as they were suspect: steel, diamonds, titanium, zirconium, gold mines in Iran, oil in Eastern Europe, oil in Africa, iron in the Gambia, shoes and leather in China, used clothing for the Third World, scrap metal, construction projects in the Gulf, and even beef and poultry in Brazil.[20] Thoughtfully for the Hezbollah investors, there was very little paperwork involved with al-Mustathmir. There were no contracts, no monthly statements, no minimum balances; there was none of the bureaucracy that coincided with investing in the stock market or in a retirement account.[21] All that Ezzedine provided was a check for the amount of the initial investment. The check, drawn on Ezzedine's al-Mustathmir corporation, could be cashed at any time if someone wanted to withdraw from the fund. Few did. The dividends were sometimes as high as 60 percent of the initial investment. Those who joined the fund included many of the top clerics in Hezbollah, who were pleased that all of Ezzedine's investments were halal, acceptable according to strict Islamic law; money in Islam is viewed purely as a medium of exchange.

The profits flowed in through Ezzedine's al-Mustathmir holding company. Hezbollah was grateful, even giddy. Salah Ezzedine suddenly found himself the guest of honor at many Hezbollah functions, seated on the dais next to the organization's top leadership.[22] As news of his financial prowess and fame spread, Ezzedine was also asked to handle investments for members of the Iranian Islamic Revolutionary Guard Corps, and clients in the Kingdom of Saudi Arabia, Kuwait, Qatar, and the United Arab Emirates. According to some reports, Ezzedine also handled money from some less-than-stellar individuals from the former Soviet Union.[23]

Many people thought that Ezzedine was Hezbollah's official financier, an investor said,[24] and they wanted in. The businessman did little to dissuade that impression. Shiites throughout the country—primarily in the south—borrowed, begged, and stole to invest their money in al-Mustathmir. Ezzedine was considered to be as close to a sure thing as anyone.

Many southerners viewed Ezzedine's interest in their welfare as an investment in a part of Lebanon that had traditionally been neglected, forgotten, and used as a battlefield. But there was newfound wealth coming into the south. Many Shiite residents traveled overseas to seek their fortunes, forsaking the slums of Beirut as the next best thing and venturing to South America, the United States and Canada, and even West Africa in search of a better life. These young men sent money home, sometimes a lot of it. Families suddenly had some cash to play around with. Peasants bought homes, and those teetering on middle class bought luxury cars. Restaurants and cafés began to open throughout southern Lebanon. The cash that Hezbollah doled out following the 2006 War also became a source of wealth. Businesses rose out of the destruction—architects, contractors, stone cutters, landscapers, electricians, and plumbers suddenly had more work than they knew what to do with. Much of that money went to Ezzedine and al-Mustathmir. The greed was infectious.

Mohammed Shour was one such investor. Shour, a young man with four children and a widowed mother, invested his family's entire life savings, roughly $45,000, with Ezzedine. Ezzedine promised the Shour family, who ran a small supermarket in southern Lebanon, a return of 25 percent on their money. Mohammed wanted to use the proceeds to purchase an orchard. "Everyone was investing," Mohammed Shour told al-Jazeera. "The man was supposed to be religious. Walk up and down this village and you'll see that everyone invested money with him. Some people mortgaged their homes to invest with him."[25] The investors thought that their money was safe. After all, investing in Ezzedine was almost the same as investing in Hezbollah. Hezbollah, these people believed, would secure their life savings.[26]

For generations the Shiites of south Beirut and southern Lebanon had lived liked poor outcasts, the lowest class in a country where they constituted the largest of the many ethnic groups. They were traditionally discarded and minimized—a schism in Islam that dated back to the founding of the religion, when Mohammed's followers split into two competing factions. Mohammed had never appointed a successor. The majority, what would become the Sunni branch, chose Abu Bakr, Mohammed's father-in-law and the first to convert to Islam, as their caliph, or leader. Another faction insisted that Mohammed's son-in-law, Ali ibn Ali Talib, lead the religion; those would become the Shiite branch. Ali was assassinated in 661 AD, and the two branches of the religion have been at odds—and sometimes at war—ever since.

The Shiites comprise only 10 percent of the world's Islamic population, but in Lebanon they outnumbered the Sunnis. Still, the Shiites were the underclass. They were called rubbish collectors; the other Lebanese religious groups routinely referred to them as the *mitweleh*, a derogatory racial slur. And now an angel had appeared promising riches. Thousands of people invested in the Shiite superstar Ezzedine. People, believing that a windfall was imminent, began spending their earnings before they arrived. As if overnight, beat-up sedans were replaced by brand-new BMW X5s or Cadillac Escalades.[27]

And then one day, just as fast as it began, the fantasy came to a crashing finale. The end came in August 2009. Ezzedine had written a check for roughly $200,000 to Hussein Haj Hassan, one of Hassan Nasrallah's closest confidants and political advisors—a check to match his investment. Hussein Haj Hassan was a Hezbollah member of the Lebanese parliament. Hassan was horrified when he learned that Ezzedine's check had bounced. His partners in the Gulf had simply emptied the accounts. Hundreds of millions of dollars simply disappeared into thin air.

Ezzedine was devastated by the discovery. Devastation soon turned to panic. His partners were nowhere to be found; their mobile phones, the BlackBerries, iPhones, and Nokias they displayed so proudly, no longer accepted calls. Panic soon turned to horror. Ezzedine feared for his life. The men who lost their money with him were not known to be tolerant of failure, especially if the cause of that failure turned out to be operatives from another country eager to harm the Shiites of Lebanon and Hezbollah in particular. Ezzedine soon realized that he had been the victim of a diabolical scam perpetrated by highly sophisticated players who had had millions of dollars at their disposal.

Hezbollah's commanders and the Shiite poor were in no position to suffer a humiliating financial meltdown. Ezzedine attempted to localize the devastation and minimize the monetary carnage. He desperately tried to borrow some money from a millionaire friend, a stopgap to plug up the astronomical losses, so that those with the most money inside the portfolio and those who were in a position to inflict punishment upon him personally could be made whole, but the word was already out. Then, in fear for his own safety, he attempted to flee. Using foreign SIM cards to camouflage his location, Ezzedine tried to negotiate his way out of the mess. He showed remorse. He was destroyed by the folly he had allowed to happen.

Ezzedine tried to summon his network of friends for help. He desperately tried to stem the tide of catastrophe with loans and gifts. But news that his fund was empty spread like a brushfire. There was a rush on the banks by the desperate and panic-stricken. But there was no money to withdraw. The banks refused to honor any of Ezzedine's checks.

Al-Mustathmir had no funds, and soon Ezzedine was nowhere to be found. Hundreds of people's life savings had simply disappeared.

People who could not afford a financial setback suddenly found themselves penniless and destitute. The anger and the outrage of the masses began to amplify. Because Ezzedine was so closely associated with many of Hezbollah's top leaders, the scandal became a political crisis for the Party of God. It is believed that ten thousand Lebanese Shiites invested with Ezzedine. "I inherited $100,000 from my father to continue my studies. I invested them with Ezzeddine, and now all my dreams are destroyed," a resident of southern Lebanon told *Time*. "I don't know what I was thinking when I invested with him."[28]

In the Lebanese press, people began to label Ezzedine as "Abu Madoff," in reference to Bernie Madoff and the multi-billion-dollar Ponzi scheme swindle he engineered in the United States, which was still reverberating in America. Al-Jazeera reported that the Ezzedine scandal had resulted in losses well over one billion dollars.[29] The damage was so significant that even Hezbollah threats and intimidation of local media outlets couldn't keep the story under wraps.

Hezbollah counterintelligence agents arrested Ezzedine as he attempted to flee the country. Officially, Hezbollah attempted to distance itself from the toxic reality of what had just transpired. The Party of God issued communiqués stating that Ezzedine was never a member of the organization and that he held no official title or capacity. It was, of course, a first stab at damage control. And an attempt doomed to fail. Ezzedine was publicly recognized as an inner-circle man who could not be erased by decree or a sermon from the mosque. It was impossible to deny the man's connection to the Party of God when nearly half the money lost belonged to Sheikh Nasrallah himself.

The Ezzedine affair quickly metastasized into Stage Three political cancer for Hezbollah. The Shiites who had been poor all their lives and who suddenly lost their life savings as a result of the scheme pointed angry fingers at Hezbollah's once untouchable leadership. They insisted upon answers and they demanded blood. Frustration and heartbreak quickly turned into furious accusations. People openly wondered why the villagers, the immaterial *mitweleh*, had once again lost and suffered while those connected to party leadership drove around in brand-new SUVs and ate in the finest restaurants in Beirut; the parking lots at these five-star eateries were packed with Mercedes-Benzes and Range Rovers. A scandal even erupted over the $300 designer head scarves that many of the Hezbollah wives were known to wear. The Arab street, the litmus test of mood and rage, demanded answers. NOW Lebanon, a news website backed by figures close to the governing March 14 alliance, put it succinctly: "Ezzedine Shows Hezbollah's Moral Bankruptcy."[30]

Even pro-Hezbollah media outlets were critical of the Party of God on television commentaries and in newspaper editorials. "Hezbollah is not the first revolutionary movement to be corrupted by money," said Sateh Noureddine in the pro-Hezbollah newspaper *As-Safir*, "and it won't be the last."[31] Other Lebanon watchers wrote that Hezbollah had finally succumbed to the "PLO Flu," a Lebanese term used to describe the Palestine Liberation Organization's indulgence of wealth and luxury during the Lebanese civil war and the corrupt abandonment of its revolutionary principles.

Iran realized that if Hezbollah were to lose the support of many Shiites, they would be seen as nothing more than a heavily armed criminal gang working on behalf of their own interests. And that worried Hezbollah's bosses in Iran as well. The noose was tightening around Iran: the United States and Israel, together, had begun to focus great espionage service and financial agency efforts against Iran and its nuclear ambitions, including harsh economic sanctions and diplomatic isolation. Iran needed Hezbollah to be ready and willing to embark on another war against Israel should the joint American and Israeli campaign reach a coordinated moment of critical mass that threatened the Islamic Republic. Hezbollah, after all, was one of the key weapons in Iran's arsenal. The Iranians, even though suffering from sanctions against their own failing economy, vowed to assist Hezbollah in making the Ezzedine fiasco right.[32] Iran pledged to assist in compensating the victims of Ezzedine's Ponzi scheme.

Meanwhile, in the wake of the scandal Nasrallah had to kick his own efforts at damage control into high gear to tamp down the outrage of the Lebanese street. Iranian support for Hezbollah was always downplayed by the Party of God's leadership. Lebanon's Shiites were Arabs, not Persians, and the Farsi invasion never sat well with many of Hezbollah's supporters who viewed the emissaries from Tehran as arrogant and meddlesome. It was important for Nasrallah to show his political base that the wars and the destruction that Lebanon had endured were not because Hezbollah was a puppet of the mullahs and Revolutionary Guard commanders in Iran.

Salah Ezzedine was interrogated inside a dark and damp holding cell somewhere inside the slums of south Beirut. Hezbollah's detainees were routinely beaten. The men who interrogated Ezzedine were counter-intelligence specialists, the most suspicious and devious minds inside the organization, who were trained in the best spy schools in Syria and Iran. They had no doubt they would swiftly get to the bottom of what had happened. If foreigners were truly involved they were determined to reveal their identities. Ezzedine was questioned for days. Specialists scoured his computers and years of e-mails. His cell phones and their SIM cards were examined. All of Ezzedine's vehicles were searched for tracking devices. His home was taken apart in search of hidden communications gear or radio receivers.

No one suspected Ezzedine of being duplicitous. He was not a liar nor was he a cheat. Had he been a swindler, Hezbollah would have disposed of the financier in an expeditious and grisly manner: a public hanging, if he was lucky. Ezzedine was genuinely a religious man. Focus soon shifted on his investment partners in the Gulf. They had all vanished without a trace.

Ezzedine was handed over to the Lebanese judiciary for investigation and adjudication. The Lebanese prosecutor general was quietly coerced into charging Ezzedine with negligent bankruptcy—a crime of stupidity rather than criminal intent that carried a short jail sentence, a public slap on the wrist. Nasrallah wanted the affair to simply go away.

Usually, when ill fortune fell upon Hezbollah, the organization was quick to blame Israel and the United States. It was a surefire formula to get the rank and file out on the streets and inside the trenches ready to fight and die. A sewer main collapse in South Beirut, a day of unseasonably cold weather, an accidental explosion at a munitions warehouse, and the Mossad and the CIA were always culpable. This time, though, there were no mentions of Israel or the United States in the Hezbollah press or even in the acclaimed Lebanese media outlets. But still, some people had a sneaking suspicion as to who was to blame. "All this happened because of the United States and Israel," a cab driver from southern Lebanon who invested $10,000 with Ezzedine commented after the crash with a theme some in Lebanon openly wondered about. "When they discovered that Ezzedine was close to Hezbollah," he added, "they ruined him."[33]

There was concern among some of the Hezbollah hierarchy that the Israeli-led war against terrorist finances played a significant role in unraveling the Ezzedine scheme. While Hezbollah leaders were clear never to lay blame on Israel's doorstep, some believed that the U.S. Department of Treasury and its effort to battle the laundering of terrorist-related funds played a direct role in making Ezzedine's funds disappear.[34] Some in Hezbollah were certain that Israel was behind the scheme. How else could it be explained, they asked?

Still, Lebanese Shiites were very wary to go as far as to openly charge Ezzedine with being duplicitous, or being a dreaded *jassoos*, an informant or operative, either willing or otherwise, on behalf of a "foreign" intelligence service.

The Ezzedine affair exposed a moral vulnerability inside Hezbollah that needed to be penetrated and exposed. Nasrallah once said of his supporters that they were "the most honorable people in the world." Nasrallah knew that these honorable people would not accept the fact that Hezbollah operated one of the largest drug trafficking and money laundering criminal operations in the world. He was wary of risking anything that might cause them to cast their suspicious eyes in Hezbollah's direction.

In the aftermath of the affair, Iranian coffers were emptied to try, once again, to compensate the believers for their faith and suffering. Just like in 2006, Hezbollah compensation came in the form of brand-new U.S. $100 bills. Like 2006, one Lebanese media website posted, "The speed with which the dollars began flying was clearly aimed as much at blunting ill will toward the party because [it] unleashed such a destructive onslaught as it was at helping people. Hezbollah knows it needs to pay these people or risk losing its more ardent followers. Once again, the party will throw money at the problem it is responsible for creating."

The Ponzi scheme exposed many chinks in Hezbollah's seemingly impenetrable armor—money being its most glaring weakness. The affair was a major embarrassment for Hezbollah and a major financial hit for the Party of God.

No one in Israel shed a tear for their pain and suffering.

CHAPTER THIRTEEN

The Cocaine Jihadis

As far back as the 1990s, the Canadian Security and Intelligence Service, the country's foreign-intelligence-gathering espionage agency better known by its acronym of CSIS, identified Hezbollah as a threat. For decades, scores of Lebanese seeking to flee the barbarous civil war sought a new life in Canada. Between lax immigration laws and French being the provincial language of Quebec, the newcomers from the Middle East felt welcome. Unfortunately, not all the newcomers were refugees seeking better lives for themselves and their families. Some had terrorist ties back home and nefarious interests in their new, adopted country.

In an internal report, CSIS identified operatives using Canadian cities as deep-cover bases, and it identified criminal activity as supporting hostile operations against Canada and the United States; Hezbollah, CSIS would later assess, was very active operationally in Canada.[1] Hezbollah operations in the United States were just as much of a concern.

In 1996, in the cigarette country of North Carolina, an Iredell County Sheriff's Department deputy passed on a tip to the local Bureau of Alcohol, Tobacco, and Firearms field office in connection with Middle Eastern males making large-scale cigarette purchases at local warehouses and then driving out of state. Truckloads of tobacco products were being bought at a time. The curious law enforcement officer had stumbled on a far-reaching and sophisticated Hezbollah operation that funneled cigarette-smuggling profits back to Lebanon. The suspicions and investigations ultimately involved the FBI-led Joint Terrorism Task Force in North Carolina, the Secret Service, the Immigration and Naturalization

Service, the Internal Revenue Service, and the State Department's Diplomatic Security Service. The Hezbollah cell purchased cigarettes in the low-tax state of North Carolina and transported them north to Michigan, a high-tax state, where the cigarettes were resold and taxes never paid. In July 2000, federal, state, and local law enforcement authorities, following the tip, executed eighteen search warrants, and seized cash, weapons, and incriminating documentation. The federal effort, known as Operation Smokescreen, was executed with the assistance of intelligence provided by CSIS.[2]

Hezbollah's cigarette smuggling operation netted a total of $8 million, which was spread among hundreds of bank accounts and wire transfer locations that sent the funds back to Lebanon. Some of the profits were used to purchase a mini-arsenal of military equipment in the United States to be shipped back to Hezbollah for the fight against Israel and, later, the United States in Iraq. The equipment included night vision goggles and sniper scopes, laser range finders, laptop computers, and very expensive digital cameras and long-range lenses. The materials also included advanced naval equipment. It is suspected—but not known—if any of this advanced equipment was delivered to the Iranian Islamic Revolutionary Guard Corps.

Charges were filed on March 28, 2001, in the U.S. District Court for the Western District of North Carolina. Twenty-six individuals were ultimately charged with a multitude of crimes including racketeering, money laundering, immigration fraud, credit card fraud, marriage fraud, visa fraud, bribery, and providing material support to a declared terrorist organization.[3] Those charged were also hit with violations of the Racketeer Influenced and Corrupt Organization Act—a lethal tool used by U.S. attorneys in major cases of a criminal conspiracy. "In a lot of ways, this case was a model for how to use intelligence information. Not only U.S. intelligence but foreign intelligence," stated Martha Rubio, a Department of Justice attorney involved in the prosecution.[4]

All those involved in the Hezbollah scheme either confessed or were convicted of their crimes. The ring leader, Mohammed Yusef Hammoud, was sentenced to 155 years in federal prison. Hammoud had, years earlier, attempted to obtain a visa to enter the United States at the U.S. embassy in Damascus, Syria. His request was denied, so he traveled to Venezuela and purchased a forged visa for $200. South America, it appeared, was becoming a Hezbollah stronghold of great concern to Israel and, ultimately, the United States.

Shai U. was born in Israel in 1960. He was seven years old when the Middle East changed forever and Israel achieved the impossible in six days in June 1967. He was of Bar Mitzvah age when Israel, once again at war, eked victory from the initial shock of surprise, overconfidence, and unpreparedness in the 1973 Yom Kippur War. Like all Israelis, Shai U. completed high school and served his mandatory three years of conscripted military service, followed by additional time in uniform as a commissioned officer. As he neared the completion of his service, Shai's mother urged him to hang up his uniform and leave the army; she wanted him to follow the dream of every Jewish mother and go to medical school. Medical school didn't work. Shai was bored and unhappy. He reenlisted, serving four years in the army in a combat unit.

At the age of twenty-four Shai was already a seasoned combat veteran eager to start a new and more interesting chapter to his life. In 1984 he entered service with the Shin Bet as a counterterrorist and counterintelligence officer. Like all junior agents, he cut his teeth on terrorist cases in the West Bank. A crash course in Arabic gave him the colloquialisms of someone who had spent much of his life in Nablus or Jenin. As he began running agents and handling operations, Shai was a natural for the spy game.

Some of Shai's work was in Israel, inside the West Bank and Gaza. He also operated far from Israel's borders. He rose up the ranks fairly quickly, developing a reputation as a thorough case officer and a cunning commander. Shai was rewarded with a plum assignment. Between 2001 and 2004 he served as the Shin Bet agent in charge responsible for the Latin and South American desk. He learned Spanish and traveled throughout the continent. Shai had an inherent talent for the assignment: He loved soccer and had a knack for coordinating multijurisdictional cooperation on a wide array of investigations and operations.

When Dagan recruited Shai to serve as Harpoon's deputy chief, his service in South America was considered a plus. Israel's intelligence services have had a long operational track record in South America. One of the early Mossad operations to inspire world attention was the legendary abduction of Adolf Eichmann, one of the chief architects of Adolf Hitler's Final Solution, from Buenos Aires in 1960. After the fugitive Nazi official—who was in deep hiding—was tracked down, he was seized by Israeli agents and whisked out of the country to stand trial in Jerusalem for his role in the genocide he had perpetrated in Europe. It was a stunning and spectacular accomplishment for the fledging Jewish state and publicly displayed the Mossad's cunning and global reach to an amazed world. The Shin Bet was summoned to Buenos Aires twice, in 1992 and 1994, to investigate the Hezbollah and Iranian connections to the suicide truck bombings of the Israeli embassy.

Hezbollah consumed much of Shai's activities in South and Latin America. Lebanese and Syrian immigrants, descendants of the great Phoenician seafarers, had traveled to the four corners of the world in the late 1800s and early part of the twentieth century to seek their fortune and religious freedom. Many of those who settled in Argentina and Brazil were Shiites. They built strong and vibrant communities, established enterprises—legitimate and other—and created hubs of commerce and religion that would attract future generations of nomads who spoke little Spanish or Portuguese but who could work hard and be trusted inside the insular ethnic ghettos that they had created.

Maicao, a city of some 100,000 inhabitants in northern Colombia, was cigarette and marijuana country, and a key area of operations for government and communist forces fighting Colombia's protracted civil war. Maicao was the northernmost city in the continent. It bordered Venezuela. Maicao also boasted one of the largest Shiite populations in South America; seventy percent of the local commerce in the city was run by

Shiite émigrés and their children.[5] The money, from sales of consumer goods and the sale of weapons and cocaine, flowed into the hands of powerful merchant clans who became millionaires ten times over in the tropical paradise. Some of the money remained in Maicao. Palatial homes were constructed, and the local BMW and Mercedes dealerships did a brisk business. The city boasted the opulent palace-like Mosque of Omar Ibn al-Khattab, built in September 1997, which is the second-largest Muslim house of worship and religious center in South America.

The local merchants proudly displayed photos of Hezbollah's leaders, such as the movement's spiritual mentor, Sheikh Mohammed Hussein Fadlallah, and Sheikh Nasrallah. The stores all had little cans or jars near the register so that shoppers could drop a coin or a few pesos for the cause back home. Larger donations were also solicited from the Shiite community. The packs of cash, converted into dollars, were sent to Lebanon—and sometimes Syria—through banks in Panama and Bogotá. These banks, the same that had made billions laundering the drug profits from the dreaded Colombian cartels, were used to handling money without asking too many questions, and they were used to handling money from Maicao.

In short time the Shiite community grew and spread out geographically, absorbing wealth and influence as it grew. There were known Hezbollah and Iranian hotbeds in South America. The tri-border region area along the junction of Paraguay, Argentina, and Brazil, where the Iguazú and Paraná rivers converge; the Paraguayan city of Ciudad del Este; the Argentine city of Puerto Iguazú; and the Brazilian city of Foz do Iguaçu, were long known to be Hezbollah's South American hubs. Shai had visited the area, known as the "Triangle," on numerous occasions, as had spies and special agents from the United States, Canada, and a half-dozen nations in the European Union. Drugs, guns, and human trafficking were the currency of day-to-day life in the region.

But Harpoon had learned, especially following the 2006 Second Lebanon War, that Venezuela was a center of Hezbollah's criminal—especially narcotics-related—revenue. The criminal money was critical to

Hezbollah. Iranian support, while guaranteed, was not as generous as in previous years. A combination of economic sanctions, a miserable economy spurned by mismanagement, and plummeting oil prices forced Tehran to send fewer dollars to Beirut. The smaller grants had a great impact on Hezbollah, and forced the organization to rely more on its criminal enterprises around the world to continue to finance its ever-expanding infrastructure and the loyalists back home.[6] Most of Hezbollah's profit stemmed from cocaine trafficking.

Israel's intelligence organizations had very little experience in crime fighting. Battling drug operations was the domain of the police. But all of Israel's intelligence service placed a newfound focus on South America and the cocaine trade and was determined to unravel the highly secretive layers that shielded Hezbollah's global drug empire from penetration and compromise.

Dagan's roundtable reviewed the intelligence carefully. The meetings were lengthy and sometimes hotly contested, as differing opinions on strategies—and jurisdictional responsibilities—were often debated with typical Israeli zeal and volume. A cloud of smoke from Dagan's pipe always fogged up the conference room. No one ever dared to complain; they simply developed alternative methods of breathing. As the roundtable assembled their data, all coming in from a variety of sources that represented the agencies they worked for, one name kept appearing in report after report: a mysterious forty-four-year-old Venezuelan named Ghazi Atef Nasser al-Din.

Ghazi Atef Nasser al-Din was born in southern Lebanon on December 13, 1962. When he was young, his family—nearly all of the collective clan, or *hamula*—migrated to Venezuela to seek their fortune and to escape the turmoil, conflict, and combat that had erupted once the Palestinian guerrilla organizations, forced out of Jordan, had taken up residence in Lebanon in 1970 and 1971. Life was difficult for the young Lebanese boy in the new country with a new language and a new culture. Ghazi's family was pious. The family worshipped at the local mosque; Ghazi attended

Islamic schools. Intelligent and ambitious, Ghazi worked with local Islamic businesses and charities that placed him as a go-to guy in Venezuela's Shiite community. The young entrepreneur minded his own fortunes as well. Ghazi developed an impressive portfolio of real-estate holdings and business ventures that made him wealthy and powerful. In time he was considered a man in good standings with some of the Lebanese émigré criminal gangs, including those who worked in narcotics.

Many of the émigrés lived on Margarita Island, a vacation spot 190 miles due east of Caracas, the Venezuelan capital. The island was a smuggler's paradise—it was a cigarette boat ride from Trinidad and Tobago; Curaçao, Panama, and the Caymans were all accessible on the wide open seas. Margarita Island was virtually a Lebanese and Syrian colony. It was a favorite vacation spot for religious Muslims, boasting resorts that catered specifically to visiting Shiites from the Middle East. Eighty percent of the businesses on the island were owned by Arabs, primarily Lebanese and Syrian Shiites; the U.S. government estimated that many of these businesses were also involved in drug trafficking and money laundering.[7] As a result of this lucrative and dangerous trade, the island was full of fortresses and heavily armed thugs who protected the drugs and the money they earned.

There were two markets that these cocaine gangs served: North America and Europe. The profits from the trade, minus the skim and expenses, were always sent back as tribute to Hezbollah, Syrian intelligence forces, and the Iranian Islamic Republican Guard. As in every organized crime enterprise, the money earners were expected to kick up the organizational chain and allow the leadership to earn its due. One method used for shipping the funds back to the Middle East was known as the Black Market Peso Exchange, or BMPE.

The BMPE is used by drug dealers to launder money and to dispatch it overseas without rousing the suspicion of international law enforcement and bank monitors. It's a simple system in which drug money is sold to South American brokers, who then deposit the cash in legitimate accounts or use it to purchase goods such as cars, appliances, or jewelry; some of the money is used to pay debts, such as rent or mortgages. The goods are shipped back South America, usually Colombia or Venezuela, and then sold on the black market in their original currency. The proceeds are then given to the narco-traffickers. Former U.S. Customs Service, and New York Police Department, Commissioner Ray Kelly called the Black Market Peso Exchange "the largest, most insidious money laundering system in the Western Hemisphere."[8]

Ghazi Atef Nasser al-Din had a partner, a Lebanese-born merchant and money launderer named Fawzi Kana'an. Kana'an was born in 1943 and hailed from Ba'albek, an ancient Roman town in the Beka'a Valley in Lebanon. He immigrated to Venezuela in 1977, years before the zealots from Tehran and Qom turned his hometown into the ground zero for Iranian military intervention in Lebanon. Kana'an was a successful businessman who had skillfully negotiated the dangerous streets of Caracas to open two successful travel agencies: the Byblos Travel Service, and the Hillal Travel Company, both on the upscale Avenida Baralt. The travel agencies were the ideal conduit for monies to be wired back to Lebanon. It was a highly lucrative enterprise.

But Ghazi's fortunes soon changed for the better. He became friends and then partners with members of President Hugo Chávez's government. One man that Ghazi grew particularly close to was Tareck El Aissami, Chávez's interior minister. El Aissami was a Druze. His father had come to Venezuela from Syria and was a successful businessman who espoused radical Arabic socialist politics.[9] He was also a major link connecting Hezbollah, Iran, and the Chávez junta. According to some reports, El Aissami's financial empire boasted front companies and properties, all shielded by accounts in banks throughout Latin America and the Caribbean. His network used the Lebanese Canadian Bank to launder untold millions of dollars and move multiton shipments of narcotics for cocaine cartels as well as Hezbollah.[10]

Ghazi also befriended Nicolás Maduro, the minister for foreign affairs and a crony of Venezuelan dictator Hugo Chávez. Venezuela had turned into an oil-rich rogue nation that stuck its middle finger in the eyes of the

United States at every turn. Although the nation was awash with petro-dollar profits, it was also a criminal state that trafficked in narcotics and maintained close ties to Iran, Syria, and, of course, Hezbollah. Maduro's Ministry of Foreign Affairs became a one-stop shop—for a hefty fee, of course—for Venezuelan passports and identity cards. The Venezuelan travel booklets soon flooded the southern slums of Beirut and the training camps of southern Lebanon.

One man who received a Venezuelan passport was an Israeli Arab named Kais Obeid; Obeid was a low-level criminal and Hezbollah opera-tive who had played a role in the kidnapping of a reservist Israeli officer, as well as the financing of certain Palestinian cells during the intifada. Obeid was a member of Hezbollah's Unit 1800, a covert force of opera-tives who recruited, funded, and led Palestinian terror squads against the Jewish state.[11] Before he fled Israel to Lebanon, Obeid had been involved in cocaine smuggling operations with Israelis, including several military officers, involving South American narcotics in Lebanon that were to be sold in Israel.[12] Other Hezbollah operatives in the Middle East—men who had never stepped foot on South American soil let alone ever uttered a word in Spanish—were also provided with genuine Venezuelan passports and *cedulas*, or identity cards courtesy of Maduro's Foreign Ministry.

Maduro had an insatiable appetite for money and skullduggery. But he saw tremendous promise in Ghazi both for his own enrichment and to advance Venezuela's foreign policy initiatives. Caracas used its oil and drug money to fund regional operations, such as providing assistance to the FARC, the Fuerzas Armadas Revolucionarias de Colombia, or the Revolutionary Armed Forces of Colombia. The Marxist FARC had waged a relentless war against the Colombian government since 1964, and drug trafficking was a major source of their income. To enhance the operation, Foreign Minister Maduro deputized Ghazi into the ranks of Venezuela's diplomatic corps. To make the growing business even more successful, Ghazi was even named the charge d'affaires at the Venezuelan embassy in Damascus. "It was a remarkable development," Uri L. recalled, "to think that a nation with an airline, an army, an intelligence service, and diplomatic outposts all over the world, was nothing more than a criminal organization was sobering. The fact that the drug business was funding Israel's enemies was a situation that could not proceed."

What became even more remarkable was the fact that commercial flights commenced in 2007 between Simón Bolívar International Airport in Caracas and Imam Khomeini International Airport in Tehran: a very unusual commercial flight path that couldn't rationally be marketed as a tourist destination. Of course the flights made a refueling stop in Damascus before continuing east. There were two sets of flights—one operated by Iran Air, and the other by Conviasa, the Venezuelan state-owned airline. The roundtrip fare was an estimated $1,450. The U.S. State Department contended that passengers boarding the flights in Caracas were mysteriously not subjected to passport and immigration controls. "The concerns are just not in the abstract," former CIA Director Michael Hayden said. "We saw people traveling who made us wonder."[13] The flights were known as "Aeroterror."[14]

With Ghazi situated as the number two Venezuelan diplomat at the embassy in the Syrian capital, the flights from South America carried drugs and cash in diplomatic pouches. It was the mother of all schemes and immensely profitable to all concerned.

Ghazi Atef Nasser al-Din became the darling of the Damascus diplomatic circuit. One American security officer who worked at the U.S. embassy and requested anonymity said that the wives of the ambassadors loved him.[15] Handsome and urbane, he represented Venezuela in Syria with an air of confidence that only a drug lord could possess. It was, of course, pure arrogance. Drugs and protection made him all-powerful. His diplomatic passport made him untouchable.

Israel's intelligence community kept a watchful eye on Hezbollah's involvement in the cocaine and heroin trade. Israel's spymasters were horrified when, in 1998, U.S. President Bill Clinton removed both Lebanon and Syria from the list of nations that trafficked in narcotics.[16] Israeli intelligence chiefs couldn't understand the American move. Not only were poppies cultivated by farmers in the Beka'a Valley, but the area was also an epicenter of criminal activity, ranging from the counterfeiting of U.S. currency and the euro to the counterfeiting of prescription medication.[17] Hezbollah's criminal reach was global.

Dagan, though, was infuriated by the Venezuelan-Syrian-Hezbollah nexus, and pushed Harpoon to act. Targeting Ghazi presented a sobering challenge to Harpoon. Regardless of his drug-dealing endeavors, Ghazi was a diplomat, protected by the Geneva Protocols; extrajudicial treatment of diplomats was frowned upon in international circles. In Damascus, Ghazi was protected by Syria's security services, Hezbollah, and agents from Venezuela's Dirección de Servicios de Inteligencia y Prevención, the DISIP.* Syria was closer to Israel's borders than Venezuela, but it was dangerous and difficult for Israeli intelligence to operate inside Bashir al-Assad's police state. Dagan remained undaunted, however. "Dagan was determined to put a serious crimp in the Hezbollah drug trade," a former Harpoon officer remembered, "but Dagan knew that this would not be something that Israel or the Mossad could do alone. It would have to enlist international support. And that meant the United States."[18]

In 2007, Syria's continuous rogue policies had earned the regime its spot in President Bush's self-declared Axis of Evil. The Mossad and other facets of Israel's intelligence community had learned of the top-secret construction of a nuclear reactor in Deir ez-Zor in northeastern Syria, near the Iraqi frontier; the facility had been designed and was being built by North Korean nuclear engineers. The intelligence-gathering operations were far-reaching and global. According to foreign reports, details of the reactor were retrieved by Mossad agents in London who swiped them from the laptop of one of the Syrian nuclear engineers involved in the project.[19] The proof of Syria's nuclear intentions was irrefutable.

Prime Minister Olmert took the intelligence to President Bush. Meir Dagan also traveled to Langley to share the intelligence findings with the

---

* In 2009, President Chávez replaced the DISIP with a new internal security and intelligence service.

CIA in the hope that the United States would see fit to take preemptive action; Dagan ventured to the White House, as well. But President Bush, embroiled in two wars already, was wary. Faced with no other choice, Israeli Prime Minister Olmert opted to go it alone and before it became operational with the threat of any nuclear material being released into the environment. At just after midnight on September 7, 2007, Israeli warplanes struck the under-construction nuclear reactor and destroyed the entire facility. The raid became known as Operation Orchard.

The possibility that Syria could build a nuclear reactor in secret underscored the danger posed by the Assad regime. "My patience ran out on President Assad a long time ago," Bush said at a White House press conference, in 2007. "The reason why is because he houses Hamas, he facilitates Hezbollah, suicide bombers go from his country into Iraq, and he destabilizes Lebanon."[20] The time was perfect for the U.S. government to support Israeli efforts against the Venezuelan and Hezbollah drug ring run out of Damascus.

Under Meir Dagan's leadership, a close-knit, never-before-exhibited relationship was forged between the CIA and the Mossad. Both agencies shared a skeptical and suspicious history. The CIA had always feared that many elements of Israel's political hierarchy—and, indeed, Israel's intelligence services—were penetrated by the KGB operatives or the Warsaw Pact espionage services. There were, of course, many inside the CIA who harbored strong anti-Semitic hatred, and they viewed American support for the State of Israel as part of a grand Jewish plot. And, of course, the arrest and conviction of Jonathan Jay Pollard, the American intelligence analyst who spied on behalf of Israel, had further strained the relationship between the espionage services of the two allies.

But both agencies also realized just how very much they had in common on the global battlefield. Meir Dagan was viewed as the larger-than-life figure whose word was rock-solid and whose ability to get the mission done knew no bounds. "He exhibits tough love," former CIA Director Michael Hayden said with a smile, in an interview for Israel's Channel

One. "There is a softness there, but there's a hard shell around it. He's a thoroughgoing professional."[21]

At Langley, or at Mossad headquarters in Israel, Dagan was always referred to as the general. The Israeli spymaster enjoyed the respect, and CIA chiefs enjoyed his company. "Dagan was always smiling and determined to tell a joke or a funny story," Uri recalled. A joke, sometimes, helped to alleviate the stress of the life and death matters being discussed in a SCIF, or Sensitive Compartmented Information Facility, behind fortified doors guarded by armed men. The intelligence file on Ghazi Atef Nasser al-Din was discussed at one of these closed-door meetings. Dagan sought the CIA's help. But Ghazi wasn't an Agency priority, and the CIA wasn't interested. But the Drug Enforcement Administration was. The agency was already working its own Ghazi file involving the nexus between Hezbollah and cocaine.

The DEA was created on July 1, 1973, by President Richard M. Nixon to replace the small and little-known Bureau of Narcotics and Dangerous Drugs. The United States, following the flower-power movement of the 1960s and its relaxed attitude toward drugs, found itself battling new society standards and a stream of heroin and other drugs flowing into the country from Southeast Asia and Southwest Asia. The DEA, part of the Department of Justice, is responsible for battling drug smuggling and use within the United States, and leading major criminal investigations—and operations—in the continental United States and overseas.

There was always an international component to the DEA. DEA representatives were stationed at key U.S. embassies overseas in nations such as Pakistan and Thailand that were either producers of narcotics or key stops on smuggling routes to the United States. During the Cocaine Cowboy years in southern Florida in the early 1980s and then in the years to follow, the DEA became an intrinsic force throughout Latin America; DEA personnel and units were embedded inside the police and paramilitary forces fighting cocaine trafficking in Colombia, Mexico, and a half-dozen other nations throughout the Caribbean. The DEA maintained a small air force and navy.

Although the DEA responded to the September 11, 2001, attacks like all other federal law enforcement entities by sending resources to newly established frontline posts in Afghanistan, as well as reinforcing agents assigned to the U.S. embassy in Islamabad, Pakistan, and the consulates in Lahore, Peshawar, and Karachi, the agency sought a more active role in what became known as the global war on terror. Frontline status in the American-led effort—especially high-profile arrests and prosecutions—meant congressional exposure and funding. Funding for an agency meant relevance and survival.

The DEA, and its special operations assets, had extensive networks in Colombia and Venezuela. Years of fighting the cocaine trade led to an intimate knowledge of the terrain and the personalities involved. All of the DEA personnel in-country, or in-theater, were fluent Spanish speakers; many were the first-generations sons—and daughters—of immigrants from those nations. The DEA also had links, through a liaison agent stationed at the U.S. embassy in Beirut, with Lebanese law enforcement and the agency that was responsible for combating narcotics trafficking. Many of those police commanders were Maronite Christians or Sunni Muslims, and they despised what Hezbollah had done to their country. The DEA also maintained excellent relations with the Israel National Police, both through the U.S. embassy in Tel Aviv and by way of the Israel National Police attaché posted to the Israeli embassy in Washington, D.C. The attaché was the conduit for information and leads going back and forth across the ocean.

Close-knit cooperation with the DEA was a powerful new weapon for the Israeli efforts. The DEA brought with it the entire might of the U.S. Department of Justice. "As we used to joke in the unit," an INP veteran explained, "the power of the American judiciary, and the other branches of government, like the Department of Treasury, wielded more force than a fleet of aircraft carriers."[22]

On June 18, 2008, the United States Department of the Treasury's Office of Foreign Assets Control (OFAC) identified both Ghazi and Kana'an as individuals operating on behalf of terrorist entities or the state sponsors of terrorist entities.[23] OFAC administers and enforces economic and trade sanctions against targeted regimes, terrorists, and international narcotics traffickers, with the power to impose controls on transactions and freeze assets under U.S. jurisdiction. OFAC's origins go back to after the Second World War, when the Department of the Treasury tried to track and retrieve assets stolen by the Nazis. OFAC's role greatly expanded following the 9/11 attacks, when the full force of the U.S. government was used to prohibit individuals and groups from having access to the U.S. financial system—which, in essence, banished terrorist groups and their financiers from global banking networks.[24]

The campaign against the Venezuelan-Hezbollah cocaine nexus was based on proactive intelligence. HUMINT (human intelligence, the use of spies and agents), SIGINT (signal intelligence, and the interception of phone calls and e-mails), and ELINT (electronic intelligence, the interception of electromagnetic signals from weapons systems) methods were used to monitor the traffickers in Latin America. Agents on the ground gathered intelligence about the sourcing of the cocaine, the methods of packaging, and how the packages were transported, all under the protection of the Venezuelan Ministry of Foreign Affairs, on the flights between Caracas and Damascus. Drug investigations were dangerous affairs. Throughout Maicao and the areas connecting Colombia and Venezuela, heavily armed men roamed the streets with impunity. Many of them spoke Arabic.

Some elements of Israel's intelligence-gathering efforts were easy. Flight arrivals were easy enough to monitor—it was easy enough for ham radio enthusiasts in the area to listen in to Damascus International Airport ground control, so it wasn't too much of a challenge for Unit 8200, the IDF's eavesdropping and technical intelligence powerhouse, to do so, as well; according to some estimates, 80 percent of the raw intelligence data that reaches A'man's Research Department for analysis originates with Unit 8200.[25] Sources and assets in Syria—the details about which cannot be extrapolated—monitored the movement of drugs and money from the airport to the Venezuelan embassy on Ibn Al Khatib Street number 5, off of Rawda Square. Syrian intelligence agents, in uniform and in plain-clothes, protected the building. The Venezuelan embassy was a mere one thousand feet from the U.S. embassy in the Syrian capital.

Ghazi Atef Nasser al-Din drove around Damascus in a vehicle with diplomatic plates. His home, his car, and his person were considered sovereign Venezuelan territory. It couldn't be stopped or searched. The drugs and money also traveled in diplomatic vehicles. The contraband arrived, sometimes several times a week, on the flights from Caracas. The loads were often warehoused at the embassy; Syrian officials had to be taken care of, and the amount had to be counted and skimmed in envelopes and bundles prepared for ruling-party insiders who were promised a cut. The Iranian Revolutionary Guard also took a cut, but their parcels of $100 bills were prepacked in Caracas and left on board the flights to Tehran to be retrieved later. The drugs, and the monies destined for Hezbollah, also had to be transported from Damascus to Beirut.

The transports to Beirut were secret and designed to avoid any unwar-ranted attention. Sometimes cars from the embassy would make the fifty-mile trek across the Beirut-Damascus Highway—men paid off on both sides of the border made sure that the vehicles were expedited. Sometimes, the vehicles would make a more circuitous overland route, attempting to avoid the prying eyes of drones, aircraft, or satellites overhead; spies, informers, and duplicitous souls were everywhere along these traditional smuggling routes through villages and crossroads controlled by rogue men. Ghazi, and the Hezbollah drug lords, thought that overland was the safest way to transport the cash and drugs; the Venezuelans and Syrians agreed. But here, of course, was where the convoys were vulnerable.

Harpoon, and other facets of Israeli intelligence, thought of innova-tive ways—mostly nonlethal—that could be used to interrupt the flow of drugs and cash. They discussed innovative ideas, such as enlisting the services of certain types of insects, namely caterpillars, that could eat the drugs or the cash before the contraband could reach a junkie in Europe and a bank in Lebanon. Dagan's spies were asked to be original and imaginative. It was a new reality for them, and in the end traditional and conventional solutions were found to make sure that not every shipment made it to the Lebanese capital.

Operations mounted against the convoys by Israel were meant to disrupt the delivery process, not kill anyone. These commando raids were late-night operations executed under the cover of darkness that intercepted the vehicles bound for the Lebanese capital; narcotics were destroyed and cash was retrieved.

But deep penetration raids into Lebanon were risky. In a nation like Lebanon, where information held unique value to militias and criminal gangs, a phone call, a tip, could often achieve the same effects as a battalion of reconnaissance commandos. There were gangs operating throughout Lebanon that made a lucrative living robbing drug traffickers, smugglers, and other criminals. These gangs came from all the ethnic groups that formed the Lebanese mosaic, but they were all heavily armed and ruthless. It is not known how many tips these gangs received from anonymous sources; the robberies, though, netted tens of millions of dollars in untraceable bills and hundreds of kilograms of drugs.

The intelligence effort—one that was passive and preemptively deterrent—was designed to let the Venezuelans, the Syrians, and Hezbollah know that the secret operation was secret to no one. It was hoped, in both Israel and in the Beltway, that the campaign against the cocaine pipeline could be stopped; if the effort wasn't going to bankrupt the endeavor, then both Harpoon and the DEA wanted it to rob Hezbollah of critical funds. When Ghazi and his partners took extra precautions to protect their loads, the DEA tipped off the Lebanese Central Office for Drug Control, the national law enforcement arm whose mission was to stifle the brisk heroin, marijuana, and cocaine trade emanating from the country. In one such major arrest, the CODC raided a house, south of Beirut, confiscated about fifty kilograms of cocaine, and arrested five members of the network; one Venezuelan national and four Lebanese were taken into custody. The drugs were worth more than $8 million and were part of 255 kilograms that the gang had planned to smuggle out of the country.[26]

The DEA was also able to tip off European law enforcement agencies about possible shipments of Venezuelan cocaine headed for the continent via Lebanese merchant ships.

The DEA's cooperation with Israel had uncovered a brand-new universe of state and hostile terrorist entities joining forces to establish global pipelines of lucrative narcotics smuggling. The interdiction—by Lebanese gangs and "others"—of narcotics and cash meant problems for Ghazi and his crew. He was ultimately pulled from his post and placed in a lesser position in Lebanon, where he lost hands-on control of the cocaine flowing in on commercial flights.

And now the DEA decided that they wanted to publicize the threat of narco-terrorism emanating from Lebanon and the threat that it posed to the United States. In 2009, Mark Braun, the head of DEA Special Operations, testified about the growing threat before a Senate subcommittee on African Affairs for the Committee on Foreign Relations. "Mark my words," Braun warned, "as we speak here today, operatives from al-Qaeda, Hezbollah, and Hamas—perhaps others—are rubbing shoulders with Latin American and Mexican drug cartels."[27]

It is difficult to quantify the dollar amount that the joint American-Israeli operation cost Hezbollah. Ghazi Atef Nasser al-Din was a pawn, a player, in a larger network involving governments but that depended on Hezbollah's vast reach throughout the world and the Party of God's dependence on criminally produced revenue as a major component of their annual operational budget. "The American-Israel cooperation shut the spigot on one stream of money," Uri remarked, "and it opened others, and those had to be attended to."[28] Hezbollah was in no position to absorb additional losses. The Party of God had absorbed a blow of shock and awe to the midsection following the Ezzedine affair, and the dilution of their cocaine portfolio through Syria now had delivered another major loss.

Ghazi Atef Nasser al-Din was a wakeup call for Harpoon and the DEA. The Venezuelan-Iranian-Hezbollah cocaine network was a stark reminder that there is an inseparable connection between terrorism and criminal activity—and both were fueled by money. In offices in Arlington,

Virginia, as well as in Israel, men and women scribbled on white boards with ideas on how to disrupt the flow of drugs and money in particular from South America into the Middle East and beyond. Questions remained unanswered for Meir Dagan and the Harpoon team. What new spigot would Hezbollah open next? What did they do with the hundreds of millions it collected from operations around the world? Once again Lebanon's banks, the ones that laundered and safeguarded much of the drug money, were placed in the center of Israel's crosshairs.

CHAPTER FOURTEEN

Follow the Money

Intelligence work has one moral law—it is justified by results.
—*John le Carré,* The Spy Who Came In from the Cold

U ri Bar-Lev was a special operations legend in Israel. A former combat engineer officer who had lost part of a leg while in service, Bar-Lev was tapped, in 1986, by the then head of IDF Central Command, Major General Ehud Barak, to establish a counterterrorist undercover unit made up of paratroopers who could masquerade as indigenous Palestinians to gather intelligence and make terror arrests. The unit was known as Duvdevan, or "Cherry," and was the first undercover counterterrorist force that the State of Israel had raised since Dagan's unit in Gaza sixteen years earlier. Duvdevan was highly active during the first intifada and incredibly effective.

In 1992, the Israeli police commissioner tapped Bar-Lev to create a Duvdevan-like unit for the Jerusalem Police District that could stem a series of destructive terrorist attacks in Israel's capital. Bar-Lev traded in his olive drab fatigues for the blue tunic of the police force and created a squad that was designated as Unit 33. The unit, made up of Duvdevan veterans and the kind of street-smart free spirits that were usually recruited by the intelligence services, was a smashing success and sealed Bar-Lev's standing in the police hierarchy. He climbed up the chain of command. In 2009, at the end of his career, Israel's minister for internal security appointed Assistant Commissioner Bar-Lev to serve as the Israeli law enforcement attaché to the United States.

For years, Israel's police attachés were stationed in New York City and the Israeli consulate on Forty-Second Street in midtown Manhattan. To Israelis, New York City was the epicenter of the world, and the New York Police Department was one of the most important departments to liaise with. It was also easy for an Israeli police representative to hail a cab to John F. Kennedy or LaGuardia Airports and fly nonstop to meet any other commissioner in the United States or Canada. The New York posting was one of the most sought after in the police—the shopping, the night life, and the dining out was considered a lottery winning assignment for a police general at the tail end of his career.

But after 9/11, Israel's police representatives to the United States worked out of the Israeli embassy in Washington, D.C. The U.S. capital was not New York City, and a town house in Georgetown or one of the other suburbs in and around the Beltway was not considered as chic as a duplex in a luxury doorman building on the Upper East Side of Manhattan. But Washington, D.C., was convenient for the police generals to meet with their American counterparts in American federal law enforcement. The 9/11 attacks turned the United States and Israel into inseparable allies in the law enforcement campaign against terror. Technologies that were standard security tools in Israel's fight against suicide bombers and active shooters were eagerly reviewed by the newly formed U.S. Department of Homeland Security; Israeli expertise, namely the sharing of counterterrorist tradecraft, for U.S. law enforcement, all traveled through the police attachés office in Washington, D.C.

Most of all, though, the posting to the Israeli embassy in Washington, D.C., made interaction with America's federal law enforcement a convenient and expedient affair. The exchange of sensitive law enforcement material was always made in person. The police attaché met with his counterparts at Federal Bureau of Investigation headquarters to discuss ongoing Hamas, PIJ, and Hezbollah investigations that fell under FBI jurisdiction; the attaché traveled to the offices of the Secret Service to talk shop concerning mutually connected investigations, such as Palestinian gangs using forged credit cards and Hezbollah cells flooding Israel with bundles of counterfeit U.S. dollars. Bar-Lev made his rounds, introducing himself to the various undersecretaries and commissioners.

Bar-Lev was quite effective as the Israeli law enforcement ambassador to the United States. Tall and lean with a shaven head, he had a fondness for fashion and the better things in life. He was a cigar smoker and was good at telling war stories. Many of the alpha males loved having a cocktail with Bar-Lev at one of the Beltway's many lounges where the men in power shared drinks and talked shop. He liaised with everyone in D.C. connected to America's war on terror and crime—from the U.S. Marshals Service to the heads of IRS enforcement.

Much of his work, though, involved the DEA. Israeli organized crime gangs were heavily involved in the Ecstasy trade that ranged from Tel Aviv to New York, with stops in Belgium and the Netherlands. Most of the mutual cooperation, however, focused on Hezbollah. "There was a lot of common interest and parallel investigations involving Hezbollah," Bar-Lev remembered, "and both the DEA and the Israel National Police were determined to join forces and do what we could to stop the terrorists from flooding our countries with drugs and then using the money to ultimately kill innocent people. We had a lot to offer."[1]

Bar-Lev was also Harpoon's police representative in the United States. When the Harpoon roundtable met, the police commander assigned to Dagan's task force would be the one to communicate with Bar-Lev in the United States requesting action and assistance. "If we needed anything from the DEA or any of the other facets of American police, we first had to sanitize the intelligence. The Americans always liked to look at what we had and names, dates, locations, and anything that would reveal our sources had to be removed," Shai explained. "The sanitized material was then transmitted from the police representative sitting with us at Harpoon to the embassy in Washington for further action. This was the protocol and it was important that we adhered to it."[2]

Meetings between Bar-Lev and his counterparts at DEA became routine. Both agencies had common interests; intelligence was shared and methods sought so that the two entities could effectively work together. Israel had extensive experience in battling terrorists, and Bar-Lev, serving in several administrative posts, had supervised operations against Hamas and against its money. Hamas was a unique criminal target; because it was an organized crime gang that wasn't in it for profit. There were few assets to confiscate as penalty for the excesses of living a criminal lifestyle, unlike the Colombian cartels that the DEA had targeted so successfully for years, which built regal palaces complete with zoos, aquariums, and gold-covered furniture, as well as other extravagances that exceeded what movie stars, star soccer players, and heads of state could ever dream of owning. Hezbollah was run differently, like a combination of Hamas and the Colombians. The profits went to fund the struggle, but the cash was used by the narco-masterminds to fund lavish lifestyles that didn't correspond with the strict restrictions of their public Shiite devotion.

The Israeli police attaché also met senior agents from the Special Operations Division, as well as the DEA's Counter-Narco-Terrorism Operations Center to convey the intelligence that he received on secure e-mail servers at the embassy from headquarters in Jerusalem. The discussions were detailed and operational. Sometimes the discussions, involving the latest intelligence on some of the most unsavory characters in the terrorism and narcotics underworld, were held in Outback Steakhouses and in Starbucks. The men always selected tables in the rear; Bar-Lev liked to sit with his back to the wall facing the entrance.

The back-and-forth flow between the Israeli police and the DEA agents was voluminous.

Federal agents and U.S. attorneys measure success and failure solely by indictments and convictions. The scuttlebutt at the federal judiciary was that cases of passport and visa fraud brought by the State Department's Diplomatic Security Service were liked the best, because those cases had a universal conviction rate; most cases were ultimately pleaded out.

U.S. attorneys loved conviction rates—it helped them get appointed to the federal bench. The combined Harpoon and DEA effort against the Venezuelan-Hezbollah drug ring was not viewed favorably by the U.S. attorney or the Department of Justice. It seemed too complicated, too costly, and too time-consuming. But the operation against Ghazi Atef Nasser al-Din was just beginning.

The joint U.S.-Israeli effort was just as much an espionage mission as it was the commencement of a criminal investigation. The bilateral exchange utilized the very best American human intelligence assets in Colombia and Venezuela. The Israelis utilized their resources outside the country, and monitored communications of the known men in the Hezbollah narcotics corporation that were responsible for coordinating drug shipments and money. As their investigations deepened, both the DEA and the Israelis were surprised to learn that all roads led to Africa.

When the "Venezuelan connection" was exposed and compromised, a very sound and seemingly economic smuggling route had been dealt a serious blow. The money and the drugs were still flown to Damascus, often in diplomatic pouches, and while in Syria, under the protection of President Assad's ruthless security forces, payouts were made for the guarantee of security. But getting the cocaine from Syria to Lebanon and then on to markets in Europe had become far riskier. Hezbollah now needed to mitigate any attempts to dilute its pot of cocaine gold.

The Party of God had proven itself to be a resourceful foe, though. The Lebanese spirit of resilience through the civil war and domestic political chaos was a Hezbollah badge of honor, as was the ability to tap into a Lebanese Diaspora spread around the world. Lebanese Shiites had settled up and down the coastal countries of West Africa in the same way that others before them had traveled to Colombia, Venezuela, Brazil, and Argentina. Lebanese were entrepreneurial and hardworking, and they negotiated their way through the local African bureaucracy of porous borders, corrupt customs officers and politicians, and lawless provinces. The terrorists discovered that in countries like Sierra Leone, Cote d'Ivoire, Senegal, and Gambia, anyone could bribe an official and employ men—or young boys—who would carry an AK-47 assault rifle on their behalf. There were even attempts by Hezbollah and Iran to gain a foothold in Nigeria—a country where Israeli diplomatic and commercial interests were strong. In 2004 an Iranian diplomat was arrested on suspicion of spying on the Israeli embassy in the capital of Abuja; later, Nigeria's dreaded State Security Service arrested members of an Iranian-trained terrorist cell planning to attack American and Israeli targets in the African nation.

The African nations of West Africa were easy marks for the shrewd and cunning Lebanese Shiites. The Lebanese businessmen quickly turned neglected plots of strewn or abandoned warehouses into brand-spanking-new construction. Iranian money was invested in the infrastructure of the many businesses, many of them mere shell companies that operated behind post office boxes and offices that were nothing more than place-holders and an address to use on a shipping manifest. The businesses, especially those that were legit, were required to kick a percentage of their earnings back to Hezbollah's coffers in Lebanon. Sheikh Nasrallah and his minions were savvy and ruthless businessmen. Shiite expatriates that didn't send their tribute back to south Beirut were dealt with harshly. In 2004, U.S. diplomats in West Africa publicly charged that Hezbollah was "systematically siphoning profits" from the region's lucrative diamond trade, in part by threatening Lebanese merchants.[3]

The most successful Lebanese business in West Africa, though, was narcotics trafficking and money laundering. International law enforcement officials have long held that the $120 million that Iran donates to Hezbollah every year was a mere pittance when compared to the billions of dollars of narco-dollar profits that the Party of God earned. Religious sentiments were given the blind eye and set aside, as the illegal contraband sales were the turbo engine that allowed the terrorists to maintain their infrastructure, their lethal operations, and their opulent lifestyles. According to the Pulitzer Foundation, "Most of Hezbollah's support comes from drug trafficking, a major moneymaker endorsed by the mullahs through a particular fatwa. In addition to the production and trade of heroin in the

Middle East, Hezbollah facilitates, for a fee, the trafficking of other drug smuggling networks, such as the FARC, in the case of cocaine."[4]

When the spigots on Ghazi Atef Nasser al-Din's Venezuelan pipeline were tightened, Hezbollah found new and remarkably clever ways to bring its cash to Lebanon via Africa. The Hezbollah scheme was simple yet ingenious. Hezbollah cocaine destined for European and Russian markets that had always been shipped through Lebanon was now sent to countries in West Africa instead. The countries were Guinea-Bissau, Mauritania, Gambia, and Sierra Leone. These nations were relatively easy prey for Hezbollah and Iranian usurpation, and the ruling dictators were always eager to align themselves with heavily armed cutthroats in positions of power who could make millions of dollars simply by looking the other way. Some of these African strongmen, like José Américo Bubo Na Tchuto, Guinea-Bissau's former navy chief of staff, were drug warlords in their own right.[5]

The money from the narcotic sales was sent to the shell companies and exchange houses in West Africa. Accra, the capital of Ghana, was the airport of choice. Lebanon's Middle East Airlines flew a route connecting Accra and Beirut. The airport was located in south Beirut, the ground zero of Hezbollah's power base, and most of the airport's employees were Shiites who had earned their positions courtesy of the Party of God. Once the flight from Africa landed in the Lebanese capital, the cargo was met by heavily armed Hezbollah squads who loaded the bulk loads of tightly packed clear plastic blocks of $100 bills into the cargo holds of shiny black Suburban and Pajero SUVs; Hezbollah shooters stuck out through the sunroofs, aiming their RPK light machine guns at anyone who looked suspicious. Lebanese customs officials were not allowed to get near the aircraft.

Billions of dollars were sent in such a manner. The remainder of the cocaine cash was delivered to Beirut by a well-oiled Hezbollah machine of money couriers, cash smugglers, *hawaladars* (those who used the informal Islamic method for transferring money across borders), and currency brokers. The cash, met at Beirut International Airport by Hezbollah units, was then transferred to money changers who deposited the drug profits into Lebanese bank accounts. From these banks the funds were transported to exchange houses and, ultimately, to Lebanese financial institutions. Once safe, the monies were then wired to the United States so that Hezbollah front companies could buy used vehicles and then ship them back to West Africa; the front companies in the United States were owned by Hezbollah operatives, or Lebanese immigrants with pro-Hezbollah sympathies. Proceeds from the car sales were intermingled with the cocaine profits and the money laundered.

This scheme netted hundreds of millions of dollars for Hezbollah. Some of the money went toward advanced technological gear, such as night vision equipment, that Hezbollah used against Israel in Lebanon and against U.S. troops in Iraq. A percentage was sent as tribute to Iranian Revolutionary Guard commanders in Tehran.

Both the Americans and Israelis were stymied by the growing global spread of this highly lucrative and national-security-threatening global narcotics-and-dollar enterprise. Whenever the DEA or Harpoon tried to box the Iranians and Hezbollah in to limit their expansion, the Revolutionary Guardsmen and the men from Beirut simply moved the boundaries. The fight became a stubborn tug-of-war on a global chessboard.

Spies, drug dealers, arms merchants, and former soldiers looking for a war of fortune were highly visible on the streets of the West African capitals, and especially inside the bars of the prominent hotels. Everything and everyone was for sale in the capitals of Dakar, Banjul, Bissau, Freetown, Monrovia, Yamoussoukro, and Abidjan: blood diamonds, stolen iron ore shipments, drugs, guns, and women of all ages. A former U.S. State Department Diplomatic Security Service special agent who had worked in American embassies in West Africa once commented that "you needed a scorecard to tell who's who amidst the unsavory characters that one would see on the streets and especially inside the hotel bars."

The local state security agents, psychopathic criminals who terrorized for the greater good, tried to maintain control over the moral void;

mostly they tried to secure a cut for themselves, and enough of a payoff to take care of their commanding officers. The rule of law, it seemed, didn't translate easily into the local West African dialects. Business disputes were settled in back alleys and usually with a gunshot to the head.

The boys from Lebanon were used to lawless chaos. They thrived in cities with checkpoints and armed thugs demanding a bribe. They didn't do much to conceal their identities. They spoke loudly in Arabic, congregated largely with each other, and ate in Lebanese restaurants. The Hezbollah money movers made a point to have a good time as they trekked across the precarious routes that connected the money pickup points and the transit hubs along West Africa's Atlantic coast. They drank alcohol even though it was strictly *haram*, or forbidden. They spent cash on prostitutes, even though HIV and other diseases were rampant among the working women. Gambling was not unheard of. For the Israelis and Americans who tried to blend in and remain inconspicuous to gather intelligence on the men and the money they moved, the Lebanese were surprisingly easy to follow. The money was easy to follow, too.

West Africa became a focal point in the discussions that Uri Bar-Lev had with his counterparts at DEA headquarters. Bar-Lev received sanitized intelligence from Harpoon. "We were careful to make sure that our sources, our methods, were concealed in the information we released to the Americans," a member of the Harpoon task force explained. "We trusted the Americans, they were our partners, but we always had to be careful to maintain the integrity and origins of our intelligence."[6] The Americans, too, were wary about sharing the true names of the operatives in the field who would slip a prostitute a few hundred dollars for information about the Lebanese man she had just been with. Spies never trusted one another.

In the information that they did share, a common denominator intrigued both Harpoon and the DEA. The profits, the skim, and the financing channels that enabled this enormous multinational operation to flourish all ran through one Beirut financial institution: the Lebanese Canada Bank, or LCB, a Beirut financial institution that maintained thirty-five branches in Lebanon and one global representative headquarters in Montreal, Québec, in Canada. Its net assets exceeded $5 billion and it had extensive interactions with the major U.S. banks in New York City.

The LCB had already sparked enormous interest in Dagan and his team. Soon, ideas for operations against the bank were being scribbled on whiteboards inside the DEA offices as well.

CHAPTER FIFTEEN

Malware and Moles

There is no place where espionage is not possible.
—*Sun Tzu*

The one rule of espionage is that there are no rules. Everyone and everything is fair game. The profession of spying is one of moral ambiguity, based on the manipulation of weaknesses and vulnerabilities. These operational guidelines are the doctrinal DNA behind the Mossad's legendary status as one of the world's top espionage services. The moments of James Bond–like daring, such as the abduction of Holocaust villain Adolf Eichmann or the exploits of superspy Eli Cohen in Syria, were awe-inspiring operations that made headlines and created *New York Times* best sellers and Hollywood blockbusters. But the day-to-day unreported grind of gathering, analyzing, and acting on intelligence is what allows people to sleep soundly in their beds.

There are numerous ways by which the spooks manipulated weaknesses and vulnerabilities in their targets. Some tools are technical. IMINT is image intelligence, the use of satellite and aerial reconnaissance photography to observe locations from national boundaries. SIGINT, or signal intelligence, is the interception of signals, either between individuals or between machines and computers, to gather intelligence. ELINT, the monitoring of electrical signals and electromagnetic signatures, is particularly effective in combat when measures and countermeasures needed to be deployed. And, of course, there is HUMINT, the classic spies-in-the-field meeting with sources and assets, engaged in the skull-duggery of breaking into hotel rooms, blackmailing targets, and abducting threats to national security.

Computer intelligence, or cyberwarfare, was the newest domain. The more the Internet becomes a center of our lives, the more vulnerable we are to others peeking in or interfering with our online activities. Accessing an adversary's computer could produce a virtual warehouse of files; tapping into their e-mails on a continuous basis could reel in a bonanza that even the most talented spy of days past would never have been able to photograph with a small Minox B spy camera. E-mails can be forwarded and manipulated. Missives with a seemingly genuine attachment can act as a Trojan horse; a hidden virus can secret its way into a computer or even enter and take over an entire network, releasing vast destruction when triggered by the click of a mouse. Manipulated properly, with the right software, an innocently opened e-mail or a strategically inserted thumb drive, can give an intelligence service the power to completely shut down multiple networks. Such a shutdown, halting operations for public services and for security forces, could paralyze a nation.

Every intelligence agency in the world, and even the terrorists they hunted, used a combination of all these means to gather information on friends and foes, and to cause mischief and mayhem. Israel did it better than most.*

For years, A'man, the Shin Bet, and the Mossad sought out men and women who displayed unique operational talents. These skills included a mastery of Arabic and Persian, tactical prowess, personalities that worked well alone and under enormous stress. People from different backgrounds, especially Diaspora Jews[1] who could work internationally using their

---

* According to published accounts (https://www.defensetech.org/2008/06/02/hezbollahs-cyber-warfare-program/) Hezbollah has been very active—and very capable—in assembling potent SIGINT and cyberwarfare capabilities. On May 8, 2008, Sheikh Hassan Nasrallah declared that the organization's communications network was its most important weapon—just as important to the group's nefarious purposes as were its missiles. Hezbollah's SIGINT and cyberwarfare capabilities include fiber-optic cable tapping and manipulation, data interception, and network and Internet hijacking.

genuine papers, always topped the lists of the intelligence service headhunters. The shooters, and those who had the right stuff for dangerous
missions on dark and treacherous nights, veterans of elite commando
units, were soon joined on the recruitment lines by computer and technology geniuses and mathematical whizzes, "jobniks," as they were once
referred to, who could, in the course of their military service, innovate
new tools and outside-the-box concepts.

Some of these brilliant men—and women—were conscripted straight
out of high school into A'man's Unit 8200. The unit had at one time been
the nation's eavesdropping force, but it quickly became something akin
to a MIT lab or even James Bond's weapons developer, Q—matching
military necessity with high-tech innovation. The men and women who
emerged from the ranks of Unit 8200 made headlines using the skills and
ideas they perfected to develop top-secret projects during their service
to create high-tech applications with far-reaching civilian uses. The unit
drove Israel's reputation as the world's leading startup nation. Veterans of
the unit include Gil Shwed, the founder of Check Point, whose net worth
today is $2.2 billion; Avishai Abrahami,[2] founder of Waze, which sold
itself to Google for $1.8 billion; Nir Zuk, founder of Palo Alto Networks,
whose company is worth $260 million; and the seven founders of NICE
Systems, which earned over $250 million in profits in 2016.

Many Unit 8200 servicemen and women who wanted to stay inside the
system were recruited by the other areas of the military or by the Shin Bet.
The war against Hezbollah—and Iran—would need all of Israel's spies,
those in the trenches and those sitting behind a keyboard.

Iran, with its nuclear weapons program, and Hezbollah, boasting a
criminal enterprise with thousands of missiles aimed at Israel's population centers, both posed an existential threat to Israel. As such, every tool,
weapon, strategy, and technology at Israel's disposal were enlisted into
the fight.

The head of a service like Dagan, according to one Harpoon veteran, faced a dilemma: "Do you follow or do you foil? Do you continue to observe a target and see where the surveillance and the intimate

interception lead, or do you wrap up an operation and stop a target being an active threat? In some cases, 'follow or foil' was a judgment call; in other cases, where the threat was imminent, there was little choice at all."[3] The combination of HUMINT, SIGINT, special operations, FININT (financial intelligence), and cyberwarfare tools at the Mossad's disposal gave Meir Dagan a new range of options when it came to this all-important question. And he wanted to use them all in an aggressive campaign against Iran's nuclear ambitions and against Hezbollah's ability to once again rain rockets down on Israel's cities. Dagan wanted to foil his foes and their finances. His American partners had a different view.

The American unit that chased terrorist money at the CIA's Financial Intelligence Operations unit (FINO) was headed by Philip Rosenberg. A thin and balding man, he was a sharp dresser with a prominent nose. FINO, established in the wake of the 9/11 attack, was placed under the National Clandestine Service's organizational chart. Rosenberg, an economist by trade, had served in a number of intelligence posts overseas, utilizing his financial skills for covert operations on behalf of the Americans. He was known among his colleagues as "Nervous Phil," for his wild enthusiasm and creative approaches, and in 2004 he was given the CIA's Directors Award by George Tenet for FINO's work.

Rosenberg was initially very suspicious of the Israelis, and he was quite reluctant to work with them. But he was eventually won over by men like Uri and Shai, and, of course, Meir Dagan. Rosenberg was impressed by the quality of the intelligence that Harpoon provided. He understood what the Harpoon boys were trying to do and realized it complemented his own efforts, while providing additional reach to the American program. There was a sharp difference of opinion, though. Rosenberg expended considerable effort to persuade the Israelis not to obstruct the flow of terror money but rather to follow it and see where it would lead them. Rosenberg's philosophy was to blend SIGINT and land-based data to track terrorists across the planet.[4] The goal, after all, was often not to immediately capture the target, but rather to see where the intelligence would lead.

This tactical disagreement had repercussions back at headquarters in Tel Aviv, inside Harpoon's staff meetings and operational discussions. The Shin Bet advocated for the quick kill, taking out the suspects right away, while the Mossad representative frequently supported Rosenberg's thesis of, according to one Harpoon veteran, "feeding a hooked whale more and giving him more line." This was the case except when it involved Hezbollah.

Dagan wanted to bankrupt the Party of God and deny it the financial means to survive. The Mossad director read the intelligence briefs coming back from Washington, D.C., and West Africa concerning the drug profits laundered in and out of Lebanon's banks, and it gave him and his team ideas. The Lebanese banking system was complicit in funding the bloodshed, earning hundreds of millions of dollars in fees and profits from handling drug money. It was itself a criminal enterprise.

Hezbollah touted itself as a highly disciplined military and political force built on strength and Shiite rage. Hezbollah military parades in southern Beirut featured rigid lines of marching soldiers, some wearing explosive vests, who goose-stepped in precise cadence. Lebanon's history of violence and factional fighting created a vacuum that enabled the Party of God to flex its military muscle—and its use of all-out terror—to achieve its political aspirations. Sheikh Nasrallah had taken Hezbollah from a terrorist army at war with the United States and Israel and turned it into the de facto ruler of the country. Hezbollah ran a semiautonomous state within a state that discarded the notion of Lebanese independence and any hope for a representative democracy. Hezbollah had its own network of social services and it had an indigenous foreign policy; Nasrallah's army could obliterate the Lebanese Armed Forces if it so desired. But for all its conventional power, the organization was still run like a ragtag band of guerrillas. Clans ruled the military wing. Greed and corruption turned the ruling elite, men who were supposed to bring about Shiite representation based on religious principles, into a gang of feuding hucksters with their own special interests, always trumping the welfare of the communities they swore to advance.

Hezbollah did not run a central bank that financed its wars and its benevolent projects. There was no party reserve into which Iranian cash flowed. Party of God commanders did not have Hezbollah-issued credit cards. All matters pertaining to money passed through an entity known in Arabic as the Hezbollah Bayt al-Mal, or the Hezbollah House of Money. The Bayt al-Mal was controlled lock, stock, and barrel by Nasrallah, and his office supervised all of the financial services for the Party of God. The Bayt al-Mal is Hezbollah's unofficial treasury, holding and investing its assets and serving as a hub for all of the group's investments and interactions—from the acquisition of state-of-the-art night vision equipment on the black market to acquiring real estate holdings.

The Bayt al-Mal national headquarters was a building nestled inside the Shiite slums of south Beirut, Hezbollah's stronghold. The structure was draped in Hezbollah flags that were positioned near billboards, some two stories tall, depicting the group's martyrs who had been killed in the wars with Israel. A small guard of heavily armed men, an elite cadre of Hezbollah special operations shooters, maintained careful watch. Heavy machine-gun positions, capable of shooting down supersonic fighter bombers or helicopter gunships, were positioned behind sandbags on the building's roof.

The Bayt al-Mal boasted other branches, of course. There were small offices in additional Lebanese cities like Burj al-Barajinah, Sidon, Tyre, Nabatieh, and Ba'albak. The Bayt al-Mal employed bureaucrats, accountants, secretaries, and auditors who made the machinery of Hezbollah's money function. The institution was slowly entering the twenty-first century by computerizing its files and systems. Israel's air raids on Lebanese banks during the 2006 Second Lebanon War resulted in damages that weren't limited to the stacks of $100 bills and Lebanese pounds that burned like dry bush in a forest fire. Ledgers, files, and notes, some written in giant notebooks that could have been used a century earlier in the Ottoman Empire and during French rule, also went up in flames. Permanent records were lost forever. Computers had to be installed and networks built from scratch. Specialists had to be brought in to run the systems, and staffers, some who conducted financial transactions the way their parents had once done in the villages of southern Lebanon, had to be retrained and certified.

The Bayt al-Mal was just one piece of the Hezbollah financial fortress. Another piece was a mysterious investment and brokerage house called the Yousser Company for Finance and Investment. The Yousser Company was used as cover for many of the Bayt al-Mal transactions, to launder loans and commercial business before they reached legitimate banks—and those used as venues by Hezbollah—for business around the world. The proxies, shell companies, Beirut post office boxes, and investment houses were nothing more than import-export companies providing a layer of cover to the complex and illegal Hezbollah financial empire.

For years Harpoon tried to convince the U.S. Department of the Treasury to take action. In fact, Harpoon tried to convince everyone and anyone in the U.S. government that both the Bayt al-Mal and Yousser were used to cover much of the facilitated terrorism, including Iranian money that flooded into the Party of God, as well as into various Palestinian terrorist groups, from Hamas and the PIJ, to the Syrian proxy, the Popular Front for the Liberation of Palestine General Command. But the State Department feared that going after these financial houses would impact the overall Lebanese economy and harm American efforts to stabilize a nation that was very unstable.

In the fall of 2006, following the summer's Israeli-Hezbollah war, Stuart Levey, the Under Secretary of the Treasury for Terrorism and Financial Intelligence, finally placed both the Bayt al-Mal and the Yousser Company for Finance and Investment on the U.S. Office of Foreign Assets Control, or OFAC, blacklist. An OFAC designation was a true legal quarantine of entities posing a threat to national security goals. It was used against foreign countries and regimes, terrorists, international narcotics traffickers, anyone engaged in activities related to the proliferation of

weapons of mass destruction, and any other threats to the national security, foreign policy, or economy of the United States.[5] Business, banks,
and organizations under OFAC sanction could have their assets frozen. It
was illegal for any U.S. business to interact with them in any way.

Levey's move angered many in Beirut. Hezbollah supporters claimed
that both institutions were apolitical, and by no means involved in any
untoward activities. But several months after the OFAC edit, a freighter
ostensibly transporting refrigerators to Beirut under an import license
from the Yousser Company was impounded when the "refrigerators" were
discovered to be actually a cargo of eighteen antiaircraft radar systems,
along with vehicles mounting specialized military capabilities.[6]

The OFAC step forced Hezbollah to move transactions it had once
concealed and openly engage with well-established banks and financial
institutions in Lebanon. Hezbollah's preferred bank, the Israelis and the
DEA learned, had traditionally been the Lebanese Canadian Bank. The
Beirut-based institution was originally formed in 1960 when it was called
the Banque des Activities Economiques SAL, and it operated as a subsidiary of the Royal Bank of Canada's Middle Eastern operations. The bank
was an empire, with a global reach and thirty-five branches throughout
Lebanon, and a North American office in Montreal. Its total assets had a
net value of nearly $5 billion.[7]

Harpoon was pleased when Hezbollah was forced to deal directly
with Lebanon's banks. It made the multi-billion-dollar institutions vulnerable. And the Israelis already had an asset* inside the Lebanese banking
system.

Israel's man inside Lebanon's banking apparatus was not someone working at the top of the corporate food chain. "The notion that a spy, in order
to be valuable, had to be someone very high up in an organization was
faulty," a former Israeli intelligence officer with knowledge of Harpoon's

---

* The State of Israel and its intelligence services do not, as a measure of policy and operational guidelines, reveal the identities of their assets.

operations explained. "Sometimes all you needed was someone knee-deep in the bureaucracy, perhaps bitter over not being considered for promotion, or perhaps angry that he was undergoing a divorce, and he wanted some measure of peace of mind. Sometimes that person just wanted to do the right thing. He or she wanted to do the patriotic thing."[8] A minor bureaucrat could have invaluable intelligence at their fingertips such as salaries, debts, secret deals; minor things, like interoffice affairs, especially affairs between office workers of the same sex and different ethnic and religious groups, could be of great value to a case officer running an agent inside an institution like a Lebanese bank. Such manipulations were classic tradecraft techniques. Identifying the vulnerabilities of targeted individuals was Lesson One in any service's spy school.

Useful bureaucrats might also be those responsible for purchasing equipment, including mobile phones, servers, mainframes, and computers. Access to those financial computers was critical. It is known that somehow, a malware cousin of what became known as Stuxnet and Flame targeted Lebanon's banks.[9] Dubbed "Gauss," the malware was discovered years after it was inserted into systems in Lebanon's banking sector; according to reports, it infected as many as 2,500 computers. The malware was strikingly similar to the worm that the world would come to know as Stuxnet, which was used against Iran's centrifuges at its Nantanz plant; according to reports, the worm was a joint operation between the CIA, the National Security Agency, and U.S. Cyber Command; the Iran Desk at Britain's Government Communications Headquarters; and, in Israel, the Mossad using the technology perfected by Unit 8200.[10]

Gauss collected configuration information of an infected machine, such as network interfaces, drives, and BIOS information. The true payload Gauss delivered was encrypted using a key derived from the information it collected from the infected machine.[11] The software gathered log-in information, allowing others to then infiltrate the accounts and monitor what was going on inside the world of electronic bank transfers and withdrawals. It was the first time that a nation-state, cyber security experts assessed, had targeted banks with malware.[12] The use of such tools underscored a line from John le Carré's novel *A Perfect Spy* that some members of Harpoon liked to quote: "In every operation there is an above the line and a below the line. Above the line is what you do by the book. Below the line is how you do the job."

The electronic insight was invaluable. But men like Dagan, old-timers who remembered typing reports on aged manual machines, often preferred the more traditional elements of espionage tradecraft: human intelligence—the art of a man observing and using his guts, instincts, and sometimes sense of honor and patriotism, in the performance of the age-old craft of espionage.

Israeli intelligence fielded an invaluable asset inside the LCB. Little has been reported about the man other than that he went by the name of Munir Z.[13] He was described as handsome yet unassuming, believed to be in his early forties and from a proud Christian family with a history of service to Lebanon. Many of the men in the family, including Munir's brother, served in the Lebanese Armed Forces, and made the military their careers. Although Lebanon had been carved to pieces by ethnic divides and then chewed up by internecine carnage, there were many in the country who viewed their allegiance solely to the flag of their nation. Munir Z. was one such individual who placed country first.

An accountant by trade, Munir Z. had been a banking bureaucrat for years, working in office branches and crunching numbers. His specialty was fraud detection. This skill set was in high demand, given U.S. Department of Treasury interests in Middle Eastern banking in the wake of the September 11 attacks and the emergence of Harpoon. Although many of the Middle Eastern financial institutions had suspicious clientele moving hundreds of millions of dollars through questionable accounts, the banks were compelled to hire money-laundering specialists to placate international audits. "It was always an issue of covering their asses," a veteran Israeli intelligence officer reflected. "The appearance of due diligence was often as important as the performance of due diligence."[14]

Munir Z. was a relatively high-ranking auditor in the bank's Beirut headquarters. Munir reviewed accounts, transactions, and a mile-long paper trail that implicated the bank in suspicious activities, a paper trail that linked it to known charities and front groups involved in supporting Hezbollah terrorist operations around the world. One such group was the Hayat al-Dam Lil-Muqawama al-Islamiya—the Islamic Resistance Support Organization, or IRSO. The IRSO raised money for Hezbollah by soliciting donations from Shiites all over the world. They pitched for the donations on Hezbollah's al-Manar television station, promising that monies raised would, according to a U.S. Department of the Treasury memo, be used to "purchase sophisticated weapons and conduct operations. Indeed, donors can choose from a series of projects to contribute to, including supporting and equipping fighters and purchasing rockets and ammunition."[15]

It isn't known if Munir was recruited by Israeli intelligence headhunters seeking someone who could be useful, or if the Lebanese accountant was what is known in the industry as a walk-in—someone who expressed a willingness to spy and volunteered his services. The information he provided, however, was of unprecedented value, in particular in exposing LBC as a main conduit of monies from all sorts of illegal enterprises—like drug dealing and criminal activities in the United States, Europe, South America, and West Africa—as well as the dispensing of those funds to the personal accounts of Hezbollah commanders or accounts used by Palestinian groups.

Munir wasn't alone. There were, reportedly, other intelligence assets working in fields that connected Lebanon's banks with the outside world. One asset, according to published accounts, was a software engineer whose main clients were banks. He helped set up DSL networks in Lebanon and was recruited, apparently without knowing that the people he was helping were actually Israeli, to complete a case study of the banking communication networks in the country.[16]

Displaying the diversity of the intelligence effort, another operative was Nasser al-Waer, a German-Lebanese citizen and an air-conditioning technician by profession. He was recruited in Europe and sent to Nabatieh, in the heart of the terrorists' zone in South Lebanon. Once situated, he found work at a Hezbollah-run hospital in town. During one of the briefings he received from his handlers in Europe, al-Waer was instructed to penetrate the IRSO, which he did successfully shortly after arriving through his connections at the hospital. The technician provided Harpoon's team with intelligence regarding money transfers and donations that were originated worldwide and transferred to Lebanon to support Hezbollah's activities.[17]

Other men recruited, the reports continued, worked for one of the country's two main cellular phone providers, a company called Alfa.[18] The data given to Harpoon was also sent to the U.S. Department of the Treasury. A month after the 2006 war, Stuart Levey's TFI office designated the IRSO as a key Hezbollah fund-raising operation.* Harpoon was delighted: Dagan wanted to use the IRSO as proof that the LCB had to be dismembered and removed from the monetary battlefield. The LCB, in Dagan's eyes, personified the evil of the terrorist financiers. The banks made record profits handling money that was dripping in blood, misery, and suffering. Rogue financial institutions like the LCB legitimized organizations like Hezbollah. The banks—and their executives—became bespoke suits of armor that shielded Hezbollah's money from the long arm of international law enforcement. Dagan wanted to make an example of the LCB, and to amputate it from Hezbollah's clutches once and for all.

The case for toppling the LCB was the most pressing topic when Israeli intelligence representatives met in America's capital with their counterparts from the Departments of the Treasury and Justice in 2007 and 2008. The intelligence from the compromised computers and industrious human assets was sanitized before it was printed out and placed in neat vinyl folders.

---

* Another such group, designated as a Hezbollah facilitator a few years later, was the Martyrs Foundation. The Martyrs Foundation was an Iranian parastatal organization that directed infusions of Iranian cash into the accounts of Hezbollah, Hamas, and the PIJ; the group, a brokerage house of sorts, maintained offices throughout Lebanon, staffed by representatives from the terrorist groups that received cash assistance, and used those offices to relay the monies gathered to the Palestinian territories and to Party of God units in southern Lebanon.

But even heavily redacted, Dagan thought that the evidence provided to the U.S. government about the bank was more than sufficient for Washington to join the offensive and take decisive action against the LCB and other financial institutions involved in bankrolling the Hezbollah apparatus. Treasury and Justice both agreed; the DEA, after all, had invested serious resources to track the cocaine superhighway spreading South American narcotics to the four corners of the world, bringing millions in profits into Hezbollah's coffers. Even the CIA agreed that something had to be done in Lebanon. Unbeknownst to the Israeli delegation, the CIA had its own human assets operating in the shadows of Beirut, collecting intelligence on Hezbollah.[19]

But even though the Treasury and Justice Departments were on board, the State Department and the Department of Defense disagreed.

Long before the term "too big to fail" entered the international vernacular, the U.S. State Department maintained, or virtually demanded, that Israel and the U.S. branches of law enforcement would not attack any financial, political, or social institutions in Lebanon that could lead the nation to the brink of collapse. "The diplomats, who we referred to as the Bow Ties, in Foggy Bottom never understood the security implications of some of their actions and the policies they pursued," recalled a retired special agent with the U.S. Diplomatic Security Service, the men and women responsible for safety at embassies around the world. "It was all about handshakes and smiles. Others had to pick up the bodies later."[20]

The U.S. Department of Defense, or DoD, wanted Lebanon to remain stable and free from a major banking disruption. It sought to reinstate Lebanon to the list of nations receiving U.S. military aid—everything from M4 assault rifles to eavesdropping counterintelligence gear for the Lebanese Armed Forces' military intelligence service, the Muchabarat-al Jaish. The DoD initiative assumed greater imperative in May 2008 when Hezbollah forces in Beirut openly clashed with the poorly trained and inadequately equipped army garrison protecting the Lebanese capital.[21]

In the end the Bow Ties and the generals won the argument, and the LCB was temporarily removed from the American law enforcement crosshairs. But Dagan was undeterred. Munir Z.'s information was too good to be wasted in the infighting of the Washington, D.C., Beltway. Sitting behind his cluttered desk at Mossad HQ, smoking his pipe, and sipping his black tea with lemon, Dagan instructed Uri L. to reach out to the lawyers once again.

Dagan despised intelligence that was not utilized operationally—especially when it was paid for in blood. Some of the intelligence and surveillance equipment that the United States provided to the Lebanese Armed Forces ultimately made its way into the hands of Hezbollah. In addition, Tehran sent counterintelligence experts to Lebanon to assist Hezbollah in its round-the-clock hunt for Israeli and American spies. Scores of men were rounded up, arrested, and interrogated by Hezbollah specialists, many of whom had trained in Iran. In May 2009, Lebanese security agents displayed some of the alleged Mossad spy gear for the press; the Lebanese spy hunters wore black balaclavas to conceal their identities. Hezbollah officials—not the Lebanese government—vowed that there would be more arrests.

Apparently Munir Z. was one of those seized and physically abused in the sweep; it is not known how he was discovered or betrayed. Little has been publicly said about his fate other than that he was executed by Hezbollah agents. He would have been tortured for information, brutally beaten, and then summarily shot in the back of the head. In some cases Hezbollah liked to make an example of traitors, stringing up the condemned men on electricity poles. But Israeli spies, to the Party of God, were the lowest form of life and not worthy of public spectacle. In all likelihood, Munir's body was thrown in a ditch by the side of some nondescript road and left there to rot.

According to Lebanese reports, members of Munir's extended family were eventually brought safely to Israel.[22] There was, after all, honor among spies.

CHAPTER SIXTEEN

Lawyers, Guns, and Money

There is a higher court than courts of justice and that is the
court of conscience. It supersedes all other courts.
—*Mahatma Mohandas Gandhi*

In the early spring the windows could still be found open in the Tel Aviv
offices of Shurat HaDin. Summer's oven-like heat had yet to arrive, and
the soothing winds left over from Israel's brief winter still blow through.
The office had grown to include steady staffers and interns, many of them
law school students and volunteers, who helped keep the wheels of the legal
proceedings spinning on all cylinders. The year 2009 had started off as a
busy year for Shurat HaDin; there were ongoing lawsuits against Hamas,
Iran, Syria, the PLO, the Palestinian Authority, and some banks. They
often received help with tips and guidance from Harpoon. Other law firms
in the United States were bringing suits against financial institutions, too.

In Israel, the impact of nearly a decade of incessant violence, suicide
bombings, and Hezbollah rockets was only beginning to sink in to the
minds of many who had lived through it. Few nations had ever been forced
to endure such a relentless wave of terror and bloodshed and still function as
a society. People went to work during the years of violence; children went to
school; the cinemas and nightclubs remained open. Those whose lives were
impacted by the bloodshed tried as best they could to persevere and continue. It was hardest around the holidays—especially the Jewish New Year.

Nitsana Darshan-Leitner was in her office one day after the holidays reviewing depositions and scheduling speaking engagements around North America. Phones were always ringing in the office, making it sound more like a telephone switchboard. One call was meant for Nitsana. "Pick up on line two," the secretary yelled to Nitsana, "I think it's the U2s."

Uri L. and Shai U. were affectionately known around the Shurat HaDin office as the U2s. They usually worked in tandem—where there was one, there was the other. Uri was on the phone, requesting a sit-down. He said it was urgent.

Meetings with the U2s were always in a public place, always where food and drinks were served, and always where a back table secured a modicum of privacy. The establishments had to be certified kosher, though food was never ordered. Uri came with a manila filing folder, some redacted paperwork, and a question. "How is the case going against the Lebanese Canadian Bank?" he asked Nitsana, hoping that the answer was good. The bank was a major conduit for Hezbollah activities, and it had financed much of the destruction that happened here two summers ago. Harpoon was pleased that the bank was in the spotlight of the legal crosshairs. The two continued to talk. What was supposed to have been a brief chat soon became a lengthy conversation. Harpoon's interest intrigued the lawyer. Taking the LCB to an American court, though, had not been easy.

The Lebanese Canadian Bank wasn't an American company, and it did not have a branch office in the United States. But the bank did work with a financial institution in the United States that enabled the LCB to conduct transactions in dollars, a relationship referred to in the banking industry as a correspondent bank. In this case, the correspondent bank was American Express Bank, a subsidiary of the American Express Company, a multinational behemoth doing $1 trillion of business per year, but with its head office located on Vesey Street in lower Manhattan. American Express's location was ironic: One would have thought that being located directly across the street from Ground Zero, the site of the largest terrorist attack the world had ever known, American Express would have been more careful about assisting terrorist money launderers. It was also less than a mile from the federal courthouse in Manhattan.

The links connecting Hezbollah to the LCB were staggering and damn-ing. The lawyers decided to proceed against LCB, but they also decided to file claims against the Democratic People's Republic of Korea (commonly known as North Korea) and the Islamic Republic of Iran in separate pro-ceedings. The opinion was that everyone complicit in the terror should be held accountable. Many of the missiles used by Hezbollah in the 2006 Second Lebanon War were produced in North Korea.[1] Other missiles, including medium- and long-range rockets, were supplied by Iran. It seemed a case could be made proving they all had to share liability for the Hezbollah missile barrages that had devastated Israel. The plaintiffs would allege that the different parties had contributed different necessary components providing material support to the terrorists, enabling them to fire thousands of rockets, packed with high explosives and ballbear-ing shrapnel, into civilian communities. Whether it was financial services, money, or the rockets themselves, they needed to be called into account. But the different pieces of the case would have to be pulled together before the bad guys could be sued. It was a daunting challenge.

Over the summer of 2008, teams of lawyers and interns of Shurat HaDin trekked from Tel Aviv to Israel's north to gather evidence from the victims. The latter came from families from every different type of background. The only common denominator was that they all had suffered the tragic fate of having been injured by Hezbollah. An Israeli-Arab attorney helped gather evidence from the Arabic-speaking victims. Experts on missiles, banking, Hezbollah, and North Korea were consulted and retained.

One of the plaintiffs was Michael Fuchs. Fuchs was forty-nine years old when Hezbollah launched the war and had just changed professions, going from being a school principal to growing a successful business that imported dinnerware from China. The married father of five was glued to his steering wheel in his new job, driving across the country to visit his close to two hundred clients and sell his wares. He was in northern Israel on July 13, 2006, driving near the city of Safed, when news reports of rocket fire prompted him to head home. He suddenly heard a menacing whistling sound followed by a massive explosion. A Hezbollah rocket landed close to his car, sending fragments through his windshield and slicing across his shoulder. His dashboard was sprayed with blood. He glanced to his right arm but all he saw was mangled flesh; a huge hole had been torn through his shoulder. He wrapped his shirt around the wound and, before going into shock, managed to kick open his door and cry for help. An ambulance picked him up ten minutes later. The Katyusha rocket from Lebanon had detached his deltoid muscle. His family learned of his situation while watching the news and then desperately searched for him among the wounded from that day's deluge of missiles. Although doctors wanted to amputate his arm, Fuchs refused. Fuchs was numbed by the fear of losing a limb, compounded by the physical pain and psychological impact of driving through a missile barrage. His injuries left him with a 90 percent loss of use of his right arm.

Another victim who joined the lawsuit was Rabbi Chaim Kaplan, a resident of Safed and an American citizen, married, and the father of eight children. Rabbi Kaplan, thirty-two years old when the war erupted, ran a camp for children from overseas near Safed. On July 13, 2006, the city came under missile fire. The rabbi's wife, Rivka, called him on his cellular phone in a panic—rockets had rained down all over the city, and the children were terrified. Once he made sure that his campers were inside their shelters, Rabbi Kaplan raced home to attend to his family. While driving, a missile impacted near the rabbi's car, and shrapnel punched into the vehicle and into his eye. It took hours to remove the fragments from his face and eye. The injuries crippled the young community leader, making it virtually impossible for him to carry out his duties. The rabbi's family, especially his sons and daughters, suffered severe psychological trauma during the bombardment—the first of what would be many attacks during the conflict.

Another victim who joined the lawsuit against the LCB was Karene Erdstein, a native of Columbus, Ohio, who was also in Safed when the missiles came raining down on her home and her family. Trained as a nurse, Erdstein had seen trauma before but had never experienced full-scale total blitz. The Hezbollah bombardments caught the family at home by surprise. A series of missiles impacted near the building where she lived with her husband and five children. A neighbor, who had not made it to shelter, was torn apart by an incoming rocket and killed instantly. Karene was pregnant at the time, and the trauma had caused her to miscarry. The Erdsteins' oldest daughter, Mayan, was also severely traumatized by the rocket attacks. The family had to move from their home and seek shelter in the central part of the country, safe from the range of Hezbollah missiles; the family, like so many others in Israel, had become refugees in their own country.

Compiling the victims' testimony was heart-wrenching. Many of the summer interns wept as they heard stories of trauma and injury. Hezbollah had launched endless salvos of rockets against the citizens of more than half of Israel. It was the first time since the Second World War that a modern First World nation had endured such a degree of indiscriminate terrorism against a civilian population. Regardless of whether one regards the conflict between Lebanon and Israel as some form of "legitimate" warfare, the wanton Hezbollah missile attacks aimed randomly at civilian areas were unmistakably terrorism. Going after the LCB and the other players was designed to make sure that such horrors never happened again.

There were two groups of clients: the first were American citizens who were entitled to sue North Korea, Hezbollah, and Iran in court because of the physical and psychological damage that they had endured as a result of the missile barrages.* These were Americans living in northern Israel— Safed and Karmiel, as well as Nahariya and Haifa. This group sued under the provisions of the Anti-Terrorism Act, and the Foreign Sovereign Immunities Act, special laws enacted by Congress that allow United States citizens and their families to bring suits in American courts regardless

---

* The families would eventually win judgments against North Korea and Iran on September 29, 2016, in the amount of $38 million in compensatory and $131 million in punitive damages. The Anti-Terrorism Act and New York City claims cases against the LCB are still ongoing at the time of this writing.

of where in the world they were targeted by terrorism. In enacting these laws, Congress expressed its intent that American families should not have to chase terrorist perpetrators and those who support them in legal actions around the world, actions that might prove logistically prohibitive and financially impossible. Many of the U.S. citizens that met with the lawyers were skeptical they would ever win a case in court, and all were certain they would never manage to collect anything. But with little to lose, and no one else offering them any assistance or hope, they all wanted to be plaintiffs, to seek a measure of closure.

The second group of families encompassed Israeli citizens. This group included residents from Israel's north—Druze, Bedouin, Christians, and Jews—who had suffered loss of life and property during Hezbollah's rocket campaign. Because this group didn't include American citizens, the lawsuit was filed in New York State Court asserting common-law claims under the laws of Israel, such as wrongful death, intentional infliction of emotional distress, assault, and battery. Suing for damages in state court was a novel approach, what lawyers call a "case of first impression." The argument was that even though the LCB was not doing business directly in the United States, the fact that it had a correspondent bank in New York and was doing dollar wire transfers through a New York bank, created enough contacts with the forum to find that the LCB could be hauled into court in New York State. The plaintiffs argued that under New York State's long-arm statute the LCB could be made to stand trial in Manhattan. The complaint alleged that the LCB had been providing financial services to Hezbollah's Yousser Company and Shahid (Martyrs) Foundation. These funds were utilized by Hezbollah to purchase rockets, pay its troops, and launch missiles into Israel. Moreover, it was alleged that the LCB processed payments to the families of the *shaheeds*, the widows and orphans of the terrorists killed while attacking Israeli civilians.

The lawyers for the LCB and the American Express Bank tried to get the cases dismissed. The LCB argued that it was a Lebanese entity and had no American presence, no branches or business offices, and, accordingly, there was no jurisdiction. The American Express Bank argued while it conducted business in the United States it was merely a correspondent, its client was solely the LCB, and it had no means of determining whose wire transfers they were processing or what they were for.

The lawsuit against the LCB was initially filed in the New York State Supreme Court at 60 Centre Street in downtown Manhattan on April 8, 2009, and was moved by the defendants to the United States District Court for the Southern District of New York. In the case of *Licci v. American Express Bank*, Harpoon permitted Shai to provide an affidavit in the case to answer the defendant's motion to dismiss. In the affidavit he explained that some of the accounts maintained by Hezbollah at the LCB's branches in Lebanon between 2004 and July 12, 2006, were titled to the Shahid (Martyrs) Foundation. The Martyrs Foundation served as an important component of Hezbollah's financial apparatus. "The organization," Shai U. submitted, "has used funds from this account to prepare for and carry out a wide range of terrorist and other violent activities, including rocket and missile attacks on Israel."[2]

The specifics of Shai's affidavit pointed to one of the Martyrs accounts, numbered 108987. During the period between 2004 and July 12, 2006, and even later, Hezbollah made dozens of dollar wire transfers in and out of account number 108987 in the LCB's branch in Beirut. These wire transfers, which totaled several million dollars, were executed by the LCB through Amex Bank in New York, which acted as the LCB's correspondent bank for these dollar transfers. The name on the account was Martyrs, so according to Shai, there was no question that Amex Bank knew that it was executing wire transfers on behalf of Hezbollah.[3]

The federal court in New York initially accepted the defendants' arguments and dismissed the case. It was a big blow to the families. The plaintiff's lawyers filed an appeal in the United States Court of Appeals for the Second Circuit. American Express Bank succeeded in its position that it was merely a correspondent bank and had no obligation to know the ultimate customer of its customer, even if it was something called the Martyrs Foundation in Beirut, Lebanon, during a highly publicized Middle Eastern armed conflict.

The case against the LCB, however, was more interesting. The Second Circuit wrote that New York State law was unclear as to whether New York courts have jurisdiction over a foreign bank that did business through a New York-based correspondent bank. Since the issue was one of first impression, meaning it had never been addressed by New York State's highest court, the Second Circuit issued a "certified question" to the New York State Court of Appeals. This appeal within an appeal was then briefed and argued to the New York State Court of Appeals. During oral argument, Judge Victoria A. Graffeo asked incredulously: "So are the banks now going to have to ask what are you using these monies for before they wire the funds?" The attorney Robert Tolchin, responded confidently, "They may. And I don't think that's a bad thing as a policy matter."[4]

The argument worked. On November 20, 2012, the Court of Appeals issued a landmark decision holding that maintenance and use of a correspondent banking arrangement in New York was a sufficient contact in New York to confer jurisdiction and that the long-arm statute provided the right to reach the LCB in Lebanon. Nitsana, shuttling back and forth between Tel Aviv and New York City, felt that the victims she represented just might have a chance in court.

The implications were astounding and immediately set the banking world reeling. No place in the world was more central to the banking industry than New York. No international bank could afford to be without a correspondent bank in New York, since without one they could not clear dollar transactions. And the highest court in New York had just ruled that even a bank that has no branch or other presence in the United States could still be reached by courts in New York when the transactions at issue involved wire transfers through a correspondent bank in Manhattan. Virtually every sizable international financial institution in the world had some U.S. correspondents, almost all of which were located in New York. Banks that had believed they could move terror funds with impunity because they were not present in the United States now understood that victims of terrorism could drag them into litigation and they could face massive damages awards. In one decision, the New York Court of Appeals had created a meaningful downside that would make international banks think twice before they turned a blind eye to doing business with terrorist organizations.

American banks were also concerned by the ruling. It meant there was a chance that they, too, could be held accountable for the actions of the unscrupulous foreign banks for which they served as correspondents. International banking had just gotten much more complicated and potentially expensive.

The plaintiffs dug in for a long litigation journey against the LCB—one that continues to this day. The bank's attorneys continued to fight.

The legal battlefield was slow-moving. The no-man's-land of motions and delays was frustrating. The LCB wasn't the only instance of justice delayed. The original case against the Arab Bank, *Linde v. Arab Bank*, had been filed in the summer of 2004 in the federal court in Brooklyn, New York, for twenty-four acts of terrorism; included among them were the Park Hotel attack, the Bus No. 19 bombing, the Sbarro restaurant massacre, the Café Moment bombing, and the double suicide bombing in downtown Jerusalem, as well as other terrorist tragedies of the intifada. All these attacks were perpetrated by Hamas. The suit was then joined by hundreds of other families, American and non-American, in similar lawsuits demanding compensation for the injuries done to their loved ones in the intifada violence carried out by a range of other terrorist organizations. The cases were brought under the Anti-Terrorism Act and the Alien Torts Claims Act.

The complaint alleged that the Arab Bank aided and abetted the terrorist organizations by transferring funds from its branch in Lebanon through its branch in New York to the leaders and senior officials of Hamas in Gaza and the West Bank, including Sheikh Ahmed Yassin. In addition, the bank was accused of moving funds for Islamic charities affiliated with Hamas—an organization that had been outlawed in Israel and the United States—and using those accounts to provide stipends to the imprisoned terrorists and to the families of the suicide bombers. The plaintiffs also accused the bank of providing financial services to the Saudi Committee for the Support of the al-Quds Intifada, which paid salaries to the terrorists and their families taking part in the ongoing Palestinian violence against Israel.

Parallel to the civil litigation, the U.S. Treasury initiated its own legal proceeding against the bank, charging that it had evaded American financial compliance regulations. In 2005 the Arab Bank was fined $24 million. The Treasury said that the bank's New York branch failed to adequately guard against the risks of money laundering and terrorist financing, and also failed to properly report suspicious activities.[5]

In the civil proceeding, the plaintiffs' lawyers sorted through the massive amounts of documents and evidence collected by the IDF in the "Green Lantern," "Destruction of Leaven," and "Defensive Shield" operations, as well as evidence the Arab Bank was compelled to turn over to the United States in its regulatory proceeding. The plaintiffs retained experts and translators to prepare reports and opinions concerning the Arab Bank's liability. The numerous depositions were taken in several different countries. During the discovery phase the bank was required by the court, pursuant to the plaintiffs' request, to disclose documents concerning the wire transfers for known or suspected terrorists that it had conducted. The Arab Bank refused and claimed that according to Jordanian, Lebanese, and Palestinian law there was bank secrecy, and turning over the documents would violate these regulations and would expose it to criminal and civil liability. The court did not accept the bank's arguments and sanctioned it for noncompliance with its discovery order. This was a dangerous and potentially devastating blow to the defense's case, and the Arab Bank's lawyers immediately appealed.

The defendant contended, in its appellate papers, that if the sanction led to a finding of liability at trial and then was reversed on appeal, the Arab Bank would suffer irreversible harm to its reputation. In its January 18, 2013, decision, the Second Circuit Court of Appeals refused to provide any relief, however, holding that this issue of whether the court's sanction was proper, could be raised only after the trial. As such, the bank's appeal, if still necessary, must wait until after final judgment was entered in the case. A year and a half later, and following ten years of preliminary preparation and proceedings, the case brought by the terror victims against the Arab Bank would finally go to trial in August 2014.

Another legal fight against terrorism dragged on, as well, in New York federal court.

In February 2004, Nitsana Darshan-Leitner and her colleagues, Mordechai Haller and David Strachman, had filed suit against the Palestinian Authority and the PLO over its involvement in terrorism. The civil action, *Sokolow v. Palestinian Authority*, bundled together the cases of eleven American families, relatives of individuals who had loved ones killed or maimed in some of the intifada's most heinous terrorist attacks carried out between 2001 and 2004, which killed thirty-three people and injured more than four hundred. These included the Hebrew University cafeteria bombing, the shooting attack on Jaffa Street in Jerusalem, a suicide bombing on King George Street, and the Bus No. 19 attack. The victims sued the Palestinian Authority and the PLO for the deaths and injuries of their loved ones, as well as the psychological trauma inflicted upon them by the defendants, demanding more than $1 billion in monetary compensation.

What bound the terrorist incidents together was the fact that they were all perpetrated, organized, outfitted, assisted, encouraged, rewarded, and financed by employees of the Palestinian Authority and the PLO. Some of the attackers, and those that supported them, were salaried members of Arafat's security forces. Some were policemen, others were PLO officials, and some were members of Arafat's notorious Praetorian guard, Force 17. Many of the terrorists acted on behalf of the al-Aqsa Martyrs Brigade, an armed militia of the PLO's Fatah Movement. The Palestinian Authority sought to distance itself publicly from the al-Aqsa Martyrs Brigades, but in fact, they were funded and directed by Yasir Arafat himself. In June 2004, then Palestinian President Ahmed Qureia openly stated this: "We have clearly declared that the Aqsa Martyrs Brigades are part of Fatah. We are committed to them and Fatah bears full responsibility for the group."

Shortly afterward, he added, "The al-Aqsa Martyrs Brigades, military wing of the Fatah movement will not be dissolved and Fatah will never relinquish its military wing."[6]

According to the plaintiffs' arguments, the attackers were on the payroll of the Palestinian Authority and the PLO. The defendants provided the terrorists with training, weapons, explosives, funding, and safe houses. When an attacker was arrested and imprisoned by Israel, he continued to receive his monthly salary in the Israeli jail. If the terrorist was killed in the course of carrying out an attack, his family would receive "martyr payments" from the Palestinian Authority. Moreover, those who sat in prison for lengthy sentences would be promoted in rank every two years, along with an increase in pay. The families also alleged that the Palestinians indoctrinated their security services to carry out violence against Israelis and Jews, labeling the struggle as a holy war. They glorified the martyrs—the suicide bombers who targeted Israeli civilians. Town squares and sports events were named after dead terrorists, and Palestinian television ceaselessly broadcast programs praising the terrorist groups and those who were killed fighting against Israel. Accordingly, the lawsuit charged that the PA and the PLO were vicariously liable for the attacks perpetrated by their employees with their encouragement, and inducement, and in the course of their duties. Moreover, they were liable for aiding and abetting terrorism under the Anti-Terrorism Act.

In response to the terror victims' suit the defendants filed a motion to dismiss, contending, among other matters, that they were a sovereign state and, thus, were protected by immunity from lawsuits. They also argued that the court lacked personal jurisdiction, as the PA and the PLO were not present in the United States. Finally, they raised the defense that the alleged terrorist attacks were legitimate "acts of war" that could not be adjudicated by a court.

In 2008, the district court handed down its decision rejecting the PA and the PLO's arguments, and the *Sokolow* case progressed into discovery and depositions. The defendants utilized every opportunity to stall the proceedings and every trick to oppose the plaintiffs' demand for

documents and evidence. The Palestinians' steely reluctance to cooperate with the discovery process was driven by a hidden secret: The Palestinian security services maintained extensive files on every terrorist who
was convicted of perpetrating attacks against Israel. The records provided
personal profiles of each individual, including his family background, his
rank, his attitude toward the "armed struggle" against Israel, the length of
his sentence, and most important, the details of each and every payment
made to him by the PA and the PLO.

Once the records found their way to the plaintiffs' lawyers' hands, they
understood their significance and magnitude, and that they had a powerful case to present to a jury. They were ready to take the *Sokolow* case to
trial.

The publicity spread like wildfire as cases like LCB, *Arab Bank*, and
Sokolow were filed and the newer cases against the state sponsors, various Palestinian organizations, and banks were launched. The personal
injury bar sprang to life and began to file anti-terrorism cases against all
sorts of financial defendants. Suddenly the same law firms that had once
declined the Israeli lawyers' invitation to become involved in terrorism
cases, because they were too speculative and they feared judgments would
be uncollectible, began filing lawsuits against every conceivable sovereign
target. Actions were filed against Iran, Libya, Syria, Algeria, Sudan, and
North Korea alleging they were providing material support for terrorism.
The proceedings against the rogue regimes moved relatively quickly.

Many of these outlaw states ignored the lawsuits, since they do not rec-
ognize the United States or its courts' authority over them, and so wound
up with multi-million-dollar judgments against them on default. Others, such as Syria, the PLO, and the Palestinian Authority, hired Ramsey
Clark, who served as United States attorney general during the Johnson
administration, as their attorney. Clark, son of former Supreme Court
Justice Tom Clark, had become the patron saint of revolutionary causes,
opposing the war on terror, and representing such scoundrels as Charles
Taylor, Slobodan Milošević, Saddam Hussein, and Lyndon LaRouche.

Clark took the position in each terror case that the defendants were entitled to sovereign immunity. The courts ruled against him every time, but even after losing the issue on appeal he quixotically insisted on his immunity arguments and refused to defend the cases on the facts and merits. The inevitable result was large judgments against his clients.

Other law firms focused on the banks and filed suits against financial institutions they believed were providing services and transferring funds for the terrorist groups. Cases were filed against banks such as UBS, Crédit Lyonnais, National Westminster Bank, Commerzbank, HSBC, Barclays, Credit Suisse Group, HSBC Holdings, Royal Bank of Scotland Group, Fransabank SAL, Banque Libanaise Pour le Commerce, Bank of Beirut, Bank Libano-Française SAL, Middle East Africa Bank, and Standard Chartered, as well as Iranian banks and some financial institutions in Asia.

Additionally, Nitsana and her colleagues continued to bring actions against the Palestinian Authority, the PLO, Hamas, the PIJ, and Hezbollah. These cases, pursued under the Anti-Terrorism Act, were frequently defended by defense firms and took many years to litigate.

Once a suit was initiated by one lawyer, several other law firms could be counted to pile on, filing their own copycat suits. A terror victim's litigation bar began to emerge, with law offices specializing in this type of practice. On the opposing side, certain law firms began to carve out a niche representing banks and other defendants accused of aiding and abetting terrorism. Once a financial institution was named in a suit, they ran to these large white-shoe firms to defend them. The billing amounts on the cases by defense counsel quickly rose to astronomical heights; indeed, in some cases the litigation costs were large enough to concern the institution's management and shareholders. The suits became a cash cow and an important source of income for certain law firms at a time when the U.S. economy was slipping toward recession.

Providing financial services to terrorist organizations proved to be outrageously expensive for banks. A Shurat HaDin lawyer joked with one of these defense attorneys about the amount of hours they were racking up in the endless motions practice, "You are in the same business as we are, bankrupting the bad guys through litigation." When law review articles about the cases and decisions were published, when law schools began to teach courses on terrorist victim litigation, and as conferences dedicated to terrorist victim litigation were organized, the attorneys knew they had arrived. Some enterprising former Israeli intelligence officers even got into the act, setting up consulting firms that specialized in advising banks and companies in best practices and how to avoid expensive terror victim litigation.

However, obtaining a favorable court decision was only half the story: The multi-million-dollar judgments were worth nothing if they could not be satisfied. Scofflaws like Iran and the terrorist organizations could not be expected to pay up. The plaintiffs now had to embark on the often even more difficult and cash-consuming task of trying to track down the hidden assets of the defendants. Little property and even fewer bank accounts were titled in the names of the outlaw states or terrorist defendants. The lawyers were left with the near-impossible job of working for years with investigators to track down property, filing liens and turnover proceedings around the world. And they were put in the uncomfortable position of having to compete with other victims of terrorism for the limited assets that could be found. As the Seventh Circuit Court of Appeals observed in one case, "Victims of terror can find themselves pitted in a cruel race against each other—a race to attach any available assets to satisfy the judgments. The terms of the race are essentially winner take all."

Sometimes information was slipped to the lawyers from friendly intelligence services or whistleblowers. It was grueling work and was a time sink that could snowball and tie up all the lawyers' working days and nights. The same defendants who defaulted on judgments, including the Iranian regime, a fake entity that called itself the Palestinian Pension Fund for the State Administrative Employees in the Gaza Strip (but was really just a slush fund created by Yasir Arafat), and others hired some of America's top law firms in an effort to stave off collection proceedings and prevent their assets from being seized—from skyscrapers in Manhattan to Persian artifact collections in a Chicago museum, to Iranian oil accounts in Italian banks, and to impounded vessels in Mexico. Attorney Robert Tolchin noted: "You have to have boundless creativity and resilience to smoke out the money on the terror cases. These are the most loathsome defendants in the world, and sometimes you have to muster the grit to pursue them down long holes for many years."

As the case continued, the terror victims became emboldened. They were no longer victims—the judgments against those who had devastated their lives gave these men and women a sense of purpose and the means by which they could fight back. It gave the families a sense of mission and a degree of closure.

Perhaps more important than the measure of justice and compensation the cases could provide to the families of the victims was that the shock waves to the banking system continued to impact as news of the suits spread. Sometimes the fear was enough. As one Harpoon member recalled, "We went to Deutsche Bank, which was administering Iranian accounts at the time, and we presented our case about the connections to terrorism and asked them to shut them down. The bank refused and we left. They were making too much money from the Iranian business. When we returned to Germany to meet again a month or so later we told them 'We were in New York recently and we spoke to some lawyers there. They told us they are planning on suing your bank for aiding terrorism. They have all these clients lined up. We have nothing to do with them, but it looks like it's going to be very bad, very expensive for the bank.' A short while later all the Iranian accounts were magically shut down."[7]

Harpoon had learned how to leverage the lawsuits against the financiers of terror.

PART III

———

LEGACY

CHAPTER SEVENTEEN

We Cannot Confirm or Deny

Where no counsel is, the people fall, but in the multitude
of counselors there is safety.
—*Proverbs 11:14 (the Mossad motto)*

Many in the Israeli intelligence community breathed enthusiastic sighs of relief when Prime Minister Sharon appointed Meir Dagan to serve as the tenth director of the Institute for Intelligence and Special Operations, the formal name for the Mossad. Dagan had a reputation for *decisive action* and as a straight shooter. Neither his views, nor his decisions, were ever influenced by political consideration. His reputation as a field officer was impeccable and defined by courage and innovation. Dagan was never reckless, though. His decisiveness was calculated by an indefinable analytical mind that measured risk and objective. The men and women he dispatched overseas to perform the most sensitive of missions knew that the director would never send them into harm's way unless the operation was absolutely essential to Israeli security and that the odds that everyone would come back to Israel safely were high.

Decisive measures—direct action—were calling cards of Dagan's view of Israel's deterrence. The State of Israel does not, as a matter of strict policy, ever admit or deny any role in the assassination of its enemies, but during Dagan's tenure as Mossad director, many of Israel's enemies ended up dead—often by spectacular means—far from Israel's borders. The first was Ghalib Awali, a Hezbollah commander who was killed by a mysterious car bomb in south Beirut in July 2004; Awali, it was later alleged, was murdered by agents, former Lebanese military officers, recruited by the Mossad.[1] Ezzedine Sobhi Sheikh Khalil, a Hamas military commander who was living and working out of the Syrian capital, was killed on September 26, 2004, when his white Pajero SUV disappeared into a fireball on an upscale street in Damascus.[2] Israel had vowed to avenge two Hamas suicide bombings in the southern Israeli city of Beersheba on August 31 that killed sixteen civilians, but Israel did not publicly take credit for Khalil's explosive end. "We have no knowledge of this incident," a spokesman for Prime Minister Sharon explained. But he added, "Our longstanding policy has been that no terrorist will have any sanctuary and any immunity. They're in a very risky business, they live in a rough neighborhood, and they should not be surprised when what they plan for others befalls them."[3]

Other assassinations followed. Mahmoud al-Majzoub, a PIJ commander, was obliterated by a bomb planted in his car in the city of Sidon, in southern Lebanon, on May 26, 2006. One of the most dramatic was the February 12, 2008, killing of Hezbollah military and global special operations commander Imad Mughniyeh in Damascus. Mughniyeh had topped the most-wanted list in many countries. The United States wanted his head for the suicide bombing of two embassies in Beirut as well as the murders of 241 U.S. servicemen in the destruction of the Marine barracks. The Hezbollah commander also kidnapped U.S. citizens in Lebanon, and he had abducted and murdered William Buckley, the CIA chief of station in Beirut, in 1984. Israel had also placed Mughniyeh it its crosshairs. He was responsible for countless Hezbollah operations against Israeli forces in Lebanon and for the suicide bombings of the Israeli embassy and a Jewish cultural center in Buenos Aires, Argentina. Moreover, the terrorist was one of the coordinators of Iranian and Hezbollah material support to both Hamas and the PIJ. Mughniyeh had a lot of innocent blood on his hands; up until 9/11 he was responsible for the deaths of more Americans than any other terrorist.

Imad Mughniyeh met his demise when a powerful explosive charge tore his head apart as he sat inside his Mitsubishi Pajero. The bomb had been planted inside the driver's-side headrest. Although no one in Washington or Jerusalem was sad to see Mughniyeh go, there were no public admissions of responsibility. It was later reported that the assassination was a joint operation between the CIA and the Mossad.[4]

Whether or not the State of Israel accepted responsibility for the string of unsolved deaths involving terror chieftains, a sense of dynamic swagger was returned to Israel, and it was all attributed to Dagan. "He was one of the best directors, if not the best one, Mossad has had in our sixty years or so of existence...Meir restored Mossad's reputation and brought the organization to new levels," Ilan Mizrahi, the former number two at the Mossad, stated. It was a remarkable admission.

The intelligence services always had an interest in targets who posed clear and present threats to the safety of Israeli citizens, either at home or overseas. Equal vigilance was invested with those who posed a threat to the Jewish state and who also had blood on their hands—men who had killed and were planning to kill again. These individuals, their identities maintained in closely guarded file folders, occupied significant blocks of times at the weekly operational meetings held at the various services. The files consisted of biographical material, last known photographs, details on their locations, and other highly classified tidbits of data that were worth recording on paper, or inside a computer. Some terrorist targets of the highest value appeared in multiple files safeguarded in numerous headquarters throughout the country. This select list of names was discussed by the soldier spies at A'man, and the names were also discussed by the Shin Bet and various units inside the Israel National Police. Of course, these archterrorists received special attention at Mossad headquarters. The fate of these men and the talk of their whereabouts topped the agenda at the Harpoon roundtable, as well.

These names were cross-tabulated on a nexus connecting intentions, capabilities, and crimes. There was no justice as long as these men were operational and until they were forced to pay for their crimes. Mahmoud al-Mabhouh was one such name.

Mahmoud al-Mabhouh was a senior military wing commander of Hamas. Once a cold-blooded triggerman, he was selected by Tehran and Hezbollah to spend the vast sums of cash that Iran and its Lebanese proxy pumped into the Palestinian Islamic resistance movement. Mabhouh was born in the Gaza Strip in 1960, one of fourteen children. Interested in weightlifting and fast cars, Mabhouh became a mechanic, even opening up his own garage, before gravitating to militant Islam. He was good with his hands, and was physically imposing; the small and secretive Muslim Brotherhood was thrilled when al-Mabhouh joined their ranks.

The Brotherhood was a small fringe group in the late 1970s when al-Mabhouh swore his allegiance, and the organization gladly welcomed anyone into their ranks who was devout and who was strong enough to win back-alley scrapes. The Muslim Brotherhood's main foe in the first years, in the early 1980s, was Fatah, and men like al-Mabhouh targeted the Gaza coffeehouses where gambling and narcotics use was common, as well as establishments that sold alcohol and trafficked ladies of the night that ultimately kicked up to Arafat and his men.

In 1986, al-Mabhouh was arrested by Israeli security services for possessing a stolen IDF M16 assault rifle. When he was released from prison he joined the ranks of the nascent Hamas. As a man whose knuckles had already been bloodied, he became one of the early commanders of the group's military wing. Al-Mabhouh commanded a highly secretive squad called Unit 101,* whose sole mission was the kidnapping and murder of Israeli soldiers.[5]

Sergeant Avi Sasportas was the first of al-Mabhouh's victims. The twenty-one-year-old served in the elite Maglan special operations airborne unit and had been outside of Gaza on February 16, 1989, trying to hitch a ride back home, as was common for Israeli soldiers traveling throughout

---

* The reference of Unit 101 was highly symbolic. Unit 101 was a controversial counterterrorist and counterinsurgency commando force that was created by a young Ariel Sharon in 1953 to mount cross-border retaliatory raids against Palestinian raiders in the West Bank and Gaza.

the country. The vehicle he entered, a white Subaru, was driven by a man dressed as an Orthodox Jew; there were other men in the car, as well. Sasportas was never seen alive again. He was beaten to death near the Gaza Strip and his body buried in a nondescript grave discovered months later.

On the evening of May 3, 1989, a Hamas team, masquerading as Orthodox Jews, kidnapped nineteen-year-old Corporal Ilan Saadon, as he hitchhiked with a friend at Masmiya Junction, west of the port city of Ashdod. There was room in the car for only one, so Saadon got in, hoping to get to his home located nearby in Ashqelon; his mother was waiting for him with dinner.

The Hamas abduction squad intended to take their captive to the Jebalya refugee camp in the Gaza Strip and demand a prisoner exchange with Israel, but the terrorists panicked. The terrorist in the front passenger seat turned around and fired a round at point-blank range into Saadon's head, killing the teenage soldier instantly.

The Shin Bet and the IDF searched every nook and cranny of the Gaza Strip for Saadon, turning the 140 square miles of densely populated neighborhoods and refugee camps inside out. The security forces arrested two hundred members of Hamas. Shin Bet and military intelligence officers assigned to the Gaza Strip were desperate—if the corporal was alive, the veteran specialists knew, then every second was precious in order to gather the information the special operations units would need to attempt a rescue. If Saadon was dead, the intelligence agents wanted to locate the soldier's body so that his parents, and the country, could have closure. The clock ticked and no information was forthcoming. "We did everything we could to find the kidnapped soldier," a former Border Guard policeman who was stationed in Gaza remembers. "We tore the place apart and we know that the bastards knew where he was, but they took pleasure in not telling us. We kept on thinking of Ilan's mother. It was all very cruel."[6]

Cruelty was part of the equation—barbarity was a calling card of the Hamas campaign against Israel. The two soldiers weren't only murdered but mutilated. "The soldiers were already dead, and what the terrorists did to them was too depraved to even imagine," the Border Guard officer remembered. "It displayed an inhumanity that we couldn't fathom."[7] According to Ronen Bergman, an investigative reporter for the Israeli daily *Yediot Aharonot*, al-Mabhouh and a coconspirator took photographs of themselves stomping on the corpses.[8]

The Hamas leadership gave strict orders to its members to remain tight-lipped about Saadon's fate. Only a handful of Hamas commanders were privy to the location of his grave and, when questioned by the Israelis, those men were not forthcoming with any information that would enable Saadon's family to bury their son. Ilan Saadon's body was recovered only in 1996. He was buried with full military honors.

Sheikh Ahmed Yassin was one of the Hamas leaders apprehended in the Israeli dragnet. He was charged with Saadon's abduction and murder for issuing the orders to al-Mabhouh to kidnap Israeli soldiers. Yassin's orders were part of a series of opening salvos to launch a war that Hamas hoped would vanquish Israel and establish an Islamic state in all of Palestine. But he soon found himself in the prisoner's dock, surrounded by Israeli military policemen, charged with two murders and a dozen other terrorist charges. He was convicted of the two abductions and murders and sentenced to two life terms in a maximum security prison.*

The Sasportas and Saadon abductions elevated al-Mabhouh in the eyes of the Hamas hierarchy. It was just the type of audacious and cold-blooded act that rank-and-file Hamas adored. Al-Mabhouh had been one of the men dressed as a pious Jew and had been personally involved in both murders. It was al-Mabhouh who shot Saadon in the face.[9] The Shin Bet never caught up with al-Mabhouh, however. He managed to evade capture in

---

* Hamas efforts to free Yassin from jail included the 1992 kidnapping and murder of Border Guard Sergeant Nissim Toledano—the crime that sparked a chain of events that connected Hamas and Hezbollah. Israel was forced to free Yassin in 1997, after a botched Mossad assassination attempt of Hamas political leader Khaled Meshal in Amman, Jordan; Jordan threatened to execute the Israeli spies unless the Israeli government released the Hamas founder. Yassin was killed on March 22, 2004, by an Israeli air strike.

1989. He was able to slink his way out of the Gaza Strip through Rafah, a border town connected to the Sinai Desert. The fugitive trekked across the desert and dodged the watchful eyes of Egyptian intelligence. He made it across Egypt and into Libya, eventually finding a temporary respite and safe haven in Algeria. From Algiers al-Mabhouh traveled to the Sudan. In his new life he now shuttled back and forth between Khartoum and Hamas headquarters in Damascus, becoming one of the most important men in the organization.

Despite his murderous past, al-Mabhouh developed into something of a technocrat inside Hamas. He became a budget and supply man. He helped negotiate the funds that Iran and Hezbollah earmarked for Hamas, and he devised plans to smuggle the funds and the weapons of war it bought into the Gaza Strip and the West Bank. Al-Mabhouh was involved in arms shipments and negotiating deals with Sinai arms merchants and shipping companies that could be bribed to ferry a load of combustible contraband. "He was part accountant, part purchasing agent, part arbitrator, part facilitator, and part banker," a former member of Harpoon commented. "Money went into one of his hands, and death came out of the other."[10]

An influx of Iranian-financed weapons would have been a game changer. On January 3, 2002, for example, the IDF/Navy launched Operation Noah's Ark, the interdiction of the *Karine-A*, a Tonga-registered freighter that had sailed from the Persian Gulf to the Sudan and then toward the Red Sea with a cargo hold of weapons destined for Yasir Arafat. Israeli naval commandos from Flotilla 13 seized the ship in open waters and diverted it to the port of Eilat, where military intelligence specialists found tons of weapons ranging from wire-guided antitank missiles to mortars and small arms; the ship carried two and a half tons of military-grade high explosives. The *Karine-A* transported weapons worth more than $15 million.

Part of the *Karine-A*'s cargo included short-range rockets. Hamas, especially after Israel's 2005 unilateral withdrawal from the Gaza Strip, realized that it could no longer engage Israeli forces with the up-close-and-personal impact of suicide bombers. The Palestinian terrorists, like Hezbollah in 2006, would need to develop short-, medium-, and long-range capability that would be both inexpensive and easy to use. The responsibility of building such an arsenal for Hamas fell upon al-Mabhouh's shoulders. He managed much of the money that Iran and Hezbollah earmarked for the organization. But in most cases that al-Mabhouh handled, the currency wasn't dollars but rather sniper rifles and hand grenades. Instead, he was the man who coordinated arms acquisition and facilitated the shipments, sometimes through the Persian Gulf and other times even through smuggling routes established in the Sudan.[11]

Following the Hamas Gaza coup against Fatah and the Palestinian Authority in June 2007, Iran was determined to change the battlefield equation and establish a foothold on Israel's southern border to complement its base of operations across Israel's northern frontier. Tehran knew from Hezbollah's success in the 2006 War that this game-changing push relied on indiscriminately launched rockets that could deliver lethal fusillades against Israeli cities. The rockets, in most cases, were fire-and-forget crude tubes constructed in local workshops that were pointed in the direction of an Israeli town or city and then launched. The know-how to construct these rockets came from outside the Strip; the tools and explosive charges to fit inside the rocket warheads were smuggled into Gaza through an endless highway of smuggler tunnels dug deep beneath the border between Rafah and the Egyptian frontier. Sinai arms merchants made a fast and furious fortune delivering war supplies and cash to Hamas.

Hamas and the PIJ launched approximately 2,700 rockets against Israel's cities between 2005 and 2007. Throughout southern Israel an air raid siren would sound and then, seconds later, an explosion would follow. The Hamas rockets, called Qassams, were crude and inaccurate. Sometimes the missiles would fall harmlessly into a field. Other times, the rockets would fall on apartment blocks, inside schoolyards, and in hospitals.

The southern Israeli town of Sderot was particularly hard hit. Close to the Gaza Strip, the residents of Sderot lived an intolerable existence of racing to fallout shelters. Several civilians were killed; scores were wounded.

The IDF responded with artillery fire. A tense and unbearable state of conflict ensued. The rocket fire ultimately resulted in 2009's Operation Cast Lead, an IDF incursion into the Gaza Strip.

Ella Abukasis was seventeen years old when she was walking with her fifteen-year-old brother on the night of January 1, 2005, in Sderot. It was Saturday night, and the alarm of incoming rockets, the "red alert," sounded a warning that a rocket had been fired from Gaza. In Tel Aviv one has ninety seconds to find his way to a shelter. In the port city of Ashdod, less than twenty miles from the Gaza Strip, one has only sixty seconds to seek shelter from the incoming rockets. In Sderot, a small desert town half a mile from the Hamas enclave, one has only fifteen seconds to find a shelter.

Ella and her brother, Tamir, were walking down a barren street when the alarm sounded. There was no bus stop to race to, no nearby buildings to hide beneath; there were no nearby parked cars to hide under. All that raced through Ella's mind was to protect her brother. She threw Tamir to the ground and covered him with her body. They were in the middle of the road when the missile launched from Gaza exploded near both their heads. The blast sent shrapnel and nails slicing into their young bodies. Ella fought for seven days before succumbing to her wounds. Tamir survived his injuries, but remains disabled for life.

Both Hamas and Iran were determined to expose Israeli vulnerability far beyond towns like Sderot that bordered Gaza. Hamas and Iran wanted to hit the strategic port city of Ashdod as well as Israel's major population centers around the Tel Aviv metropolitan area. The missile arsenal they assembled was diverse and lethal: the Qassam 1 rocket, with a warhead weighing a pound, had a range of two and a half miles; the Qassam 2 rocket had a range of just over six miles and yielded a warhead of nearly five pounds; the Qassam 3 carried a warhead of more than thirty pounds with a range of seven and a half miles; and the Grad rocket carried a warhead packed with forty pounds of high explosives and had a range of nearly thirteen miles from launch. The Iranian-financed weaponry was a make-or-break component of this deterrence power for Hamas.[12] Al-Mabhouh's smuggling operations from Iran to Sudan, and then from Sudan to Sinai and underground into Gaza, were the lifelines of this endeavor.

But what made the Israeli intelligence community particularly nervous was the development of an Iranian-designed missile called the Fajr. The Fajr, "dawn" in Farsi, was a long-range ballistic missile by Arab-Israeli standards. With a reach of nearly forty-seven miles and a payload of two hundred pounds of military-grade explosive, the missile could hit Tel Aviv and the capital Jerusalem; Ben-Gurion International Airport, Israel's lifeline to the outside world, was in range of this fairly advanced rocket. Components of the missile were, according to reports, manufactured in Iran or developed, under a loose license, in concealed factories in and around the Sudanese capital or close to the water so that shipment to Sinai would be easily facilitated. Like one giant Lego puzzle, the rocket components were then smuggled across the desert, underneath the Egyptian border, and brought into Gaza where they were assembled in makeshift factories—some of which were underground.

The Sudanese element of al-Mabhouh's operation was particularly troubling to Harpoon and the Mossad, because it was so far from Israel's frontiers and because the complicated system had to be built by educated and experienced technicians, and they were in short supply in Gaza.[13] In January and February 2009, Israeli warplanes attacked trucks that were transporting Fajr-3 rockets, which had been brought by Iranian Revolutionary Guard Corps to Port Sudan and then handed off to smuggling gangs who would ready the rockets for transport to Sinai. The Israeli F-15 and F-16 fighter bombers flew more than eight hundred miles to hit their targets.[14]

The entire endeavor, tunnels and all, consumed an inordinate percentage of the money that Iran budgeted toward Hamas. Al-Mabhouh watched over how these funds were allocated and spent. He had great skill as a logistician. It made him a lethal foe. It made him a legitimate target.

There was, according to reports, an attempt to assassinate al-Mabhouh when he traveled to Dubai on official business in November 2009. Israeli intelligence had managed to insert a Trojan horse into al-Mabhouh's laptop and monitored all of his transactions and his many movements.[15] A Mossad operation was immediately launched. Reports indicate a Mossad hit team met al-Mabhouh at a five-star hotel in the city and even succeeded in slipping the Hamas commander a toxin into a cocktail he was drinking. The Hamas official drank the poisoned beverage, but much to the Mossad's surprise, he wasn't killed by the agent. It just made him very sick.[16] The opportunity had been lost.

Two months passed until al-Mabhouh's next trip. This time, the Mossad learned that his final destination was China. Al-Mabhouh, once again, would be spending a few days in Dubai. Dagan, according to reports, proposed an intricate operation terminating the Hamas commander in the Emirati city. Prime Minister Netanyahu, who succeeded Ehud Olmert on March 31, 2009, gave his Mossad director the green light to proceed.[17]

Dubai, one of the seven emirates that constitute the United Arab Emirates, is one of the most dazzling and lavish city-states in the world. The city-state's skyline is science-fiction-like, boasting the tallest building in the world and more luxury cars on the smoothly paved roads than there are camels in its outlying desert. Dubai is a remarkable experiment in free-wheeling economics in a region where a bomb under one's car is usually the currency of day-to-day existence. Dubai was supposed to be a neutral city—a bastion of commerce and pleasure that was off-limits to the violence of the region. It was strictly forbidden for the Iranians, the Saudis, the Arabs, and the Israelis to use the city-state as a battlefield for their own petty little wars and disagreements. The Jihaz amn a-Dawleh, or State Security Service, the UAE's intelligence agency, went to great lengths, in bilateral meetings and in covert sit-downs, to make sure that the regional players knew and respected the rules. State Security, of course, encouraged the warring factions to conduct business in Dubai. The hotels and restaurants were more than enough reason for the spies to conduct their affairs there.

Only Iran and Hamas ignored the pleas to keep the city clean from nefarious players. But by 2010 the global real estate bubble implosion had hit Dubai. The sheen of gold and platinum was threatened by overpriced properties that were abandoned and underwater. Dubai's economy was in a nose dive. The Iranians stepped in. They used the vacated office complexes as convenient addresses from where to set up shell companies to skirt Israeli-urged and Western-led economic sanctions against the Islamic Republic over its nuclear ambitions.[18] UAE State Security was incensed by Iran's ambivalence toward the unwritten rule, but the small intelligence service was wary about angering Tehran to the point of Hezbollah operatives being unleashed inside the malls and luxury hotels.

One of the lures of Dubai—to friendly spies using the emirate as a meeting ground and for more suspect operatives with less than honorable intentions—was that it was so accessible. Dubai International Airport was a marvel of size, scope, and shopping. In 2009, 40 million people flew in and out of Dubai; 140 airlines serviced the city. Emirates, the city-state's airline, had gone from a small regional connector to one of the largest intercontinental carriers in the world.

Mahmoud al-Mabhouh booked his own travel from Damascus to Dubai. He used a credit card in his own name and booked a ticket on the Emirates Airline website. Al-Mabhouh was senior enough in the organization to have a complement of bodyguards who traveled with him at all times, but the flight from the Syrian capital to Dubai was nearly sold out. Apparently the Hamas commander thought it more important to secure a ticket for the flight rather than wait for a later one that would have seats for his security detail. Al-Mabhouh abandoned many protocols of survival tradecraft. Unlike the top leaders of Hamas, he didn't utilize charter services, where a Gulfstream and a crew of pretty flight attendants were at a warlord's beck and call.

The ticket al-Mabhouh purchased, Emirates Airlines flight 912, departed Damascus on January 19 at 10:05 AM. EK912 was the daily morning flight to Dubai—one that made sure its passengers could be in their hotel lounges for afternoon cocktails. The alcohol always flowed in

Dubai. Al-Mabhouh's security detail would have to meet their principal in UAE the following day. They'd be forced to fly on SyrianAir, an airline without the charm or style of Emirates, but one that allowed them to carry their sidearms on the plane.

On the morning of January 19, 2010, a car picked al-Mabhouh up from his Kfar Sousah home in Damascus to drive him to the airport. The neighborhood was the exclusive section of the Syrian capital reserved for Palestinian and Lebanese militants and friends of the ruling Assad regime. Syrian intelligence agents at the airport took care of the check-in process for al-Mabhouh; such VIP respect was customary. He had five fake passports at his disposal. For this trip he used an Iraqi travel document in the name of Mahmoud Abdul Raouf Mohammed; some reports claimed he used a forged Palestinian travel document.

The Hamas commander was ushered through passport control and then brought to the business-class lounge. The Emirates air hostesses, in their tan blazers and skirts and characteristic red caps, made sure that the passengers were well attended to during the three-hour flight. The Emirates Airline flight landed at precisely 3:15 PM. One of the airport's perks was a quick turnaround from landing to city adventure. Al-Mabhouh dragged a black carry-on bag across the polished marble floors until he reached the stand where an airport shuttle car would take him to the al-Bustan Rotana. Mahmoud al-Mabhouh was at the check-in desk before 4:00. Closed-circuit television cameras taped virtually every moment of al-Mabhouh's arrival in Dubai—from passport control to hotel check-in. It seemed every nook and cranny of Dubai was under a protective blanket of video surveillance. Ironically, it is believed that Israeli firms were the ones who put the systems in place.

There were human eyes on al-Mabhouh, as well. A significant-sized force of men and women, all young, all between the ages of twenty-five and thirty-five, had arrived in Dubai the previous day. Some had arrived earlier that morning. The men and women arrived on flights from Europe's hubs of commerce—Frankfurt, Paris, Rome, and Zurich—and they carried genuine European and Australian passports. The tourists were dressed neatly, in the kind of casual clothing that young urban professionals in Europe would wear when traveling; their carry-on bags and laptop bags were top-of-the-line.

They had arrived on separate flights and ventured to separate hotels. There was some question as to where al-Mabhouh would end up, and the hit team decided to spread out throughout Dubai in anticipation of where the Hamas man might eventually check in. Some members of the team took rooms at the al-Bustan Rotana located adjacent to the airport. Surveillance footage later showed some of these young European travelers following Mabhouh from the airport to hotel check-in.

The top leadership of Hamas would never have agreed to spend a night in a hotel like the al-Bustan Rotana. It was a five-star hotel, and its lobby was a beautiful combination of dark, clean, and crisp angles, but the hotel wasn't überluxurious by Dubai's standard. Still, so close to the airport, it had rooms under $125 a night and it was a convenient and comfortable stop for weary travelers. The man handed the clerk his passport in the name of "Mahmoud Abdul Raouf Mohammed" and his credit card. He requested a suite with windows that could not open and one that had no balcony. He was issued two white plastic card keys and a smile from the young woman at the front desk. Mabhouh declined the offer to receive help with his bags.[19] He rode up to his second-floor room with a man who, surveillance footage revealed, was wearing a fake moustache and glasses. He carried a tennis racket and watched as al-Mabhouh opened the door to Room 230. The tennis player then glanced across the hallway and noticed that the room number directly across the hall from al-Mabhouh's was 237. A call was soon made on his cell phone to book the room.

Al-Mabhouh showered, but he didn't change his clothes. He left his bag on a small folding table near the dresser but grabbed a small spiral notebook. (Fellow travelers in the economy section of Flight EK912 remember al-Mabhouh deep in thought as he jotted down notes in the small journal during the flight from Damascus.) Reportedly, he placed a few items in the safe located near the room's entrance by the bathroom.

Al-Mabhouh left the hotel and walked a little more than a kilometer to the City Centre Deira shopping mall. He was still in good physical shape, and he made it to the mall in fifteen minutes. There he bought sneakers and met with two individuals. He then traveled to the Iranian consulate on al-Wasl Road for high level talks. His first discussions were with an Iranian banker, and it is believed the discussion was about the money Hamas needed from Tehran to continue its missile program. Al-Mabhouh then met with his Iranian intelligence handler from the Iranian Islamic Revolutionary Guard Corps. It is believed that the two men discussed the logistics of getting the Iranian-financed missile parts into the Gaza Strip. The Revolutionary Guard officer had flown in from Tehran specifically for the meeting.

Rotating surveillance teams followed al-Mabhouh's every step during his time in Dubai.

While al-Mabhouh was meeting with his Iranian contacts, additional surveillance teams, most in disguise with poor-fitting hairpieces and fake glasses, staked out the lobby of the al-Bustan Rotana. One member of the crew had already checked into Room 237. Four members of the team, men who appeared to be the muscle on the closed-circuit TV surveillance, had made a copy of the key card to enter al-Mabhouh's room.[20] The killers sat silently and waited for the Hamas commander to return to his room. The four men, reportedly, wore rubber gloves and masks to shield their DNA.[21]

Mahmoud al-Mabhouh was last seen alive on CCTV cameras as he returned to the hotel at 8:24 PM. It is believed that he was overpowered in his room, given a muscle relaxant, and then suffocated to death. He was still wearing the same checkered shirt, jacket, and blue jeans when he returned, though the assassins quickly stripped him down to his black jockey shorts and placed him on the bed and under the covers. There were no reports of a scuffle, and the intruders took great care to make sure there were no signs of a struggle to be found in the neatly arranged hotel room.

Mahmoud al-Mabhouh's killers left the room unnoticed. It is still unexplained how they managed to exit the room and still leave it locked on the inside. Over the next few hours, twenty-seven men and women checked out of their Dubai hotel rooms and headed for Dubai International Airport. The al-Bustan Rotana was an ideal place for a team of intelligence agents to carry out a stunning hit and then escape the country in a hurry. The hotel was a stone's throw from the departure areas where one could grab flights to anywhere in the world twenty-four hours a day.

Some took flights to Hong Kong, Johannesburg, and Frankfurt; others traveled to other hubs in Europe, where they doubled back, perhaps carrying new passports. Apparently, everyone involved in the operation made it back home safely.

The operation's success depended on al-Mabhouh's death being made to look as if he died of natural causes. Past assassinations attributed to the Mossad, such as those responsible for the Munich Olympics massacre, were carried out with silenced .22 Beretta pistols and bombs placed in cars under the driver's-side cushions. Dubai wasn't a safe city for a Blue and White, or purely Israeli, operation; there was no Israeli embassy where the team could hide if the local authorities came after them. It was imperative for the team to depart the UAE before word of al-Mabhouh's death was revealed and be safe outside the UAE, en route back to Israel, according to reports.

The maids, women from Pakistan and the Philippines, knocked on Room 230 for a good ten minutes at just about noon the following day. The night crew had tried to get into the room the evening before. Turndown service was common, but the hotel was used to passengers, some from the Gulf States, who frequently called a service for female companionship, and who craved privacy. A DO NOT DISTURB notice was on the doorknob. But Mabhouh was supposed to stay only one night, and at noon the cleaning staff still couldn't get into the room with the master key. The hotel security officer was summoned. The lifeless body of the man in possession of the Syrian passport in the name of "Mahmoud Abdul Raouf Mohammed" was found under the covers. His body was cold. He had been dead for several hours. The hotel immediately called the police. When detectives searched the room, they found al-Mabhouh's fake passport and his clothing; a white bag and a pair of brand-new Adidas running shoes were on the floor.

The briefcase that al-Mabhouh had brought with him from Damascus was nowhere to be found.

At first, the Dubai Police assumed that the man, who had expired sometime between six o'clock on the evening of January 19 and noon the next day, had died from natural causes. A heart attack was suspected. But when investigators dug deeper, and realized that the decedent was actually a high-ranking Hamas commander, an autopsy was ordered and a criminal investigation was launched. According to some with close ties to the security services inside Dubai and the UAE, the Jihaz amn a-Dawleh was furious that al-Mabhouh and the Iranians were using the emirate as a meeting place.[22]

Al-Mabhouh's killers would most certainly have known that every step they took in Dubai was covered by CCTV surveillance. The cameras didn't seem to bother anyone involved. Still, the Dubai Police force, famous for having vehicles such as the Lamborghini Aventador LP700-4 and the Ferrari FF on patrol, did an extraordinary job of piecing together what must have looked like a Hollywood epic's worth of footage to build a case that nearly thirty men and women were involved in the al-Mabhouh assassination.

The Dubai Police, in fact, counted twenty-seven suspects who they believe were involved in the killing. Twelve of them carried British passports. Six of the alleged perpetrators carried Irish passports; four of them carried French travel books, four carried Australian passports, and one entered the country on a German passport. Sixteen of the passports belonged to names of dual citizens who lived in Israel but whose identities had been cloned and borrowed.

There were close to 684 hours of CCTV to review and analyze.[23] Perhaps the Mossad, or whoever carried out the operation, had underestimated the ability and the sophistication of the Dubai Police to collate and review the CCTV footage from so many diverse sources and create a singular time line[24] that linked the twenty-seven foreign visitors to the events that transpired inside and outside of Room 230. Perhaps, if it was the Mossad behind the operation, the Israelis really didn't care what the fallout would be.

The Dubai Police were able to triangulate the cellular phone traffic, all through an exchange in Austria, of the participants, as well. There was also an incriminating American connection discovered. Thirteen of the twenty-seven suspected individuals used prepaid MasterCards from a prepaid credit card company based in New York City called Payoneer;[25] the CEO of the company, Yuval Tal, was reportedly a former member of the Israeli special operations community.[26] Payoneer produces customized and prepaid MasterCard credit cards that companies can issue to their employees. The cards used in Dubai were drawn on MetaBank, a financial institution based in the Midwestern United States.[27] The prepaid credit cards were used to pay for flights and hotel stays.

The intelligence-gathering capabilities that the Dubai Police displayed in assembling this matrix were, indeed, impressive. According to one Palestinian security expert, the men who worked for the Dubai Police reviewing the CCTV footage were all foreign—expatriates, mainly retirees, working as contractors in the emirate city after they had completed successful investigative careers for Scotland Yard or some of the other English-speaking nations where tax-free retirement often coincided with freelance security work.[28]

But the al-Mabhouh assassination wasn't the first time an intelligence service had carried out a hit operation in Dubai. On March 30, 2009, Sulim Yamadayev, a former Chechen general, was shot and killed by anonymous assailants as he left a car park in Dubai, where he had been living in secret for several months under an assumed identity; his brother had been shot and killed in Moscow months earlier. Dubai police apprehended two assassins, an Iranian and a Tajik, who they believed were working on behalf of the Russian government and its FSB intelligence service.[29] But, clearly, the al-Mabhouh "hit" was the most spectacular murder to ever be perpetrated in the city.

Police chief Lieutenant General Dahi Khalfan Tamim, commander of general security for the Emirate of Dubai, was the point man leading the investigation into al-Mabhouh's death. Correspondents from all over the world rushed to Dubai to cover the assassination, and the fifty-nine-year-old police commander relished the media spotlight. General Tamim joined the force in 1970 when the emirate city was a small and forgettable dusty fishing village, and now he led the law enforcement force responsible for protecting one of the world's most important international business centers. A born actor with a dramatic flair, he appeared in press conferences in a wide array of costumes: In one briefing, he wore neatly pressed khaki fatigues displaying his rank, a chest full of medals, and the swagger of a man who ruled with an iron fist, and in other gatherings of the press he wore traditional gray Bedouin garb showing that he was a man of the desert.

Tamim's presentations to the international media were polished and highly impressive. In one case, he broadcast an eleven-minute compilation showing the alleged Mossad agents arriving in country and assembling in some of the city's other hotels, as well as in a shopping mall, and, of course, the same hotel where al-Mabhouh was staying. In one press conference, he said, "Israel must not carry out assassinations on our land. This is an insult to Britain and to Australia and to Germany and to New Zealand. If the Mossad dipped their hand in blood and wiped it on European passports, our treatment of Europeans will remain the same. In the future those who we suspect of carrying dual nationality will be treated very carefully."[30] The investigation and accumulating details were turning into a freewheeling circus.

General Tamim used to be criticized for being aloof to the local media, but now with cameras all over the world following his every word, the Dubai Police chief became a star. He enjoyed, in the papers at least, the appearance that he could go toe to toe with Meir Dagan. Tamim urged Meir Dagan to "be a man" and admit that Israel and the Mossad were behind the killing of Mahmoud al-Mabhouh, according to the Emirati newspaper *al-Khaleej*.[31]

Pundits in Israel, columnists for the nation's vibrant press, and even some former members of the country's intelligence and special operations community, claimed that "if" Israel was involved in al-Mabhouh's killing, then the operation was sloppy and errant. Amir Oren, a columnist for the left-of-center *Ha'aretz*, called for Meir Dagan's resignation. Ben Caspit, from the *Ma'ariv* newspaper, described the incident as "a tactical operational success, but a strategic failure."[32] No one in the country cared that al-Mabhouh himself had met an untimely death; privately, many wished that the man with blood on his hands suffered like the two soldiers he had killed in cold blood. Most concerning was the diplomatic fallout over the use of forged and genuine foreign passports in the execution of a targeted assassination operation.

Israeli ambassadors were called to the carpet in Berlin, Paris, and London; Israeli diplomats were even expelled in a public show that the Mossad—or any intelligence service—would not be able to carry out espionage activity on the back of forged and genuine indigenous passports. Kevin Rudd, the Australian prime minister, was harshest in his criticism of Israel. "As a longstanding friend of Israel, I repeat what I said before, any state, any state, which uses or forges Australian passports let alone uses or forges Australian passports for the purpose of assassination is of the deepest concern to Australia, and we will not let the matter rest," Rudd expressed during a radio interview with the Australian Broadcasting Corporation.[33] The politicians had to huff and puff for the benefit of the cameras to show the Arab world that they would not tolerate the abduction of genuine identities for the convenience of an intelligence operation. Al-Mabhouh wasn't a man who was going to be missed by any of the countries whose passports had been used. Once the furor over the passport issue died down, the matter was soon forgotten.

Meir Dagan chuckled when asked if he thought the "Dubai Job" was a disaster for Mossad. "I never heard of any Israelis being arrested," he joked.[34]

*　　*　　*

From a clearly end-result perspective, it's hard to label the Israeli operation as a failure. Mahmoud al-Mabhouh was buried in the Yarmouk refugee camp in Damascus on January 29, 2010.[35] It was a cold and windy Friday morning when his coffin, draped in the green Hamas flag, was lowered into the ground at Martyrs Cemetery. The Syrian intelligence services saw to it that there was a decent turnout at the burial.

From a regional perspective, the Iranian Islamic Revolutionary Guard Corps and al-Quds Force operatives who set up shell companies in Dubai for the purposes of supporting groups like Hezbollah and Hamas thought twice before sending a representative to a hotel bar or a Russian-populated strip club in the city without constantly looking over their shoulders. That constituted the sort of preemptive deterrence that an agency like the Mossad was famous for.

Hamas would have to find someone who possessed al-Mabhouh's experience and knowledge of the financial and armament pipeline that flowed from Tehran to the Sudan to Sinai and Gaza. The Palestinian Islamic Resistance Movement would have to find someone capable who knew that his predecessor had been spectacularly killed and that now he himself would be stepping into the enemy's crosshairs. Men like al-Mabhouh were not replaced with a job posting on craigslist.

The al-Mabhouh assassination sent the powerful message that even those merely involved with the financing of terrorist operations no longer enjoyed safe harbor. They would be aggressively hunted down and eliminated just the same as those that built the bombs and carried out the attacks. The al-Mabhouh assassination operation—the size, the scale, and the investment into the operation—exposed the irrefutable fact that obstructing the flow of money had become a national intelligence service priority, one as crucial as targeting the terrorist chiefs. Despite the media storm that would ensue, the al-Mabhouh operation was a game changer. His murder gave those who moved money for terror reason for pause. Those players were now on notice. Their seemingly innocuous role in facilitating terror had become a very high-risk profession.

It took Hamas nearly four years to recover from al-Mabhouh's death—
four years for the organization to find a replacement that had his network, experience, and ability to coordinate Iranian money and smuggling
routes into a cohesive and effective rockets and armaments program.
Those four years were a period of relative peace and quiet along Israel's
southern border with Gaza. They were four years in which Israeli civilians
weren't killed by rocket attacks and suicide bombers. From that perspective, regardless of who gave the order, the operation in Dubai was a rousing success.

CHAPTER EIGHTEEN

The Final Victories of an Old Soldier

The unforgivable crime is soft hitting. Do not hit at all if it can be avoided; but never hit softly.
—Theodore Roosevelt[1]

Meir Dagan relished his reputation as a fierce warrior who could be counted on to lead a daring mission deep behind enemy lines, dagger nestled firmly in his hands. But Dagan hated war. His subordinates and friends knew just how much he despised senseless bloodshed. His family, his closest friends, knew how much the loss of friends and comrades pained him. His barrel-chested toughness concealed a wounded heart made up of scar tissue. Much of the pain he carried with him was caused by the bloodshed he participated in during the 1973 Yom Kippur War, when Israel was caught by surprise by a simultaneous attack on two fronts by the Syrian and Egyptian armies. But whenever Dagan's friends and family spoke about war, they inevitably spoke of Israel's 1982 conflict in Lebanon.

Dagan commanded the 188th Armored Brigade in the fighting, leading three battalions of Centurion tanks into southern Lebanon in the bitter combat around cities like Sidon and in refugee camps, like Ein el-Hilweh. In the war's first days, one of his junior officers, Captain Uzi Arad, was killed in front of him. Dagan was fond of Arad; Arad's brother had been killed in action, and Dagan had to assure Uzi's mother that her other son would be okay as a company commander in his brigade.[2] Dagan failed to fulfill his promise. But the war continued. The 188th Armored Brigade pushed north deeper into Lebanon.

The 188th, along with infantrymen from the Golani Brigade, fought in the battle of Kfar Sil, a close-quarter bare-knuckle brawl against well-entrenched Syrian commandos who were propping up Hezbollah's forces; the battle was described by many as the toughest of the war.[3] There were cease-fires and skirmishes, and sometimes all-out hellacious fighting. At the end of July the brigade was ordered to get ready to enter Beirut. It was the first time that Israeli forces were poised to seize an Arab capital. Days later, the 188th brigade advanced on Beirut International Airport. The control tower became Dagan's headquarters. From there, according to one of his battalion commanders, he conducted and choreographed the opera of war.[4]

The battle for the airport was hard fought. At dawn on the morning of August 4, Syrian commandos unleashed a lethal barrage of antitank missiles against one of Dagan's battalions near the main terminal. Later that day, toward afternoon, Palestinian and Syrian artillery poured a deadly and pinpointed rain of fire onto the Israeli positions. Thirteen soldiers were killed in the barrage, including Captain Tuval Gvirtzman, the commander of a company of tanks codenamed "Crusher"; he had been killed rushing to the aid of an armored personnel carrier that had suffered a direct hit and had burst into flames.[5]

Gvirtzman, known by the nickname of "Tuli," was Dagan's favorite officer in the brigade. "Dagan loved Tuli very much," a former officer in the brigade remembered. "He was the most beloved officer in his command." Lieutenant Colonel Eyal Ben-Reuven was Tuli's commanding officer and had to break the news to Dagan. Under fire, Ben-Reuven climbed up the stairs leading to the control tower toward the brigade command post. Dagan was peering through high-powered field glasses; marked-up maps were strewn about the floor amid broken glass. When Dagan heard that Tuli had been killed, he stopped what he was doing and his body slumped inward. He broke down in a loud and gut-wrenching cry that could be heard amid the gunfire.[6] No one had ever seen Dagan cry before news of Tuli's death reached him. Even though Dagan's brigade lost twenty-five men in the conflict, and he had seen his men killed and wounded before, Tuli's death changed Dagan forever.

Other events during his service in Lebanon made a lasting impression as well. Upon Dagan's return home on leave in 1985, he informed his wife, Bina, that as a result of the fierce carnage he had witnessed in the fighting he no longer felt able to eat meat. It simply disgusted him, brought up difficult memories and images, and he insisted that he and his family become vegetarians. Just like that he swore off meat forever.

Thirty years had passed since the battle for Beirut International Airport. Israel endured numerous intifadas and suicide bombing campaigns, SCUD missiles from Iraq, and a second war in Lebanon against Hezbollah. The country also endured a ceaseless terrorist campaign of attrition in between. But the biggest threat Israel had to face now was Iran.

Meir Dagan hated war and wanted to do whatever he could to avoid it; this was part of the genius behind Harpoon—an effort to shock and awe the bankbooks of terror and not the crowded refugee camps where the perpetrators hid shielded by women and children. This revolutionized how nations waged war on terror. There were some in Israel pounding war drums to keep Iran from becoming a nuclear power. Israelis well understood that much of the terrorism being waged against them was being funded directly by the mullahs in Tehran, and they had no illusions what kind of threat the Islamic Republic would pose with nuclear capabilities. Dagan knew when war was necessary and when it could be avoided. In the eighth year of his tenure as Mossad director, Dagan was in a position to put actions in motion that could prevent war—even if it meant that some had to die as part of a larger and more important policy of preemptive deterrence.

It was a little before 8:00 AM on the morning of January 12, 2010, when Dr. Masoud Alimohammadi left his modest but comfortable home in the northern Tehran suburb of Gheytarieh. He had just completed breakfast, a quick bite of flatbread and goat cheese drizzled with honey, and had finished his third cup of tea when he grabbed his car keys and headed out the door. The fifty-year-old, an Iranian quantum field theorist and elementary-particle physicist, was a revered and distinguished professor at the University of Tehran's Department of Physics. He was also a player in Iran's nuclear program, and he was already late to work. He didn't notice the motorcycle with its concealed cargo, parked near his small Japanese-made sedan. Before he could unlock his car, neighbors saw a blinding flash of light followed by an ear-splitting blast that lifted him into the air. Alimohammadi was killed instantly when he was cut to pieces by the force of the powerful explosion and the shrapnel that chewed through his body. More than one thousand mourners attended Dr. Masoud Alimohammadi's state funeral. The pall bearers were all members of the Revolutionary Guard.[7]

The Iranian security services scrambled to investigate the assassination and hunt down the perpetrators. At all costs the regime needed to project the image that it was firmly in charge, that it could safeguard national security, and that the public was protected; having a senior nuclear scientist cut down in the street outside his home generated widespread fear among ordinary Iranians. The culprits needed to be found and punished immediately. The regime became obsessed with identifying the cell that carried out the hit.

Iran's security services ultimately made an arrest in Alimohammadi's murder. The suspect's name was Majid Jamali Fashi. Following a thorough and brutal interrogation, he allegedly confessed to having been a Mossad spy trained in Israel.* Fashi admitted to traveling to Tel Aviv for specialized Mossad training; he said that Israel's intelligence service had planned and paid for the entire Alimohamaddi operation.[8] He was ultimately convicted and executed—hanged in a prison courtyard.

---

* Fashi was apprehended after documents, released by WikiLeaks, revealed his name in a cable from the U.S. embassy in Baku, Azerbaijan. Iranian investigators believed that Fashi, a twenty-four-year-old kickboxer, had been recruited in Baku, during a martial arts tournament and that he ultimately traveled to Israel. The State of Israel—and particularly the Mossad and the national defense industries—enjoyed close-knit relations with Azerbaijan.

The close-quarter ground war against the Iranian nuclear program was now well underway.*

Traffic was moving at a snail's pace in the northern neighborhoods of Tehran on the morning of November 10, 2010. Traffic in the Aghdasieh district was particularly maddening. An endless number of cars maneuvered in and out of their lanes in a slow-moving crawl while the drivers, many chain-smoking, honked their horns violently in a serenade of Persian anger. The only vehicles that moved freely in this morning mess were of the two-wheeled variety. The mopeds and the motorbikes weaved in and out of the maze with few obstacles. In Tehran it was the only way to travel.

Majid Shahriari was a passenger in a silver Peugeot 504 sedan trying to get to this university job through the frustrating mess on Artesh Boulevard. Shahriari, forty-three years old, was a quantum physicist and a major player in Iran's nuclear program. According to some accounts, the professor was also one of Iran's foremost experts investigating the Stuxnet worm attack.[9] Shahriari sat in the back seat with a female passenger, witnesses recalled, and both looked anxious by the morning's heavier-than-usual gridlock. The two were driven by a middle-aged man pounding his horn in boredom and anger. Shahriari didn't notice the motorcycle coming up behind him and then slowing down as it passed the Peugeot. Shahriari's chauffeur didn't see the motorcyclist's brief dalliance along his vehicle's side nor the small but potent explosive device that had been attached to the rear door with an adhesive strip. The motorcycle sped up as it proceeded forward and disappeared into the morning's rush hour. Minutes later a powerful explosion punched through the Peugeot—Shahriari was killed instantly, along with the woman and the driver.

As sirens blared and emergency service personnel rushed toward Artesh

---

* The first Iranian nuclear scientist to be killed was Dr. Ardeshir Hassanpour. He was murdered on January 15, 2007, in an operation that the Israeli newspaper *Ha'aretz* claimed had been carried out by the Mossad.

Boulevard to aid the victims, and the chaos played out on the crowded rush-hour highway, another car and passenger were being targeted in a similar incident just a few miles away to the west. A two-man motorcycle team had affixed an explosive device to the car driven by Dr. Fereydoon Abbasi as he traveled slowly through Tehran traffic. Dr. Abbasi was a senior scientist in the Ministry of Defense. According to reports, he worked side by side with Mohsen Fakhrizadeh, an officer in the Islamic Revolutionary Guards Corps, and believed to be one of the pillars of Iran's nuclear efforts.[10] This time, though, the bomb failed to accomplish its goal. Abbasi survived.

The State of Israel did not confirm nor deny any role in the attacks targeting Iran's nuclear scientists. But Israel—and the Mossad—was determined to slow Tehran's march toward nuclear weapons capability any way that it could short of all-out war or a preemptive strike—options Dagan and others inside the IDF believed would have disastrous consequences for Israel and the region. Dagan wanted to use every tool in his arsenal to delay and deter the Iranians. He urged that the same tactics—covert and devious—that Harpoon had used against the Palestinians and Hezbollah be used against the Iranian nuclear program. "Bankrupt them," Uri L. remembered Dagan saying. "Make it impossible for them to do business. Make it unviable for them to buy the material and pay the scientists. Bankrupt the ayatollahs and force them to abandon the dream."[11] The goals and tactics of Harpoon had now become the norm throughout Israel's intelligence services.

Operations against the Hamas and Hezbollah gave Dagan ideas. According to one account, the Mossad director wanted to ruin the reputation of Mohamed El-Baredei, the former director general of the International Atomic Energy Agency, who Israel considered to be biased toward the Iranians and hostile to the Jewish state and its security concerns. A plan was considered to deposit large sums of money into El-Baredei's bank account and then leak the word that the Iranians were paying him off in exchange for lenient reviews of their reactors.[12] The operation was never executed, but it telegraphed the Mossad's steely determination to resort to classic manipulation and dirty tricks against anyone involved in advancing Tehran's perilous ambitions.

The political winds had changed in the winter of 2010, though. Some wanted war. According to accounts of heated debates that occurred inside Israel's security cabinet, Prime Minister Benjamin Netanyahu and Defense Minister Ehud Barak openly called for the Israel Air Force to conduct a preemptive strike against Iranian nuclear facilities. Israel had, after all, destroyed Iraqi strongman Saddam Hussein's own fledgling reactor back in June 1981, in a spectacular air force operation that brought blistering public condemnations and quiet, relieved congratulations from the international community. The Israeli raid on the Osirak reactor had obliterated Saddam's nuclear program in its infancy, and it was never relaunched. Many were insisting that the IAF take the matter into its own hands once again. Dagan, however, vehemently opposed the notion,[13] as did others, including Yuval Diskin and many generals. According to Dagan's thinking, at best an Israeli bombing run would provide an illusory solution, perhaps destroying the facilities temporarily only to have them be rebuilt, next time in deeper, more secretive, and better fortified underground bunkers.

The back-and-forth inside the closed-door sessions was heated and impassioned. Israel, many understood, couldn't take out the nuclear program on its own. There was great concern that the United States wouldn't conclude what Israel had started and finish off the Iranian facilities once and for all. "Our belief was that if they [the Israelis] went on their own, knowing their limitations, they are a very good air force but it's small and the distances are great and the targets are dispersed and hardened," former CIA Director Michael Hayden said. The American fear was that if Israel put events in motion, the United States would be drawn into completing the job, and that was not an option.[14] President Barack Obama, elected in 2008 in part to extract the United States from Middle Eastern wars, was not an enthusiastic supporter of unilateral Israeli action that would draw American forces into the fray. And he certainly wasn't going to undertake the task on his own.

Israeli pilots continued to train for the mission that might or might never be sanctioned. Tactics were honed and flight paths were examined. In the end, like so many times before, Dagan's argument proved to be persuasive. The financial effort that Dagan and Harpoon favored took on an aggressive new energy as the United States now led the effort to isolate Iran economically; this could have become a leverage tool to get Tehran to the negotiating table and agree to halt its nuclear weapons program. Dagan wanted the United States to strangle the Iranians into financial submission. The Mossad director felt that economic warfare was the only way to prevent a war that he personally viewed as destructively unwinnable. "Military action against the Iranian nuclear program," Dagan argued, "was the final option."[15]

The job of Mossad *Memuneh*, or Director, was one of the most challenging and tension-filled posts inside Israel's pressure-packed security establishment. It was the type of responsibility that could give someone with even superhuman resolve a case of high blood pressure, chronic insomnia, and an endless surge of stomach ulcers. The stress of the job—on a personal level and on a national geopolitical level—was numbing. The decisions made while sitting at the director's chair could get agents killed in far and distant lands. The director has to look his subordinates in the eyes and convince them that the mission is worth the risk, worth their lives being in danger. The Mossad director once explained, "People on these missions don't have aircraft waiting to rescue them if they get in trouble, they don't have tanks and soldiers waiting to back them up, most of the times they don't even have weapons. All they have is a piece of paper in the form of a passport, a cover story, and their ability to think sharply on their feet to stay alive."[16] And, as Mossad director, Dagan had to warn these dedicated agents that if they were caught, if an operation turned disastrous, it might be very difficult for Israel to get them out—worse, it might be downright impossible to rescue them or barter for them at all.

The operations that had the director's signature could end up costing more than the life of an agent or an asset. Intelligence operations could place the nation at war. The job and the decision made at the top had a direct impact on the day-to-day lives of Israel's citizens, as well as for Jews around the world. Dagan remembered what Prime Minister Shimon Peres once said: that he read about the failures of the Mossad in the newspaper and he read about its successes in classified reports.[17]

Most Mossad directors served for a term of four or five years. Exhaustion and burnout were common denominators among outgoing chiefs. As one of Dagan's men in Harpoon put it, "There was only so much political hubris and bullshit that one man could handle."[18] Isser Harel, one of the legendary spymasters of Israel, spent ten years sitting behind the chair, at Mossad headquarters. Harel had raised the Mossad from a small and insignificant service to one of the world's major intelligence arms, operating globally to protect Israel's precarious security. The Mossad thwarted Arab intentions during Harel's term, and Israel's spies captured Nazi Final Solution architect Adolf Eichmann in Argentina, but Harel's decade-long service tenure was considered extraordinarily long for a spy chief. Yitzhak Hofi, a former general who rehabilitated the Mossad following the disastrous 1973 War and had scored some major successes for the service, including the assassination of Munich Olympic massacre mastermind Ali Hassan Salameh,[19] served eight years. As 2011 approached, Meir Dagan was entering his ninth year as Mossad director.

It was time to call it a day.

Dagan's stint as Mossad director had been extended twice. The first time was in 2006, after Ehud Olmert's ascension to the prime minister's office, and then again, in 2009, following Netanyahu's election victory. The politicians wanted Dagan by their side. It made them look decisive and maverick. The voting public felt assured by having Dagan at the helm of the Mossad. But Dagan was tired. It was an odd reality for the chief of an espionage service, but up until a few years before he assumed the post, the identities of the Mossad and Shin Bet directors were classified and referred to in the press only by the first initials of their names. The culture in Israel had progressed rapidly, and now that the names were well known, there was a demand for more transparency, oversight, and scrutiny. As such, it seemed everyone was scrambling, constantly, to cover their behinds.

The years of work at the Mossad had caught up with Meir Dagan. The grueling pace of eighteen-hour days, covert travel, and political nonsense had taken their toll. Journalists and politicians from across the political spectrum speculated that because Netanyahu and Dagan were openly at odds over Iran, the Mossad director had been forced out. "It wasn't true," Bina Dagan commented on her husband's status. "He was tired, eight years going on nine was too long. He wanted the chance to do other things."[20] He was a grandfather. He wanted to paint and earn a CEO's salary. He had dedicated forty-eight years in service to his country. It was time to sleep in mornings after 7:00 AM and eat breakfast with his wife, maybe read stories to his grandchildren.

Dagan, interviewed for Israeli television after he left office, refused to speak openly about the successes he was proudest of as Mossad director— the man was not one to ever discuss anything that could even hint as leaking classified information. But he did say what his two greatest disappointments were. The first was not definitively determining the fate of Ron Arad, an Israeli Air Force F4E Phantom navigator held by Hezbollah and possibly Iran. The second was the failure to bring back the body of Eli Cohen, the agency's legendary spy who provided Israel with invaluable intelligence on the Syrian military and who was hanged in Damascus; his body, at the time of this book's writing, remains in Syria.[21]

Meir Dagan had gone from a newcomer to Israel, the son of a family that paid a terrible price in Hitler's Holocaust, to a man in charge of one of the country's most important pillars of defense. In Harpoon, he defined a new way in which intelligence could be used to deplete a terrorist army of its means, and not only its men. Dagan's journey was an improbable one but, as Dagan once commented, it was "proof that anything was possible."[22] In January 2011, in a quiet ceremony at the prime minister's office, Netanyahu hugged his spymaster and thanked him for his many years of service. When Dagan left Mossad headquarters, many of the cool-thinking and courageous intelligence agents quietly wept to see their chief leave the building. It had been a golden age for Israel's espionage service.

Meir Dagan woke up the morning after as a civilian for the first time in nearly half a century. The old soldier and spook, though, Meir Dagan had no intention of fading away.

Dagan's view that terror funding was a new battlefield, and his belief that Iran should be strangled financially rather than hit by aircraft in a sure-to-fail attempt at shock and awe, left behind another legacy.

Shortly after the September 11, 2001, attacks against the United States, the Central Intelligence Agency was authorized by the Bush administration to embark on one of the most secretive programs of the American-led war on terror. The initiative, known as the Terrorist Finance Tracking Program (TFTP), entered the highly secure Society for Worldwide Interbank Financial Telecommunication (SWIFT) network to monitor bank transfers made all around the world. Virtually every bank, every financial institution of note, is connected to SWIFT, which is a Belgian-based, highly secure network that allows banks to safety and confidentially interact and do business with one another. SWIFT provides the mechanism by which some 7,800 financial institutions around the world transfer money.[23] SWIFT is a cooperative, consisting of more than two thousand organizations, and virtually every financial institution uses its codes and services. Any bank, from a major icon of global finance in midtown Manhattan to a small Islamic credit union on the byways of Peshawar, can communicate with any other bank and transfer and receive money courtesy of the SWIFT network. Banks have to have SWIFT codes to wire money. It is an essential tool of international commerce; SWIFT enables over eleven million transactions a day.[24]

The joint CIA-Treasury operation was carried out with the assistance of the National Security Agency's massive eavesdropping program, which monitored telephone calls, facsimiles, e-mails, and text messages—without warrants—of more than five thousand Americans who were suspected of maintaining terrorist ties.[25] The two programs worked in parallel and complementary directions, each often enhancing the efforts of the other. Phil Rosenberg ran it for the Agency; Undersecretary Stuart Levey's Terrorism and Financial Intelligence unit ran Treasury's half.

The Israelis maintained close relations with FINO and urged them to target the Iranians and place pressure on SWIFT not to allow the Islamic Republic's banking sector to utilize its services. Unlike Harpoon, with its emphasis on going after the street-level cash and the specific banks, the United States finally decided to go after the Holy Grail of financial information—the system itself. TFTP was run out of CIA headquarters in Langley, Virginia, and overseen by the U.S. Treasury Department, and it functioned without ever asking the Belgians for permission. "The Agency simply managed to break into SWIFT's databases and monitor all the financial moves that everyone, everywhere, around the world made," a former Harpoon officer commented. "It was a masterful coup for American intelligence and they were determined to keep it to themselves and use it only in the most sensitive areas, and even then they were always quick to cover up the fact that intel from financial information had anything to do with a major operation, seizure, or extrajudicial killing."[26]

Because the intelligence that TFTP produced was unique and so secretive, the Americans used it sparingly. Most of what the CIA and the Department of the Treasury did with the data remains classified. One success reported from the program was the capture of Riduan Isamuddin, the head of the Indonesian al-Qaeda affiliate known as Jemaah Islamiyah. Isamuddin, who was also known by his nom de guerre of Hambali, was called by many the Osama bin Laden of Southeast Asia. He had fought with bin Laden in Afghanistan against the Soviets and then created one of the largest Muslim terrorist armies in Asia. Hambali was behind the October 12, 2002, terrorist massacre targeting tourists in nightclubs on the tropical paradise of Bali; 202 people were killed in the multiple bombing strikes, and another two hundred seriously wounded. Hambali was arrested a year later in Thailand by counterterrorist police.[27] He was renditioned to a CIA black site and then incarcerated in Guantanamo Bay. Hambali was located and apprehended as a result of the financial back-and-forth that helped to finance the Bali operation the TFTP program intercepted through SWIFT traffic. Another known TFPT success was the 2003 arrest of a Pakistani national, Uzair Paracha, who was wiring money back to banks in Pakistan in conjunction with supporting al-Qaeda. Paracha laundered in excess of $200,000 for terrorists in Pakistan.[28]

The Americans didn't tell their other allies in the Five-Eyes network of intelligence agencies about TFTP. The Five-Eyes arrangement was the sharing of intelligence between agencies from the United States, Canada, Great Britain, New Zealand, and Australia. The CIA and the Department of the Treasury did not share word of the program's existence with Harpoon, either. "There were some, many, at the CIA who didn't trust us," a Harpoon veteran admitted, "even though the sharing of intelligence often originated from the most sensitive and clandestine of sources, sources that were always redacted."[29] The arrangement was, of course, bilateral. The Israelis sanitized the raw data that they exchanged with the CIA and other agencies in the U.S. intelligence community. "We never knew who the spy chiefs would share the information with," the Harpoon officer explained, "and we were always concerned that somehow a U.S. government official who read the material would share it with eyes we had never intended to look at the information."[30]

Still, when Meir Dagan visited CIA directors George Tenet, Porter Goss, and Michael Hayden from 2002 to 2005—and enjoyed one-on-one conversations inside the director's office at Langley—TFTP was never mentioned, even though the heads of the two services discussed some of the most compelling secrets vital to their nation's security. Some Harpoon veterans believe that it was U.S. policy not to share the TFTP intelligence with Harpoon, because the Bush administration was adamant that the Israelis not bring down the entire Palestinian Authority's economy.[31] In 2005, the CIA disclosed some of its capability to access banking intelligence to Harpoon in a meeting in Washington, D.C. However, the Americans insisted that the intelligence could not be used without prior authorization of the United States. Secrecy was a must.

Nothing remains secret in the Beltway for very long, however. In June 2006 the *New York Times*—followed by the *Washington Post*, and the *Los Angeles Times*—caught wind of the program and ran with exposés. Forced to react, Stuart Levey spoke to the press and explained that TFTP was legal and made use of proper authorities, offering a unique and powerful window into the operations of terrorist networks. He stated, "Data from the Brussels-based banking consortium, formally known as the Society for Worldwide Interbank Financial Telecommunication, has allowed officials from the CIA, the Federal Bureau of Investigation and other agencies to examine 'tens of thousands' of financial transactions."[32] The public revelation of the U.S. hacking the SWIFT database caused an international storm for Treasury, the CIA, and the Bush administration. The Europeans, unsurprisingly, were enraged, demanding explanations, resignations, breast beating, and reassurances. Levey's half-hearted mea culpa did little, at first, to temper their bruised sense of indignation and betrayal.

Harpoon officials were at their desks at headquarters on the morning of June 23, 2006, when the *New York Times* exposé broke. Agents and officers assigned to the task force sat open-jawed and in shock reading about the revelations. Uri L. and Shai U. simply couldn't believe it. The American effort was a masterstroke, a piece of technological espionage mastery worthy of accolades and, the Israelis hoped, increased sharing from Langley and from the Department of the Treasury's terrorism intelligence unit.

It took great diplomatic skill—most of it covert—for the U.S. intelligence community to restore relations and the trust of the SWIFT conglomerate in Europe. There were apologies rendered and promises that such violation of secure networks would never happen again. TFTP continued, albeit not in so covert a manner. Still, the program was credited with assisting federal and local law enforcement in the investigations that followed the 2013 Boston Marathon bombing, as well as other plots around the world involving members of the al-Quds force of Iran's Islamic Revolutionary Guards Corps.[33]

U.S. apologies to SWIFT following the *New York Times* article and international cooperation enabled a strong and united western front against Iran. Following the 2006 Second Lebanon War, Israel—led by men like Dagan—succeeded in convincing the U.S. government and others in the west that one of the surefire ways to slow down Iran's nuclear pursuits was to strangle it economically. This was financial warfare as Dagan envisioned it—to use money instead of the lives of young soldiers—as a battlefield weapon, and it led to a vigorous and persistent effort to press financial institutions to remove the Islamic Republic of Iran from its network. The idea was to simply choke the Iranian economy so thoroughly that diplomacy and negotiations could transpire and so that Israel would not be compelled to go to war against Iran and its nuclear program. Lázaro Campos, SWIFT's chief executive officer, described the move as "extraordinary and unprecedented and is a direct result of international and multilateral action to intensify financial sanctions against Iran."[34]

The tactic worked. Negotiations between the United States and Iran commenced shortly after Iran's banks were disconnected from SWIFT and isolated from the rest of the world. It was just before the mullahs in Tehran realized their country would face financial collapse unless it reached an accord with the west. The effort culminated in July 2015 with the controversial Joint Comprehensive Plan of Action, known as the Iran Deal.

CHAPTER NINETEEN

Operation Pegasus

At the age of fifty-three Tamir Pardo replaced Meir Dagan, and became the eleventh director of the Mossad in January 2011. He arrived with an impressive résumé. Born in 1953, to parents who hailed from Turkey and Serbia, Pardo was a native-born Israeli who was raised in Tel Aviv. He had served in the paratroopers and later as a communications officer in the elite Sayeret Mat'kal commando unit; he participated in the legendary rescue raid on Entebbe. In 1980, following a brief stint in the IAF's top-secret Shaldag special operations targeting unit, Pardo was recruited into the ranks of the Mossad. His specialty was electronic intelligence, and he rose quickly up the chain of command; eventually becoming Meir Dagan's deputy.[1]

The Mossad continued its swashbuckling and saber-wielding ways under Pardo's leadership. "Pardo wasn't Dagan," a former member of Harpoon commented, "but the Mossad was still the Mossad."[2] The enemies of Israel, those who threatened the security of the Jewish State, continued to die mysterious unattributed deaths.

On July 23, 2011, Darioush Rezaei, a thirty-five-year-old scientist working on Iran's nuclear program, was shot and killed by men on motorcycles as he returned home from picking up his daughter in a nursery near his suburban Tehran home. Rezaei, a physicist, was reportedly an expert in electronic switches, needed for the triggering of a nuclear device. Iranian counterintelligence specialists searched Tehran and the countryside for the gunmen, but the men who pulled the trigger simply vanished. The assassins left no clues, not even a spent cartridge. Publications around the world labeled the assassination as the first Israeli hit of Pardo's term.[3]

With Dagan no longer at the helm, Harpoon was never the same. Uri L. remained behind for a short while, but with his mentor and friend gone, he, too, retired from national service. Lavi left for the private sector, and Shai was hired to serve as the general manager for one of Israel's premier soccer teams.

The United States, now, took the lead with a terrorist financial center that Dagan had long wanted to see destroyed: the Lebanese Canadian Bank.

Shurat HaDin's 2009 lawsuit against the LCB coincided with what would be the culmination of the massive U.S. law enforcement effort against Hezbollah and its laundering of drug and terror money. Hezbollah and their global cash-cleansing operation was a challenge to the DEA—an agency that had an impressive track record in bringing down Colombian cartels, Afghan poppy growers, and the heroin armies of Southeast Asia. The investigations against Hezbollah's networks were conducted in the shadows for the most part—in treacherous locations that were far from home. The agents themselves were often at great peril. Their mission was to witness crimes and to gather prosecutable evidence that an assistant U.S. attorney could use in a federal courtroom. The material they gathered was extensive, including wiretaps. A small army of agents who were fluent in Spanish, Arabic, African dialects, and a half a dozen other languages, spent countless hours turning the raw data into actionable intelligence that could be utilized as evidence by the prosecutors. The process was painstakingly slow: five years and counting. Justice was often delayed, but it most certainly wasn't denied. Assistant U.S. attorneys never went to court with cases they weren't certain they'd win. Their careers were made by conviction rates and plea bargains.

The DEA effort against Hezbollah had two objectives: indict and convict those who were guilty of crimes, and to dismantle and crush the ability of the Lebanese Canadian Bank to launder the proceeds from Hezbollah's operations. The effort was global in nature.

The first aspect of the DEA investigative offensive began in 2006–2007 with what was codenamed Operation Titan, a joint U.S.–Colombian investigation that focused on cocaine distribution and money laundering. The target of Titan was Chekry Harb, a Lebanese national and a narcotics kingpin who enjoyed being referred to by his nom de guerre of "El Taliban." Harb was based in Bogota, and he was what might be called a connector. He brought together multifarious players like Hezbollah, the cocaine cartels, and local terrorist groups like FARC so that they could all engage and prosper together. Harb supervised a highly complex and highly effective money-laundering operation that cleansed hundreds of millions of dollars a year in banks and shell corporations stretching from the Panama Canal to Hong Kong. A percentage of the money that Harb's ring earned, believed to be 12 percent, went straight back to South Lebanon. Gladys Sanchez, one of the Colombian investigators working side by side with the DEA in Bogota, confirmed, "The profits from the sales of drugs went to finance Hezbollah."[4]

Both the DEA and the Colombians were tight-lipped concerning the number of agents they deployed for the operation, but courts in Colombia and the United States issued warrants for 370 wiretaps that taped 700,000 conversations. In one of the phone taps, Harb boasted that he could arrange a cocaine shipment of 950 kilograms, made in coordination with Syrian intelligence, that were sent via the Jordanian Red Sea port of Aqaba, then smuggled north overland, first into Syria and then into Lebanon, on a moment's notice.[5] Harb, along with two other Hezbollah operatives, were arrested on October 3, 2008—the DEA and the Colombians raided numerous locations and arrested 130 people.[6] Agents also seized $23 million in cash. Harb was ultimately extradited to the United States.[7]

Operation Titan sharpened the focus into Hezbollah's wider operations out of South America and West Africa—a pipeline of drugs, cars, and cash that both Harpoon and the DEA discovered jointly. One name emerged repeatedly in all aspects of the criminal enterprise throughout the wiretaps and the electronic intercepts: Ayman Joumaa. Joumaa was what the DEA and the U.S. Department of Justice called a Significant Foreign Narcotics Trafficker. The designation was reserved for the mightiest drug kingpins—men like Pablo Escobar and Mexico's Joaquín Guzmán, also known as "El Chapo," who controlled vast narcotics empires.

Ayman Saied Joumaa was born in 1964, in the village of Qaraoun, in the Beka'a Valley, over fifty miles east of Beirut. Little is known of his early years other than that he gravitated toward a career of crime and narcotics. Joumaa, also known as "Junior," traveled with a complement of machine-gun-toting thugs who were handsomely paid so that rivals as well as law enforcement were kept at a safe distance. Although he worked side by side with Hezbollah, Joumaa was believed to be a Sunni Muslim. The terrorist group's leaders usually trusted only those from within their own Shiite faith, where clans and family loyalty allayed fears of betrayal, but Joumaa made up for his religious shortcomings by bringing Hezbollah lots of drugs and cash. According to Brian Dodd, head of counternarcotics operations at DEA headquarters, Joumaa couldn't have survived without Hezbollah, and he was a source of revenue for the terrorist group.[8]

Joumaa also connected Hezbollah with Mexico's drug cartels. He worked closest with the Los Zetas. Known in Mexico simply as "Z," many law enforcement experts view Los Zetas to be the most ruthless, and the most globally sophisticated, of all the Mexican cartels.[9] Joumaa also worked with the Mexican Sinaloa Cartel, considered by U.S. intelligence agencies to be the most powerful drug-trafficking organization in the world.[10]

The DEA estimated that Joumaa laundered as much as $200 million in narcotics proceeds per month. Joumaa's network shipped cocaine to Africa, where it was parceled and later shipped to the Middle East and Europe. The profits from those sales were then sent back to Lebanon, where they were processed through exchange houses, like the Hassan Ayash Exchange Company and the Ellissa Exchange Company in Beirut. The money was sent via wires transfers from the Lebanese Canadian Bank, to businesses in the United States, where used cars were purchased.

Hezbollah's West African operation would never have been possible without the LCB laundering the proceeds. The DEA speculated that a small portion of the money from this scheme was diverted to Iranian intelligence and the Iranian Islamic Revolutionary Guard as tribute to the mullahs and the intelligence services in Tehran.

By early 2011, the sheer might of the American judicial system came crashing down on Hezbollah and the LCB. The overall effort of American law enforcement to finally shut down the LCB "money-washing machine" was codenamed Operation Pegasus.

On February 10, 2011, the U.S. Department of the Treasury's Financial Crimes Enforcement Network officially identified the Lebanese Canadian Bank as a money-laundering institution. The declaration forced U.S. financial institutions to immediately cease all interactions and transactions with the LCB; the bank was prohibited from sending money to the United States. The LCB had enabled Hezbollah-related operations and interests to conduct massive cash transactions, in some cases as much as $260,000 per day, without disclosing the source or purpose of the money.

The U.S. Department of the Treasury declaration turned the LCB toxic. Bankers, especially in the litigious atmosphere that the terror-victim lawsuits had created, were wary of any connection to a financial institution that openly did business with the likes of Hezbollah. The upside of doing business with the terrorist organizations had finally sunk deep below the potential downside of criminal prosecutions: massive fines and menacing civil actions. The seventy-one-year-old, venerable financial institution was beginning to gasp its last breaths.

On November 23, 2011, Ayman Joumaa himself was indicted in the Eastern District of Virginia on charges of conspiracy to distribute narcotics and conspiracy to commit money laundering related to drug trafficking by Mexican and Colombian drug cartels. Well protected in Lebanon by an army of drug soldiers, Joumaa has, at the time of this book's writing, yet to be brought to face justice before a U.S. federal judge.

Finally, in December 2011, two years after Shurat HaDin helped sue the bank and after Lebanese Central Bank Governor Riad Salameh publicly declared that his banking system wasn't connected to the Party of God, the U.S. attorney for the Southern District of New York unsealed a $483 million civil forfeiture action against the LCB. The pursuit of the money came under the provisions of the International Emergency Economic Powers Act, which allowed the U.S. government to demand civil money-laundering penalties. "Hezbollah, like any other criminal enterprise, wants to convert cash into usable funds that can be transferred through the formal financial system," David S. Cohen, the undersecretary for Terrorism and Financial Intelligence at the Treasury Department, would later say.[11]

The LCB never recovered from Operation Pegasus. The bank ceased operations in 2012. The Lebanese Canadian Bank's assets were ultimately acquired by the Société Générale de Banque au Liban. Known as the SGBL, the bank could not commence business until it settled with the U.S. government, paying a penalty of $102 million. The SGBL also undertook to pay off the debts of the LCB, including a reserve for claims made against the bank. Claims against the Hassan Ayash Exchange Company, one of the companies that took the drug sales receipts and laundered them through LCB wire transfers, forfeited more than $720,000 to the United States. Preet Bharara, the U.S. attorney for the Southern District of New York, would later comment, "Money is the lifeblood of terrorist and narcotics organizations. We will use every resource at our disposal to separate terrorists and narco-traffickers, and the banks that work with them, from their illicit funds, even those hidden in foreign accounts."[12]

The DEA's partnership with its partners in Israel had reaped enormous rewards. The connection between drug traffickers and terror networks was clear, and the end of the Lebanese Canadian Bank was a severe body blow to Hezbollah, enhancing both American and Israeli national security.

CHAPTER TWENTY

Money in the Crosshairs

*Supreme excellence consists of breaking the enemy's
resistance without fighting.*
—*Sun Tzu,* The Art of War

Hussam Qawasmeh was a member of perhaps the most powerful clan in Hebron. The Qawasmehs were a prominent force when the city was under British rule, and their influence continued after the West Bank was annexed by Jordan in 1950. When Israel took control of the West Bank following the 1967 Six Day War, the large Qawasmeh family remained well respected; people from all over sought their counsel. The family passionately opposed Israeli control over their lives, and, as devout Muslims, many had taken senior leadership positions in the local Hamas organizations in recent years. Hussam, thirty-nine years old, was a regional commander in the terrorist organization; devout, he wore a long and full black beard and glasses, and his scholarly appearance hid a stocky frame and a muscular build that made him look like a brawler. Hussam felt it was his obligation, as one of Hebron's first citizens, to lead the struggle against the Zionist enemy. This pressing sense of obligation and duty weighed heavily upon him when he caught up with friends or talked to his brothers in Hamas at daily prayers.

One night in early June 2014, Hussam Qawasmeh met with his young nephew Marwan, and a family friend named Amer Abu Aisha, at his home. The three sat around the dining room table eating sunflower seeds and drinking tea. They spoke softly, fearing that the Israelis might be listening, but in heated discussions the three shared ideas for an operation against Israel. They wanted to perpetrate something spectacular. The talk turned to kidnapping an Israeli soldier so that he could be exchanged for Palestinian prisoners serving lengthy or life sentences in Israeli jails. The three discussed the Gilad Shalit operation and how that abduction had rocked Israel to its inner core. Shalit was kidnapped in 2006, and Hamas held Israel captive for five long years until Prime Minister Netanyahu's government agreed to release 1,200 prisoners in exchange for the one Israeli serviceman; Hussam's brother had been one of the prisoners released in the lopsided deal and then deported to the Gaza Strip.[1] Hussam and his cohorts plotted well into the night.

The kidnap plan that the three conjured up was simple but daring. Hussam Qawasmeh was responsible for intelligence. He selected Gush Etzion junction, a remote crossroad frequently used by off-duty soldiers to hitchhike rides to Jerusalem, as the kidnap location. He also found several safe houses, isolated and easy to defend, where the abducted soldier could be held and moved in case Israeli security forces came too close. Marwan Qawasmeh and Amer Abu Aisha would kidnap the victim. The two would masquerade as Orthodox Jews and once the soldier was lured into the car, they would subdue and secure him.

The plan required two vehicles: one for the abduction and the other to move the soldier from house to house after the kidnapping. The first car was disposable, and would be destroyed to ensure that the kidnappers left no evidence behind. The team also needed weapons, two M16s they assessed, in case the soldier was armed and tried to resist. Finally they needed two pistols, in case something went wrong in the car.

Hussam conducted a cost analysis of the plan, and he assessed he'd need $65,000. He approached the al-Nur Foundation in Gaza, a well-established charity that supported the families of the Hamas suicide bombers, and paid their monthly families stipends to live on. Al-Nur was known to finance attacks against Israelis, and the charity's administrators agreed to grant Hussam the money in order to carry out such a noble mission. Qawasmeh's mother, who had permission to travel to and from Gaza, retrieved the money, and smuggled the funds to them in Hebron. The weapons were purchased. The two cars were paid for. Hussam found a few isolated homes that he could rent with no questions asked.

The kidnappers set out on their operation on Thursday evening, June 12, 2014. They dressed as Orthodox Jews, and played Israeli music on their car radio. They drove to the Gush Etzion junction and looked for a soldier. But it was already the beginning of the weekend and it was getting late; there were no soldiers in sight.

But the kidnappers did see some individuals at a bus stop as they slowed down. They were three Israeli teenagers who had finished school late and were heading home. Two of the boys, Naftali Frenkel and Gilad Shaer, were sixteen; the third, Eyal Yifrah, was nineteen. When the car door opened, all three of the teenagers surprised the Hamas men by jumping into the back seat together to hitch a ride. The Palestinian brothers did not expect three healthy young people, and they briefly panicked. Pulling themselves together and pointing their pistols, they yelled at the teens that they were being kidnapped and ordered them to put their heads down. Shaer had managed to dial 100 on his cellular phone, the number to summon police, and whispered to the police operator: "They kidnapped me." His plea for help was followed by shouts in Arabic, then by the sounds of gunfire, all of which was recorded by the police switchboard.[2]

The terrorists didn't plan to kill their captives, but the operation hadn't gone as they intended, and they improvised. Marwan Qawasmeh and Amer Abu Aisha drove to the rendezvous point where the second vehicle was waiting. They loaded the bodies to the new car and set fire to the first. They nervously drove around the Hebron hills looking for a place to hide the three murdered teens so that the Israelis wouldn't find them. By morning, though, all of Israel had heard the news reports that the three teenagers were kidnapped.

The Shin Bet, the IDF, and the Israel National Police launched a Herculean effort to locate the three boys. They found the burned-out car and feared that the three were already dead. The IDF launched Operation

Brother's Keeper to find the three teens and to apprehend those responsible. IDF commanders enlisted the services of Bedouin soldiers, famed trackers who usually patrolled Israel's frontier, to search for footprints or any other telltale clues in the Spartan terrain of hills and caves.[3] For almost three weeks all of Israel stood on edge awaiting news of the kidnapped students. On June 30, an Israeli volunteer, one of hundreds that joined the search, discovered the bodies of the three boys in a field northwest of Hebron. Their bodies were buried under a pile of rocks.[4]

The security forces realized that their suspicion was true: The teens had been shot at close range—murdered shortly after being seized. Prime Minister Benjamin Netanyahu vowed a decisive Israeli response.

Hamas rocket fire commenced shortly after word was released that three Israeli teens had been abducted. Throughout June, Hamas launched hundreds of mortar rounds and missiles into Israel. The IDF responded with air strikes designed to destroy Hamas launching sites and to obliterate a sophisticated and expensive network of tunnels that were used to transport terrorists into Israel. The fighting once again forced the population of southern Israel into air raid shelters. At just after dawn on the morning of July 12, a large force of Hamas terrorists emerged from a tunnel into Israel proper; the gunmen, many carrying RPG antitank rockets, suddenly came out of an opening burrowed in a field inside a kibbutz a few hundred meters from the Gaza frontier. Israeli forces killed the raiders, thwarting what would have been a disaster—the terrorists had planned to perpetrate a mass shooting in the kibbutz and then bring abductees back into the Strip to be held hostage, no doubt used as bargaining chips for Hamas to negotiate the release of its prisoners.[5] The situation had become untenable. Prime Minister Netanyahu had had enough.

The following day Israeli forces entered the Gaza Strip. The operation was codenamed Protective Edge.

Since it seized control of the Gaza Strip in a bloody coup in 2007, Hamas had spent seven years reinforcing the home to over one million Palestinians into an urban fortress. Neighborhoods were ringed by improvised explosive devices; booby traps were everywhere and Hamas fighters hid behind the civilian population almost daring Israeli forces to engage them. The fighting inside the neighborhoods of northern Gaza was fierce. Much of it was house-to-house and hand-to-hand. Operations were mounted underground, to root out the tunnels and the men who deployed inside them. But casualties mounted on all sides.

Israeli forces had learned, through the intelligence it had gathered, that the elite of the Hamas force, the men on the front lines battling Israeli infantry and reconnaissance units, were rumbling to their wives and families over not being paid and that morale was low. The men doing the fighting hadn't received their salaries in weeks. Their anger was close to undermining the entire military campaign. It was a cash economy. Each fighter had to sign for his stipend inside a notebook ledger, complete with carbon paper. The archaic system was akin to how the old Turkish pasha paid his soldiers and policemen during Ottoman times.

It was nearly impossible for Hamas to get cash into the Strip during wartime. Israeli aircraft flew constant sorties overhead, and ground forces maintained a determined vigil over key access points. The lack of money meant that the families of the fighters couldn't buy food and clothing. Many inside Gaza began to openly mock their political leadership— especially the jet-setters who lived in Doha and were worth billions. Hamas leaders worried of an insurrection. Calls were made for an emergency delivery of dollars. The Israelis learned that the money would be routed through the Sinai Desert.

On August 23 the intelligence services picked up the trail of a man in his twenties traveling across Sinai with $13 million in cash packed inside four large leather suitcases. The cash had come from a money changer in the town of El Arish on the Mediterranean coast who, after receiving confirmation that covering funds had entered a bank account in the Persian Gulf, prepared the stacks of $50 and $100 bills. Bribe money helped the man make it across the barren deserts without running into the Egyptian secret police or packs of Bedouin gangsters. The senior Hamas leadership thought it wise to send him without a heavily armed contingent of body-guards; groups of men attracted attention, and the spies were everywhere. The man would have to protect the money with his life. If it was lost, he knew, his entire family would be killed.

It took the courier just under a day to cross the twenty-eight miles to the Egyptian side of the border. He took a circuitous route toward the rendezvous point and changed his car a few times, always making the switch under an awning to fool the Egyptian and Israeli drone operators whose devices were constantly overhead. When darkness fell, he was driven to a safe house, a nondescript two-story home where an elite Hamas bodyguard squad awaited him. The suitcases were removed from the car and brought to the center of the room, where prayer rugs were rolled out and a small meal of rice and poultry prepared. A tunnel, well illuminated and ventilated, had been dug underneath the safe house. The man would have to wait until dawn, however, before making his move: Israeli warplanes owned the darkened skies over Gaza and watched everything that moved.

At just before dawn the envoy sent a brief SMS message to his patrons, who were impatiently waiting for the money on the Gaza side of the tunnel in Kishta, a Hamas stronghold in the town of Rafah. The text consisted of a code word indicating that the courier was coming across; the phone, like the man, was a throwaway, the SIM card, from Etisalat—one of the largest carriers of international voice traffic in the Middle East and Africa—was destroyed immediately after the message was sent. It took him and his bodyguards nearly an hour to cross the tunnel into Palestinian Gaza. The tunnel was narrow, and movement inside the confining space was slow and uncomfortable. As the man neared the exit, a smile came over his face. The cash had been delivered. His mission was over. He would be allowed to return to his family.

A black Mercedes, parked under concealment of a grape arbor, was waiting for the luggage. Inside the car was Mohammed el-Ghoul, Hamas's head of payroll. El-Ghoul was short and thin, with an oval face and a spotty beard. He was a member of the Hamas ruling council and a diplomat, maintaining a dialogue with members of the ruling clan in Qatar, and with the finance offices of the Iranian Revolutionary Guards' ultrasecretive al-Quds special operations force in Tehran. He negotiated with money changers in the Gulf and middlemen in the Arab world with banking connections. El-Ghoul was one of the most important men in Hamas: He decided who was paid and when.

The four suitcases were hurriedly placed into a different car, a Chinese-made BYD sedan that was waiting nearby. Once the money was loaded into the car, the trunk was tied down with bungee cords. El-Ghoul sat in a rear seat, sandwiched in between two bodyguards. Speaking into a mobile phone whose SIM card he would destroy by sunset, he gestured to the driver to head north, through the rubble of the night's Israeli air strikes, in the direction of the fighting near Beit Lahiya. Hamas forces battling Israeli commando units had not been paid in a month, and it was urgent to get the cash to them before the nighttime operations commenced.

Several miles away an Israeli Air Force AH-64D Longbow attack helicopter hovered over the Mediterranean Sea, awaiting word from a command center near the front lines confirming that the money had been loaded into the vehicle. The weapons officer locked his sights on the fuzzy image of the sedan over the horizon, awaiting the code word to green light the launch. It came. With the push of a button, a single AGM-114 Hellfire antitank missile accelerated to supersonic speed and slammed into El-Ghoul's Chinese-made car. The sedan evaporated into a fireball and a cloud of black smoke. Chunks of the vehicle, and shards of flesh and bone, were blown hundreds of feet away.[6]

Most of the $13 million that el-Ghoul had waited for, the lifeblood of his men in the trenches, was destroyed in the missile strike. Once the smoke cleared, the skies turned green as a storm of singed $100 bills cascaded onto the dusty streets of Gaza City like strips of confetti in a Wall Street tickertape parade. The payroll's incineration was a major blow to Hamas. Without the cash they couldn't maintain the struggle. Hamas asked for a cease-fire, and the summer war in Gaza ended forty-eight hours later.

Meir Dagan had been right all along. If you choke off the money, the bloodshed will end.*

It has been reported—neither confirmed nor denied by the U.S. government—that in 2015 David S. Cohen, the former undersecretary of the Treasury for Terrorism and Financial Intelligence, chaired a meeting at a CIA black site in 2015, somewhere in an allied nation to assemble a task force to deal with the new terrorism scourge that confronted the West and the United States: ISIS. Known as Daesh in Arabic, the Islamic State of Iraq and Syria, or ISIS, was born out of al-Qaeda in Iraq and achieved prominence in 2013 in the chaos of the Syrian Civil War where its fanatical fighters captured large swaths of territory. ISIS became a regional concern when it declared itself a caliphate and seized major cities in western Iraq, including Mosul. Flush with oil money stolen from the lands it captured, ISIS attracted fighters from all over the world, including many disillusioned young people from Western Europe. The western fighters were considered the most fanatic and bloodthirsty. After fighting in Iraq and Syria, some of the westerners returned home and established operational cells in their home countries. One of these cells was responsible for the November 2015 multipronged attacks in Paris that resulted in 130 dead and scores more wounded.

David Cohen had taken over from Stuart Levey at Treasury in 2011, and he had now been tapped personally by President Barack Obama to serve as CIA deputy director. Cohen's appointment sent shock waves through the ranks at Langley—deputy directors were usually promoted from within. Cohen had served as Levey's deputy, and he had seen Harpoon operate up close and personal. He wanted to assemble a similar entity at CIA.

---

* Marwan Qawasmeh and Amer Abu Aisha were killed in a shootout with Israeli counterterrorist forces in September 2014. Hussam Qawasmeh was arrested by the Shin Bet and sentenced to three life sentences. He was also ordered to pay $63,000 to the families of the murdered teenagers pursuant to a new law that required the terrorists themselves to pay for the crimes they committed.

At the black site, Cohen spoke to his operational heads in the clandestine service. Some of the people at the roundtable were computer wizards, some were accountants and lawyers, others were shooters, operators from the Agency's Special Activities Division who had spent the better part of the last fourteen years fighting al-Qaeda all around the world. Cohen knew, like Meir Dagan before him, that the war on terror wasn't simply one of shock and awe. It was one of finesse and guile. And he knew that targeting a terrorist group's sources of income and its ability to acquire the tools of war was just as important as, if not more important than, impressive body counts from aerial bombardments and drone strikes.

The CIA wanted to establish a unit that could track terrorist money in real time, not in monthly statements, but from the field. And the CIA wanted a unit that could focus on the moneymen, the currency launderers and the financiers who profited from the bloodshed and who enabled operatives to travel across borders, rent safe houses, and perpetrate attacks in Europe and the United States.

Cohen had no experience in an intelligence organization, but his appointment signified the focus that the Agency, as well as other western intelligence services, now have in the war on terror: namely "follow the money."[7] In order to meet and defeat the threat of ISIS and other groups that were bound to follow, the CIA wanted to replicate the template that Harpoon had produced.

In the field, in the blood-soaked towns of Iraq and Syria, the new policy was proving to be highly effective.

Throughout its advances into Iraq and Syria in 2014–2015, as ISIS fighters took over a territory, the Islamic State began to fill its coffers. Everything that could be stolen was stolen. Everything that could be taxed was taxed. The group seized local banks, stripping their assets, emptying personal accounts, and claiming all the cash reserves as their own. They pillaged museums and libraries, selling off precious antiquities and national treasures as quick swag. Christian and Yazidi girls, along with those of other religious minorities, were abducted and auctioned off as sex slaves. This systematic robbery yielded massive amounts of money used to expand the group's reach and cement its hold over captured populations. Water, electricity, and even cell phones were subject to taxation by ISIS. Any withdrawals from banks under ISIS control were subject to a 5 percent fee.[8]

This larcenous policy was employed to great effect in Mosul, the northern Iraqi city captured by ISIS in June 2014. The group took control of Mosul's Central Bank, a move that brought in $480 billion for ISIS.[9] It also engaged in massive theft from the terrified local population. The group seized anything of value, anything that could be sold, and its revenue used to further its objectives. This included cattle, jewelry, and even machinery used by Moslawi craftsmen. Antiquities were confiscated and auctioned off. Experts estimated that this yielded the group an additional $500 billion in assets from this wide-scale looting.[10]

But ISIS was far from finished. The hundreds of thousands of Christian residents of the city were given three options: leave, convert to Islam, or die.[11] Most fled. Their deserted homes and other properties were seized, and daubed with the Arabic letter *Nuun*, indicating that it belonged to Christians. The *N* stood for *Nasrani*, or *Nazarene*, denoting members of the faith whose founder had once lived in Nazareth.[12] When the effects of the United States targeting its finances began to bite, ISIS put these Christian homes up for auction, with the group pocketing the profits.[13]

ISIS also earned millions from kidnapping for ransom and from donations from the Persian Gulf. Money was also raised from fund-raising, especially through Internet promotion and social media.[14]

Money poured in from every corner of their callous empire, which quickly stretched across swaths of Iraq and Syria. But the real money, the cash cow that never stopped giving, was the oil, a natural resource that had long been a cause for brutal conflict.

At its height, the Islamic State held hundreds of oil fields, controlling more than 60 percent of Syria's oil production and 10 percent of Iraq's. Despite draconian international restrictions on ISIS, there was no shortage of buyers for the oil; even Syria's embattled leadership was willing to pay for the privilege of using its own stolen natural resources.[15]

Like Israel at the height of the second intifada, U.S. President Barack

Obama realized the most effective way to defeat ISIS was to separate it from its revenue stream. The cost of running an empire is steep; without money, the group could not pay its fighters, buy munitions, or even keep the lights on.

In October 2015, the U.S. and coalition forces launched Operation Tidal Wave II, named in honor of a Second World War mission to decimate the oil capabilities of Nazi Germany and its Axis. Tidal Wave II's objective was to take out the oil fields that were the central source of ISIS income, and, for the first time, focus on the entire mechanism that kept the oil flowing. The air raids conducted by the United States and its allies targeted oil distribution, trucks, brokers, and even middlemen who were hitherto largely ignored in previous bombings.[16] The Americans were using intelligence gathered during a May 2015 raid that yielded deep insight into the workings of the highly lucrative ISIS oil industry.[17]

By December 2015, the U.S. military announced that it had destroyed almost all ISIS oil assets.[18]

Faced with a military onslaught now coupled with a direct assault on its primary source of funding, ISIS was left shell-shocked and weakened. Its once fierce grip on large areas of territory in Iraq and Syria was now under real threat of annihilation. Its oil fields, which had once brought in estimated profits of USD $50 million per month, were smoking ruins.[19] The organization was now also cash-strapped, limiting its ability to send fighters back to their home countries to perpetrate catastrophic attacks, such as the November 2015 attacks in Paris that killed 130 people and wounded close to five hundred, and additional strikes in Brussels and Istanbul.

By the close of 2015, ISIS fighters who had been used to lavish monthly wages began to feel the pinch, as the group scrambled to compensate for its dramatic loss of revenue. These salaries once averaged USD $500 per month or even more. Foreign fighters were the highest paid—often earning more than USD $1,000 a month.[20]

This was higher than the remuneration offered by Syria's civil service, or even rival Islamist group Jabhat al-Nusra.[21] ISIS needed to keep its fighters happy or face mass defections—and to do that, it needed oil.

Ultimately, ISIS's fear of losing its fighters came to pass once the stipends dried up. The local populations, emboldened by the swift, shocking blow to their captors, began to resist the now-depleted ISIS presence. This paved the way for the local and international coalition to reclaim territory once thought lost.

A policy birthed in Israel had again proved its effectiveness in combating a terrorist scourge in the Middle East, bringing the greatest threat to the region in modern history to its knees. But the Americans and their coalition partners also borrowed a specific tactic. On January 10, 2016, U.S. air strikes hit a key facility in Mosul where ISIS stored its cash reserves—making it impossible for the fighters in the field to be paid. The air raid destroyed the site, incinerating close to USD $45 million in irreplaceable cash.

Legacy

For by wise guidance you can wage your war, and in
abundance of counselors there is victory.
—*Proverbs 24:6*

M ore than two decades have passed since the tourists from Chicago
arrived at an Israeli airport with suitcases brimming with money
and malicious intentions of financing bombs and murdering innocent
civilians. In the years since the Oslo Accords—which purportedly settled
the Arab-Israeli conflict—were signed, the Middle East, and the world
beyond it, has grown more violent and lawless as terrorism has metastasized, and religious rage has been weaponized. Hate and extremism
have been exported to every corner of the globe, evolving into a pandemic
plague.

The war on terror financing, pioneered in the Jewish state as a radi-
cally unconventional but desperately needed start-up, has grown into a
standard and vital component of every nation's national security strategy.
Most of the original Harpoon members have retired from service, and
have pursued civilian careers, while others have passed away. The private
sector—attorneys and others, who rose to wage their own battles against
the terrorist organizations, their patrons, and the financial institutions

that aid and abet them—continue pursuing these villainous miscreants with lawsuits and legal actions in courtrooms around the world. While the names and faces of many of those killed and injured in the terrorist attacks quietly fade with time from memory, the pursuit of justice on their and their families' behalf continues on.

On a chilly and cloudy afternoon in September 2014, a federal jury in a Brooklyn courtroom found that the Arab Bank was liable for supporting Palestinian terrorism, in connection to a slew of attacks in Israel.[1] The decision followed a fiercely fought five-week-long trial and set a historic precedent that sent shock waves through legal—and banking—systems around the world. It was the first time ever that a bank had been held responsible for aiding and abetting terrorism in a civil suit. There were 297 plaintiffs in all. They represented victims of Hamas terror who had loved ones killed or injured, during the second intifada. It was another stinging defeat for the Arab Bank. Years earlier, in 2005, the U.S. Department of the Treasury forced the Amman-based institution to pay a hefty $24 million fine for failing to adequately initiate anti-money-laundering controls; in that ruling, the Treasury Department's Office of the Comptroller ordered the Arab Bank to cease transferring money or opening new accounts from its midtown Manhattan branch.[2]

The court battle had taken nearly a decade. Sitting through the trial had been heartbreaking for the victims and their families, who were forced to relive the horrors of the suicide bombings and shooting attacks. The victory, though, was an important milestone in the war on terror. Throughout the trial, the bank's officials had insisted upon their innocence, that they knew nothing about the terror funds moving through their accounts. The Brooklyn jury wasn't buying it. "Terrorist organizations are dependent on the financial system to operate," one of the plaintiffs' lawyers, Gary Osen, explained outside the courthouse. "They've been able to thrive largely because folks like Arab Bank and others have turned a blind eye."[3] Reportedly, the parties entered into a settlement just before the damages portion of the case could be heard.[4]

Shortly after the Arab Bank decision, another landmark counterterrorism verdict was received. In the federal courthouse in lower Manhattan, the civil case against the PLO and the Palestinian Authority came to a close. On February 23, 2015, a federal jury found the PLO and the Palestinian Authority liable for supporting, financing, and perpetrating murderous terrorist attacks that killed thirty-three people and wounded close to five hundred, including American citizens, in Israel.[5] During the seven-week-long trial the jury heard compelling evidence in regard to a series of shooting and bombing attacks carried out by Fatah's al-Aqsa Martyrs Brigade, Hamas, and the PIJ between the years 2001 and 2004—the height of the second intifada, when the Palestinian leadership launched an all-out terror war against Israeli civilians. In a unanimous decision, the twelve-member jury found the Palestinians liable on all twenty-four counts of terrorism. The representatives from the PLO who were in court that morning, along with their lawyers, looked crushed and defeated as the jury answered "Guilty" to each and every count.

Unlike the Arab Bank trial, the verdict came with a damages award. The PLO and the PA were ordered to pay $218.5 million in damages to the ten American families who were represented in the case; under the provisions of the 1992 Anti-Terrorism Act, the damages were automatically tripled to $655.5 million. The U.S. State Department officials worried that the court decision could bankrupt the Palestinian Authority.

Lawyers for the victims' families were jubilant. If the Palestinian Authority and the PLO had the money to pay the imprisoned terrorists and families of suicide bombers, they asserted, they certainly could pay the court judgment to the victims. As lead trial counsel, Kent Yalowitz had stated passionately in his closing arguments just days before: "Money is oxygen for terrorism. The anti-terrorism law hits those who send terrorists where it hurts them most: in the wallet." Outside the courthouse, standing with the other lawyers and wearing an overcoat to protect her from the harsh New York winter, a smiling Nitsana told reporters, "Now the PLO and the PA know there is a price for supporting terrorism."[6]

Lawyers for the Palestinian Authority quickly left the courthouse, despondent and silent, trying desperately to avoid the press. One man was happy, though. Meir Dagan knew that lives could be protected and terrorism could suffer serious setbacks on new battlefields without shots in anger having to be fired.*

Meir Dagan was diagnosed with liver cancer shortly after leaving the Mossad. His doctors told him that he had two options: get a transplant or, as he would explain, "clean his desk so that others wouldn't have to." He was a year past the age limit to get a transplant in Israel, so he tried to find a match in the United States. Finally, he underwent surgery in Minsk, the capital of Belarus.[7] Dagan fought like a soldier to make it through the difficult medical procedure and the precarious post-op period. According to his wife, Bina, the monarch of a nation that Israel does not have formal ties with offered Dagan the use of one of his palaces so that he could recover from the difficult operation.[8] The Middle Eastern leaders respected Dagan, and they felt safer while he was at the helm of the Mossad. An Egyptian newspaper, remarkably, even called him Superman.[9]

Meir Dagan never allowed his medical condition to interfere with his daily routine. For the next four years, Dagan traveled the world speaking at conferences and making the kind of money soldiers and spies can only dream of. He painted and he read. Dagan spent time with his children and grandchildren, and he enjoyed the company of his friends and former comrades in arms. Those who had served with Dagan, those who he had counted on in dangerous moments, adored their former commander. These men and women made sure that Meir Dagan always knew exactly how much he was revered.

To the surprise of some, Dagan used his time to be an outspoken critic of any unilateral Israeli military action against Iran. He sincerely believed

---

* On August 31, 2016, the United States Court of Appeals for the Second Circuit reversed the district court's verdict in *Sokolow v. Palestinian Authority* on purely technical grounds. The court held that the plaintiffs did not have adequate jurisdiction over the defendants. The families have filed for review from the United States Supreme Court.

that any effort to take out the Islamic Republic's well-fortified and strategically positioned reactors, laboratories, and factories would end in failure. His position, which he determinedly shared with news organizations around the world such as CBS, was viewed by many as a direct challenge to Prime Minister Benjamin Netanyahu; some in Israel accused Dagan of leaking classified information for political gain. Dagan would have none of it. He was a private citizen, he told Ilana Dayan, one of Israel's premier investigative journalists, in an interview given in his Tel Aviv apartment, and it was his right to speak on what he believed."[10]

Dagan appeared at rallies, and he was a featured guest of honor at symposiums and forums around the world. In early 2016, however, his medical condition worsened. He lost weight, and he began to lose the bombastic energy that he had displayed throughout his entire military and Mossad career. Meir Dagan died on March 17, 2016 at the age of 71.

The former soldier and spymaster was buried the following day at a military ceremony in Rosh Pina, his beloved home in northern Israel near where he fought so many battles in the hell of Lebanon. His coffin was carried by six senior IDF officers; an honor guard fired a volley of rifle rounds over his grave.[11] Prime Minister Benjamin Netanyahu, President Reuven Rivlin, and scores of Dagan's former comrades in arms attended the funeral, held under gray skies and a cold, light rain. The Mossad was forced to hold a private ceremony, behind closed doors, so that the men and women that Dagan had led in the shadows could mourn without being subjected to the media spotlight. Condolences flooded Mossad headquarters from espionage services from all over the world. The CIA, the U.S. Department of the Treasury, and many who were on the front lines of America's war against terror mourned the passing of a partner and a legend.

Mossad Director Yossi Cohen eulogized Dagan by saying that "he taught us to take chances and to take responsibility."[12]

Dagan did so much more than that. He spent a lifetime in his country's service, going above and beyond to fight for Israel's security and for its future. He continuously planned new and innovative tactics that could be used to defeat the enemies of Israel, conventional and other, that threatened the country he loved and fought for. Dagan understood that military might would never defeat the armies that surrounded Israel, and that diplomatic negotiations would never change the minds of those dedicated to marching into the fires of a holy war. But by going after the money that funded terror, by making it difficult for terrorist armies to launch suicidal campaigns, Dagan established a new dimension to the asymmetrical battlefield that revolutionized how Israel—and the west—would combat terror.

The terror, of course, would continue.

In the autumn of 2015, Israeli security forces encountered a new and disturbing wave of what appeared to be Palestinian terror attacks targeting civilians, police officers, and soldiers. Palestinian men and women approached people on the street, removed knives from their bags or jackets, and then proceeded to hack away, hoping to kill and wound as many people as possible before being killed by security forces. In other attacks, Palestinian motorists used vehicles as battering rams to run over pedestrians. The attacks were random and bloody. Dozens of Israelis were killed in these strikes, and scores more were injured.

Even so, Israeli intelligence chiefs were relieved that, for the most part, the suicide bombings hadn't returned. Counterterrorist efforts against Hamas and the PIJ had been very successful; the follow-the-money campaign against the terrorist groups had deprived them of the funds vital to carrying out the catastrophic bombing campaigns from the second intifada. Perhaps, the spymasters and generals believed, the Palestinians were inspired by the bloody knife and beheading videos that ISIS broadcast on the Internet? There was one heinous common denominator linking all of the bloodshed: Video footage from the stabbing and ramming attacks was quickly broadcast online and in social media. In many cases, on such platforms as Facebook, Twitter, and YouTube, the perpetrators discussed their intentions on social media before perpetrating their attacks.

The modified asymmetrical battlefield had changed once again. Social media, Harpoon veterans and Shurat HaDin realized, was a new form of currency with a unique and ominous value that had none of the counterterrorist preventive controls of the banking world. "Why is it illegal for a major bank to block a known terrorist, on a black list, from opening and maintaining an account," Shai asked, "but it's permitted for that same person, that same organization, to maintain active accounts on social media?"[13] Social media, like money, had become a new form of oxygen keeping terrorism alive.

Lawsuits against social media platform giants such as Facebook, Twitter, and Google have been filed by Shurat HaDin's lawyers and others in federal courts across the United States. The plaintiffs in the cases, the families of victims of recent terror attacks such as Tel Aviv, Brussels, Paris, Istanbul, Orlando, and San Bernardino, contend that the Anti-Terrorism Act prohibits the provision of any material support or resources, including services, to any designated terrorist or organization, and imposes civil and criminal liability. The Internet and specifically social media have become a necessary and vital component in international terrorist operations, no less so than weapons, explosives, training, safe houses, and funding. Terrorist use social media to recruit volunteers, disseminate their messages, raise funds for their activities, publish training manuals, and organize their deadly operations.

How then do the wealthy social media platforms in Palo Alto justify providing Facebook pages, Twitter accounts, and YouTube channels to designated terrorist organizations such as Hezbollah, Hamas, and ISIS? How is it that designated individuals such as Ismail Haniyeh and Hassan Nasrallah—along with Iranian and Syrian outlaws, who could not receive visas to visit the United States and are prohibited from any contact with American businesses or citizens—are provided social media services by American high-tech companies? How do commercial ads on YouTube's sites accompany videos of ISIS beheadings?

Today, the Internet stands at the center of virtually all human endeavors and has become a necessary societal component that provides limitless opportunities, continuous advancements, and uncharted technological possibilities across all global borders.

It has also become the next battlefield to conquer.

ACKNOWLEDGMENTS

Seldom in life does one have a chance to faithfully realize the hopes and dreams of their early years. Often, intervening events, unanticipated obstacles, and the riptides of destiny pull us far away from the course we had once imagined we'd travel. As a young law student, I envisioned a career representing society's underdogs, battling for important causes and pursuing the path of justice wherever it would lead. I was fortunate to meet up with wise mentors, talented colleagues, and innovative co-conspirators on my journey who allowed me to realize much of the dream. Somehow it all worked out.

Embarking upon the writing of this book provided me a long overdue opportunity and deep breath from the whirlwind of legal practice, distant travels, and public speaking I'd been engaged in for almost two decades. It gave me pause to review many of the dramatic challenges and activist street fights my colleagues and I navigated as young lawyers, as well as some reflection upon the wild successes and sometimes heartbreaking setbacks we garnered. The research allowed me to revisit with some long-ago colleagues. Most important, writing this story furnished me with an important reminder of why we had set out together years back to fight so fiercely on behalf of the State of Israel and the world Jewish community.

First and foremost I'd like to express my appreciation to my family who supported and encouraged me throughout the many long days and late nights of the work on this book. My husband, Aviel, who toiled tirelessly with us on the manuscript, watched over every word. To my children Yarden, Elia, Bar

Yochai, Ateret, Zimrat, and Shaked, I'm sorry that Imma wasn't around so often. Thank you for your understanding and support. Please always know that I love you all very dearly. My parents, Esther and Rachamim Darshan, allowed me never to have to choose between my career and my family. They kept the home front secure whenever I was away. My mother-in-law, Adina Leitner, provided much encouragement and wisdom for our work.

My bestselling co-author, Samuel Katz, provided superhuman energy, virtuoso skill, and calm counsel as he undertook so much of the heavy lifting of the research and writing (and rewriting) of the manuscript. Sam, you indeed are a trouper.

We were fortunate to have the opportunity to conduct an extensive interview with the late, great Meir Dagan in his apartment in Tel Aviv. Sam and I were moved by his still-buoyant enthusiasm and lucid insights about the work of Harpoon and the vitality of the financial war on terrorism. A Jew of charm, courage, commitment, and daring, he provided depth to his legendary warrior philosophy and filled in many of the gaps in our story. Our deep appreciation also goes to his lovely wife, Bina Dagan, and their daughter, Noa, who graciously provided us their friendship, encouragement, and insights, along with much personal material for the book.

We were told that we cannot mention by name the officers and spies of the Harpoon unit that we had the good fortune to meet and work with over the years. These dedicated patriots were our jungle guides through the dark world of the terrorist organizations and rogue regimes that armed and trained them. From the agents we received instructions in the *krav maga* of combating terror financing and learned how bold creativity can always triumph over evil. They personified the old-school ethos of Zionist sacrifice and are living examples of soldiers who place the interests of the country and the Jewish community before their own, frequently at a heavy personal cost. The heroic Harpoon veterans provided us so much of their personal time and acumen, sitting for interviews and encouraging us to write this story. Could not have done without you guys!

My top-tier agent Jim Hornfischer offered his leadership and advice, and was a guiding beacon throughout the project. My editor Paul

Whitlatch and the expert team at Hachette provided unparalleled support, critical review, and uncommon patience. Paul was a fantastic champion for the project, contributing his counsel and experience—everything a first-time author needs.

Many of the attorneys with whom I have had the privilege to work with over the years succeeded in pioneering the practice of terror-victim litigation in courtrooms around the world. Their faith, innovation, and skills have inflicted damage on the terrorist groups and sent a shock wave throughout the international banking system. The world is safer place because of them. My special thanks to Mordechai Haller, Robert Tolchin, David Strachman, Roy Kochavi, Meir Katz, Nathan Tarnor, Kent Yalowitz, Abbe Lowell, Mark Abelson, Gary Osen, Naomi Weinberg, Asher Perlin, Asaf Nebentzal, Avi Segal, Asaf Chen, Jeff Miller, David Schoen, Alberto Mansur, Maurice Hirsch, Ed Morgan, the late Eddie Greenspan, and Alessio Vianello.

The staff of the Shurat HaDin Law Center in Tel Aviv are among the leading legal activists and dedicated advocates for Israel in the world. On a daily basis they are vigilantly fighting the good fight, frequently without the recognition or praise they deserve. My deep public appreciation then to everyone, past and present, who assisted with this book, including Alona Zohar, Rachel Weisner, Avi Guez, Dina Rovner, Liora Blum, Gideon Israel, and Yifat Segal. Much thanks as well to Sara Miller for her editing assistance and to Ronn Torossian for all his encouragement.

The experts who we employed in the various courtroom proceedings throughout the years utilized their knowledge, experience, and scholarship in the service of justice for the terror victims. They include Patrick Clawson, Ronni Shaked, Arieh Spitzen, Noa Meridor, Bruce Bechtol, Mathew Levitt, Udi Levi, Uzi Shaya, Yossi Kuperwasser, Echud Levi, Daniel Reisner, Israel Shrenzel, Eugene Kontorovitch, Avi Bell, Jonathan Schanzer, Nick Kaufman, Alon Evyatar, Peter Raven-Hansen, Rael Strous, Allan Friedman, Marius Deeb, Berti Benedetta, David Pollock, Itamar Marcus, Claudia Rosett, Clive Ansley, Gordan Chang, Donald Clark, and the late Barry Rubin.

Special thanks as well to my personal fixer, Margalit Gordon of ISRAM Tours, for her love and friendship and ability to arrange pretty much anything anywhere.

It's an emotional experience for any author to have her work reviewed by government censors. No one likes their words being toyed with or told what they can or can't say. It can be a difficult and thankless task safeguarding the secrets of the state, however, and we greatly appreciate the speed and fairness with which the IDF censors carried out their work. They asked not to be mentioned by name, so thank you, ladies.

Finally, the families and victims of terrorism provided all of us with the inspiration and strength to launch our battle in the uncharted and high-risk arena of courtroom warfare worldwide on their behalf. With their courage and noble determination they turned the tragedies so unfairly inflicted upon them and the open wounds that don't heal into powerful weapons in the pursuit of justice. It was these beautiful families that personally paid the full price of the reckless gamble of the Oslo Accords. They chose not to be merely victims any longer, honoring their loved ones by fighting back. "For if you remain silent at a time like this."

—Nitsana Darshan-Leitner, July 2017

A book of this kind that covers the most secretive and sensitive operations of intelligence work could never have been written without the assistance of a great many people—most of whom, for reasons that require no further explanation, cannot be named. To do the jobs that they have sworn to carry out, they have had to work and live in the shadows. But still, these secret soldiers knew of the importance of this story and they offered what they could, providing a brief glimpse into the imagination and courage that went into the effort to deny the terror masterminds the funds needed to maintain a murderous campaign whose sole mission was to kill innocent people. I am grateful for the trust these anonymous men and women have invested in me. I am honored for the friendships that subsequently developed. I would like to thank Brigadier-General (Ret.) Danny Arditi and Uzi Arad, both former heads of Israel's National Security Council, for their time and insight. I would also like to thank the man known as Lavi S. for his generous time and his patience in explaining to me the intricate world of Israel's neighbors. I would also like to offer a special word of thanks to Deputy Commissioner (Ret.) Uri Bar-Lev for his assistance and friendship.

It was a great pleasure and privilege to have been able to meet and talk to Meir Dagan. I met Meir Dagan at the end of his life, yet his brilliant mind was sharp and his unique brand of charisma beamed with great power. His infectious smile and mischievous sense of humor were inescapable. Talking to Dagan for even a few moments was a lesson—there was so much I wanted to ask and so much I wished he would and could tell. Even ill, fighting cancer, Dagan was the commando, the general, the spymaster: He was the man who knew all the secrets. It was easy to see why he was both feared and highly respected by his enemies. The moment I was in Dagan's company I realized why he was adored by his friends and revered by those who worked for him. He was truly a legendary figure.

The men who worked for Dagan were of similar swagger. I am grateful to these spies and soldiers for sharing their insight and experiences—they are the embodiment of the words *chutzpah* and *genius*. They must remain anonymous though they are the true heroes in Israel's war against terror. I would like to personally thank the "U2," the men known as Uri L. and Shai U., for their assistance and friendship, and for offering me a fascinating glimpse into this covert world.

Finally, a very special word of thanks to my co-author, Nitsana, and her husband, Aviel. Nitsana's energy and dedication in the roll-up-your-sleeves, in-the-trenches legal fight for the rights of terror victims is absolutely inspiring. Nitsana, Aviel, and the team at Shurat HaDin are very much on the front lines of the war on terror, fighting tirelessly for the rights of everyday people whose lives were devastated by extraordinary evil. I am grateful to have had the chance to be part of this book and to have been included in their campaign.

There are other heroes, of course, and some provided me with unofficial assistance. The war against terror was not limited to the State of Israel and its intelligence services, of course. The war is fought by Americans, Brits, Germans, Jordanians, and many others. Over the course of my writing career I've come to know many of these frontline spies, soldiers, and special agents working diligently for their countries, and I am grateful to a great many of them who provided me with some background and guidance in my writing. A special thanks to former special agents with the U.S. State Department's Diplomatic Security Service for their international perspective and the use of their knowledge and contacts.

I would like to thank my terrific agent, Jim Hornfischer, for making sure that this book became a reality. I would also like to thank Paul Whitlatch, our editor, for his guidance and sharp eye, and I would like to thank the team at Hachette Books who turned this mixture of words and images into a finished product. I'd like to thank my three children for their tolerance amid the chaos and endless hours that the travels and late-night writing sessions warranted. You kids are the best! Last but certainly not least, I'd like to thank my wife, Sigi, for being very patient, very tolerant, and ultimately, very proud.

—Samuel M. Katz, July 2017

NOTES

Preface

1. Kimberly Dozier, "Taken Out: Haji Imam, ISIS's 'Second in Command,' Killed by U.S. in Syria," *Daily Beast*, March 25, 2016.
2. Kyle Orton, "Obituary: Abd al-Rahman Mustafa al-Qaduli (Abu Ali al-Anbari)": https://kyleorton1991.wordpress.com/2016/03/25/obituary-abd-ar-rahman-mustafa-al-qaduli/.
3. Barbara Starr, Ryan Browne, and Laura Koran, "Pentagon: ISIS Finance Minister Killed," CNN, March 25, 2016.
4. U.S. Department of Defense, "Department of Defense Press Briefing by Secretary Carter and General Dunford in the Pentagon Briefing Room," March 25, 2016.
5. Barbara Starr, Laura Smith-Spark, and Ray Sanchez, "Abu Sayyaf, Key ISIS Figure in Syria, Killed in U.S. Raid," CNN, May 17, 2015.
6. Ronen Bergman, *The Secret War with Iran: The 30-Year Clandestine Struggle Against the World's Most Dangerous Terrorist Power*, New York: Simon & Schuster, 2008, p. 284.

Chapter One: The Tourists from the Windy City

1. Danny Sadeh, "Darsu Et Toledano, Sahvru Et Raglav, U'Belayla Ratzhu Oto," Yediot Aharonot 24 Sha'ot, June 7, 1993.
2. Joel Greenberg, "Israel Arrests 4 in Police Death," *New York Times*, June 7, 1993.
3. Michael Parks, "Arab Militants Kidnap Israeli, Demand Swap," *Los Angeles Times*, December 14, 1992.
4. http://mfa.gov.il/MFA/ForeignPolicy/Terrorism/Palestinian/Pages/Ahmed%20Yassin.aspx.
5. Interview with Unit 33 veteran "F.," name withheld for security reasons, Tel Aviv, September 29, 2016.
6. David Johnston, "U.S. Prosecutors Suspect an American Citizen of Financing Hamas Terror," *New York Times*, June 14, 1998.
7. Tom Hundley, "Chicagoan Is Charged by Israel With Heading Hamas Militants," *Chicago Tribune*, October 23, 1993.
8. See affidavit signed by "Nadav," September 26, 1995, used in the deportation proceedings against Musa Abu Marzook from the United States in 1995.
9. Ibid.
10. Ibid.

11. Terrence McCoy, "The Enigmatic Hamas Leader Allegedly Behind the Israeli Kidnappings That Ignited War," *Washington Post*, July 10, 2014.

12. See Tom Hundley, "Chicagoan Is Charged by Israel With Heading Hamas Militants," *Chicago Tribune*, October 23, 1993.

13. Joel Greenberg, "Israel Holding 3 U.S. Arabs It Links to Militant Group," *New York Times*, February 1, 1993.

14. Ronen Bergman, *The Secret War with Iran: The 30-Year Clandestine Struggle Against the World's Most Dangerous Terrorist Power*, New York: Simon & Schuster, 2008, p. 249.

15. Ehud Ya'ari, "The Metamorphosis of Hamas," *Jerusalem Report*, January 14, 1993.

16. See Danny Sadeh, "Darsu Et Toledano, Sahvru Et Raglav, U'Belayla Ratzhu Oto," Yediot Aharonot 24 Sha'ot, June 7, 1993.

17. Michael Rotem, "Arrest of Hamas Terrorists Foiled Massive Car Bomb Attacks," *Jerusalem Post*, June 7, 1993.

Chapter Two: Da'wa

1. Interview, Tel Aviv, May 30, 2015.

2. Ibid.

3. Ibid.

4. Ibid.

5. Interview, December 13, 2016.

6. Amos Harel, "Ha'Matkefa al Hamas: Mivtza Raava She'A'lul La'hafoch Le'Pe'ulat Serek," *Ha'aretz*, June 6, 2014.

7. https://www.youtube.com/watch?v=UZd_jlHdVRg.

8. https://www.youtube.com/watch?v=DWcAyWEnD3I.

9. Ibid.

10. Interview, with Bina Dagan, May 9, 2017.

11. Ibid.

12. Amir Oren, "Meir Dagan: The Outsider Who Blocked Netanyahu and Barak's Adventurousness," *Ha'aretz*, March 17, 2016.

13. Ronen Bergman, "How Meir Dagan Restored The Mossad to Its Former Glory," *Ynet Magazine*, March 20, 2016.

14. Yossi Melman, "Ha'Kesher Im Sharon Hithil Be'Yamei Hakamat Sayeret Rimon," *Ha'aretz*, September 11, 2002.

15. Itamar Eichner, "A Fighter to the End: Meir Dagan's Daring Life," *Ynet Magazine*, March 19, 2016.

16. Amir Oren, "Meir Dagan: The Outsider Who Blocked Netanyahu and Barak's Adventurousness," *Ha'aretz*, March 17, 2016.

17. http://www.gvura.org/a4839-%D7%A1%D7%A8%D7%9F-%D7%9E%D7%90%D7%99%D7%A8-%D7%93%D7%92%D7%9F-%D7%94%D7%95%D7%91%D7%A8%D7%9E%D7%9F.

18. Dr. Uri Milshtein, "Rimon Helem: Kach Husla Yisrael Et Ha'Terror Be'Retzu'a," *Ma'ariv*, January 23, 2016.

19. See https://www.youtube.com/watch?v=DWcAyWEnD3I.

20. See interview, with Bina Dagan, May 9, 2017.

21. https://www.youtube.com/watch?v=1HKq_qt0748.

22. See Amir Oren, "Meir Dagan: The Outsider Who Blocked Netanyahu and Barak's Adventurousness," *Ha'aretz*, March 17, 2016.

23. Clyde Haberman, "Arab Car Bomber Kills 8 in Israel; 44 Are Wounded," *New York Times*, April 7, 1994.

Chapter Three: Closed Accounts

1. https://www.youtube.com/watch?v=K7PAOlxjd24.

2. Elie Rekhess, "Khomeinism in Gaza," *Jerusalem Post*, January 11, 1991, p. 8.

3. http://www.cfr.org/israel/palestinian-islamic-jihad/p15984.

4. Gustav Niebuhr, "Professor Talked of Understanding But Now Reveals Ties to Terrorists," *New York Times*, November 13, 1995.

5. Mary Curtius, "Bombings Kill 6 Israelis, Hurt 47: Mideast: Suicide Attackers Set Off Two Explosions near Isolated Gaza Strip Settlements. Rabin Says Peace Talks Will Continue, but Demands Arafat Disarm Violent Militias," *Los Angeles Times*, April 10, 1995.

6. Ibid.

7. Clyde Haberman, "Arafat's Police in Gaza Widen Crackdown on Muslim Radicals," *New York Times*, April 12, 1995.

8. Samuel M. Katz, *The Hunt for the Engineer: How Israeli Agents Tracked The Hamas Master Bomber*, New York: Fromm International, 1999, p. 123.

9. Joel Greenberg, "Islamic Group Vows Revenge For Slaying of Its Leader," *New York Times*, October 30, 1995.

10. Serge Schmemann, "The World; Shhh! That's a (Not Very) Secret," Week in Review, *New York Times*, January 14, 1996.

11. Yossi Melman, "Kidon, the Mossad Within the Mossad," *Ha'aretz*, February 19, 2010.

12. Yassin Musharbash, "Tourists with a License to Kill: A Look at the Mossad's Assassination Squads," *Der Spiegel Online*, February 18, 2010.

13. Yossi Melman, "The Assassination in Malta: The Professional Skills of the Agents vis-à-vis the Negligence of Shaqaqi. No Bullets Were Found At the Killing Location. The Motorcycle Was Brought Especially to the Island," *Ha'aretz*, October 30, 1995.

14. See Joel Greenberg, "Islamic Group Vows Revenge For Slaying of Its Leader," *New York Times*, October 30, 1995.

15. John Battersby, "World Honors a Shepherd of Peace, Players Vow to Keep Rabin's Legacy," *Christian Science Monitor*, November 6, 1995.

16. https://www.mossad.gov.il/heb/history/Pages/dagan.aspx.

17. Joel Greenberg, "Islamic Group Vows Revenge For Slaying of Its Leader," *New York Times*, October 30, 1995.

18. Interview, Tel Aviv, May 28, 2015.

19. See interview, with Uri, December 13, 2016.

Chapter Four: The Head of the Table

1. Interview with "O" (identity withheld for security considerations), September 28, 2016.

2. Interview, New York City, December 7, 2014.

3. Interview, with INP Superintendent (Ret.) Gil Kleiman, December 12, 2016.

4. Interview, Tel Aviv, September 26, 2016.

5. Interview with Uri L., December 13, 2016.

6. Ibid.

7. Interview, Lod, December 31, 2013.

8. Amnon Kapeliouk, "A Summit Clouded by Suspicion," *Ha'aretz*, November 23, 2001.

9. George J. Mitchell, "The Sharm el-Sheikh Fact-Finding Committee Report," May 2001.

10. See interview with Uri L., December 13, 2016.

11. https://www.youtube.com/watch?v=DWcAyWEnD3I.

12. Ibid.

Chapter Five: Khalas

1. http://israelspy.com/turn-the-clock-back-32-years-lebanon-was-the-battleground/.

2. Jim Newell, "Jeb's 'James Baker' Problem: Why Hawks Are Turning on the 'Anti-Israel' Bush," *Salon*, March 25, 2015.

3. Interview with Harpoon representative, Tel Aviv, May 31, 2016.

4. http://www.jewishvirtuallibrary.org/jsource/Peace/ehrenfeld.html.

5. David Hoffman, "Arafat Denounces Conditions Imposed on Foreign Aid," *Washington Post* Foreign Service, July 2, 1994.

6. https://www.ynet.co.il/articles/0,7340,L-2058616,00.html.

7. Interview, Washington D.C., December 25, 2016.

8. Alexander Cockburn, "Why Say No?," *Nation*, October 4, 1994.

9. David Samuels, "In a Ruined Country: How Yasir Arafat Destroyed Palestine," *Atlantic*, September 2005.

10. Ibid.

11. Interview, Washington, D.C., January 11, 2017.

12. http://www.cbsnews.com/news/arafats-billions/.

13. Ibid.

14. Yossi Melman and Arnon Regular, "Yossi Ginossar, Ex-Senior Shin Bet Official, Dies at 58," *Ha'aretz*, January 13, 2004; available at http://www.haaretz.com/news/yossi-ginossar-ex-senior-shin-bet-official-dies-at-58-1.110762.

15. John Kifner, "All Sides Resist Plan by Clinton for the Mideast," *New York Times*, December 31, 2000.

16. See David Samuels, "In a Ruined Country: How Yasir Arafat Destroyed Palestine," *Atlantic*, September 2005.

17. Ben Caspit, "How a Former Official of Israeli Intelligence, Yossi Ginosar, Managed a Secret Account for Arafat," Behind the News in Israel, December 5, 2002.

18. See David Samuels, "In a Ruined Country: How Yasir Arafat Destroyed Palestine," *Atlantic*, September 2005.

19. Inigo Gilmore, "Arafat 'Diverted $300m of Public Money to Swiss Bank Account,'" *Telegraph*, November 9, 2003.

20. https://georgewbush-whitehouse.archives.gov/government/jzarate-bio.html.

21. Joel Greenberg, "Victims' Accounts of a Night of Horror," *New York Times*, June 3, 2001.

22. Clyde Haberman, "At Least 14 Dead as Suicide Bomber Strikes Jerusalem," *New York Times*, August 10, 2001.

Chapter Six: Money Kills

1. Serge Schmemann, "Mideast Turmoil: The Outlook; Dire Day: Trying to See Beyond Sure Revenge," *New York Times*, March 28, 2002.

2. Shaul Mofaz, "Operation Defensive Shield: Lessons and Aftermath," Washington Institute, Policy no. 387, June 18, 2002.

3. James Bennet, "Mideast Turmoil: Mideast; Israelis Besiege a Defiant Arafat in His Office," *New York Times*, March 30, 2002.

4. "Provisions Supplied to PA Chairman Arafat-2-Apr-2002," available at http://mfa.gov .il/MFA/PressRoom/2002/Pages/Provisions%20Supplied%20to%20PA%20Chair man%20Arafat%20-%202-Apr-.aspx.

5. Efraim Karsh, *Arafat's War: The Man and His Battle for Israeli Conquest*, New York: Grove/Atlantic, 2003, p. 156.

6. Dror Moreh (writer, director, producer), *The Gatekeepers* (documentary film), Sony Pictures Classic, 2012.

7. Bruce Hoffman, "The Logic of Suicide Terrorism," *Atlantic*, June 2003.

8. Ibid.

9. Ibid.

10. Interview, Ra'anana, September 7, 2015.

11. Matthew Levitt, *Hamas: Politics, Charity, and Terrorism in the Service of Jihad*, New Haven: Yale University Press, 2006, p. 4.

12. Ibid.

13. Vered Lubich, "Hugash Katav Ishum Neged Mitcanen Ha'Pigu'a Be'Malon Park," Ynet, August 1, 2002.

14. Hebrew translation of interview transcript of Abbas al-Sayyid in Kishon Prison, May 12, 2002.

15. Juan C. Zarate, *Treasury's War: The Unleashing of a New Era of Financial Warfare*, New York: Public Affairs / Perseus Books Group, 2013, p. 87.

16. Ella Levy-Weinrib, "Meet the Hamas Billionaires," Globes, July 24, 2014.

17. Interview, December 13, 2016.

18. Ari Shavit, "The Waiting Game," *Ha'aretz*, May 14, 2005.

19. Presentation by Efraim Halevy, Director of the Israeli Secret Intelligence Service ("The Mossad") for the NATO–Israel Nineteen Plus One Dialogue, June 26, 2002.

20. Interview, Tel Aviv, September 27, 2016.

21. Ibid.

22. Yossi Melman, "Kidon, the Mossad Within the Mossad," *Ha'aretz*, February 19, 2010.

23. Ronen Bergman, "Ba Le'Mossad Bahur Hadash," *Yediot Aharonot*, April 22, 2003.

Chapter Seven: Blood Money

1. "(Almost) Everything You Wanted to Know About Arab Bank Following Settlement with Terror Victims," Jewish Press, August 18, 2015.

2. Lawrence Joffe, "Abdul-Majid Shoman," *Guardian*, August 18, 2005.

3. Ibid.

4. http://addustour.com/ViewarchiveTopic.aspx?ac=\localandgover\2000\10\local80 .html (October 28, 2010).

5. Christopher M. Blanchard and Alfred B. Prados, "Saudi Arabia: Terrorist Financing Issues," Congressional Research Service, September 14, 2007.

6. Ibid.

7. http://www.osenlaw.com/case/arab-bank-case.

8. Interview, Tel Aviv, May 30, 2016.

9. Amos Harel, "IDF Arrests Most-Wanted Hamas Bomb Mastermind in West Bank," *Ha'aretz*, May 23, 2006.

10. Tracey Wilkinson, "Blast Kills 7 at University in Jerusalem," *Los Angeles Times*, August 1, 2002.

11. Elliot Abrams, "After Fayyad," *Weekly Standard*, April 16, 2013.

12. http://www.presidency.ucsb.edu/ws/index.php?pid=64915&st=&st1=.

13. https://it.ojp.gov/PrivacyLiberty/authorities/statutes/1286.

14. http://www.osenlaw.com/case/arab-bank-case.

15. Janine Zacharia, "U.S. Freezes Arab Terror Groups' Bank Accounts," *Jerusalem Post*, November 4, 2001.

16. Juan C. Zarate, *Treasury's War: The Unleashing of a New Era of Financial Warfare*, New York: Public Affairs / Perseus Books Group, 2013, p. 105.

17. Interview, with Harpoon officer, Tel Aviv, May 31, 2017.

Chapter Eight: Operation Green Lantern

1. http://www.mfa.gov.il/mfa/foreignpolicy/terrorism/palestinian/pages/suicide%20 and%20other%20bombing%20attacks%20in%20israel%20since.aspx.

2. Interview, May 30, 2016.

3. Ibid.

4. Interview, with Uri, February 14, 2017.

5. Ibid.

6. Interview, with Colonel (Res.) Maurice Hirsch, May 9, 2017.

7. Efrat Weiss, "Gormei Bitachon: He'Hramnu ce-40 Milyon Shekel Be'Ramallah," *Ynet Magazine*, February 26, 2004.

8. Ibid.

9. Interview, with Mohammed Najib, Ramallah, February 11, 2017.

10. http://www.justice.gov.il/Units/HalbantHon/docs/-20%בישראל20%הטרור20%במימון20% אברבוךהמאבק20%אלכס20%משפטיים20%היבטים20%.pdf.

11. Interview, Tel Aviv, September 25, 2016.

12. Ibid.

13. See interview, with Mohammed Najib, Ramallah, February 11, 2017.

14. Matthew Kalman, "'Armed Robbery' Israeli Troops Raid Palestinian Banks, Take $9-Million," *Globe and Mail*, February 26, 2004.

15. Interview, Lod, October 1, 2016.

16. See Efrat Weiss, "Gormei Bitachon: He'Hramnu ce-40 Milyon Shekel Be'Ramallah," *Ynet Magazine*, February 26, 2004.

17. See interview, with Uri, February 14, 2017.

18. https://wikileaks.org/plusd/cables/04TELAVIV1392_a.html.

19. Gal Brenner, "Gormei Bitachon: Ha'Bank Ha'Aravi Ke'Tzinor Ha'Mimum Ha'Merkazi Shel Ha'Hamas Ve'Ha'Jihad," News1, July 11, 2004.

20. See Matthew Kalman, "'Armed Robbery' Israeli Troops Raid Palestinian Banks, Take $9-Million," *Globe and Mail*, February 26, 2004.

21. Ibid.

22. Ibid.

23. Ibid.

Chapter Nine: The Letter of the Law

1. Interview, Haderah, March 28, 2014.
2. Interview, Tel Aviv, May 18, 2017.
3. Interview, Ramat Gan, September 30, 2016.
4. https://www.govtrack.us/congress/bills/102/s740.
5. https://www.govtrack.us/congress/bills/102/hr2222.
6. Interview, September 29, 2016.
7. Dan Levine, "In Anti-Terrorism Lawsuits, Verdicts Are Just the First Battle," Reuters, April 29, 2015.
8. Yossi Melman, "Hatzatza El Ha'Maavak Ha'Mishpati Be'Terror: 'Menasim Le'Hochiach Zika Le'Reshut," *Ma'ariv*, July 2, 2015.
9. Interview, February 16, 2017.
10. Interview, May 28, 2016.

Chapter Ten: The Higher Cost of Murder

1. Caroline Kennedy-Pipe, Gordon Clubb, Simon Mabon, *Terrorism and Political Violence*, London: Sage Publishing, 2015, p. 185.
2. http://laad.btl.gov.il/Web/He/Victims/112.aspx?lastName=&firstName=&fatherName =&motherName=&place=&year=&month=&day=&yearHeb=&monthHeb=&dayHeb =&region=%20מרכזית20%תחנה&period=14&grave=.
3. https://news.google.com/newspapers?nid=1755&dat=20061215&id=BvMeAAAAIBAJ &sjid=eoYEAAAAIBAJ&pg=6771,5191936.
4. Interview, Tel Aviv, May 29, 2016.
5. https://wikileaks.org/plusd/cables/05TELAVIV1013_a.html.
6. Ibid.
7. Ibid.
8. Greg Myre and Dina Kraft, "Suicide Bombing in Israel Kills 9; Hamas Approves," *New York Times*, April 18, 2006.
9. Interview, Tel Aviv, May 26, 2016.

Chapter Eleven: The Party of God

1. Interview, Tel Aviv, September 30, 2016.
2. Interview, Tel Aviv, May 8, 2017.
3. Interview, Bina Dagan, Tel Aviv, May 9, 2017.
4. David K. Shipler, "Lebanese Tell of Anguish of Living Under the PLO; Thefts by PLO Are Described," *New York Times*, July 25, 1982.
5. Ibid.
6. Eli Ashkenazi and Yoav Stern, "New Film Leaves Parents in the Dark on Sons' Fate During Kidnap," *Ha'aretz*, September 5, 2006.
7. Hassan M. Fattah and Steven Erlanger, "Israel Blockades Lebanon; Wide Strikes by Hezbollah," *New York Times*, July 14, 2006.
8. Ibid.
9. Uzi Rubin, "Hizballah's Rocket Campaign Against Northern Israel: A Preliminary Report," Jerusalem Center for Public Affairs, *Jerusalem Issue Brief* 6, no. 10, August 31, 2006.

10. David B. Green, "1973: Moshe Dayan Allegedly Suggests Israel Demonstrate Its Nuclear Capacity," *Ha'aretz*, October 7, 2016.
11. See Hassan M. Fattah and Steven Erlanger, "Israel Blockades Lebanon; Wide Strikes by Hezbollah," *New York Times*, July 14, 2006.
12. Interview, Tel Aviv, September 25, 2016.
13. Interview, Tel Aviv, September 28, 2016.
14. Adam Ciralsky, Lisa Myers, and the NBC News Investigative Unit, "Hezbollah Banks Under Attack in Lebanon," *NBC News Investigates*, July 25, 2016.
15. Ibid.
16. Matt M. Matthews, *We Were Caught Unprepared: The 2006 Hezbollah-Israel War*, Long War Series Occasional Paper 26, Fort Leavenworth, KS: U.S. Army Combined Arms Center Combat Studies Institute Press, 2008.
17. "Retired Israeli Generals Vent," *Washington Times*, September 26, 2006.

Chapter Twelve: Greed

1. Interview, Tel Aviv, May 31, 2016.
2. "Factbox: Costs of War and Recovery in Lebanon and Israel," Reuters, July 9, 2007.
3. Ibid.
4. Andrew Lee Butters, "Lebanon's Bernie Madoff: A Scandal Taints Hizballah," *Time*, September 16, 2009.
5. Interview, Tel Aviv, September 29, 2016.
6. Interview, Hadera (Israel), September 5, 2015.
7. Joshua Hersh, "Follow the Money," *National*, February 4, 2010.
8. Robert Fisk, "'Lebanon's Madoff' Bankrupted After Bouncing $200,000 Cheque to Hizballah," *Independent*, September 7, 2009.
9. "Hezbollah Chief Sheikh Hassan Nasrallah," Ynet News, July 31, 2006.
10. "Iran: Ensuring Hezbollah's Loyalty," Stratfor, October 6, 2009.
11. https://now.mmedia.me/lb/en/commentaryanalysis/ezzedine_shows_hezbollahs_moral_bankruptcy.
12. Yossi Melman, "Should Retired IDF Officers Do Business in Arab States or Not?" *Ha'aretz*, September 18, 2008.
13. Jonathan Ferziger and Peter Waldman, "How Do Israel's Tech Firms Do Business in Saudi Arabia? Very Quietly," *Bloomberg Businessweek*, February 2, 2017.
14. Shuki Sadeh, "The Badly Kept Secret of Israel's Trade Throughout the Muslim World," *Ha'aretz*, January 19, 2012.
15. See Jonathan Ferziger and Peter Waldman, "How Do Israel's Tech Firms Do Business in Saudi Arabia? Very Quietly," *Bloomberg Businessweek*, February 2, 2017.
16. "Secret Israeli Business Deals with Gulf States May Herald Public Ties," Tower, February 3, 2017.
17. See Jonathan Ferziger and Peter Waldman, "How Do Israel's Tech Firms Do Business in Saudi Arabia? Very Quietly," *Bloomberg Businessweek*, February 2, 2017.
18. "Salah Ezzedine, le «Madoff» Libanais," *Libération*, September 14, 2009.
19. Robert F. Worth, "Billion-Dollar Pyramid Scheme Rivets Lebanon," *New York Times*, September 15, 2009.
20. See Joshua Hersh, "Follow the Money," *National*, February 4, 2010.

21. Ibid.

22. Doron Peskin, "Miliard Ha'Me'Kurav Le'Hezbollah Hashud Be'Hona'at A'anaq," Ynet, August 31, 2009.

23. See "Iran: Ensuring Hezbollah's Loyalty," Stratfor, October 6, 2009.

24. See Andrew Lee Butters, "Lebanon's Bernie Madoff: A Scandal Taints Hizballah," *Time*, September 16, 2009.

25. https://www.youtube.com/watch?v=XjFDybGduiI.

26. Ibid.

27. See Joshua Hersh, "Follow the Money," *National*, February 4, 2010.

28. See Andrew Lee Butters, "Lebanon's Bernie Madoff: A Scandal Taints Hizballah," *Time*, September 16, 2009.

29. See https://www.youtube.com/watch?v=XjFDybGduiI.

30. See Joshua Hersh, "Follow the Money," *National*, February 4, 2010.

31. Alia Ibrahim, "Investment Scandal Damages Hezbollah," *Washington Post*, November 26, 2009.

32. See "Iran: Ensuring Hezbollah's Loyalty," Stratfor, October 6, 2009.

33. See Robert F. Worth, "Billion-Dollar Pyramid Scheme Rivets Lebanon," *New York Times*, September 15, 2009.

34. See "Iran: Ensuring Hezbollah's Loyalty," Stratfor, October 6, 2009.

Chapter Thirteen: The Cocaine Jihadis

1. Colin Freeze, "Canadian Spy Secrets Exposed in WikiLeaks Dump," *Globe and Mail*, November 29, 2010.

2. Tim Whitmire, "Two Convicted in Hezbollah Smuggling," Yahoo News, June 21, 2002.

3. https://www.atf.gov/our-history/operation-smokescreen.

4. "Man Gets 155 Years For Leading Hezbollah Smuggling Scheme," *Ha'aretz*, March 1, 2003.

5. Library of Congress, "A Global Overview of Narcotics-Funded Terrorist and Other Groups," May 2002.

6. Matthew Levitt, "Hezbollah as a Criminal Organization," Washington Institute for Near East Policy, *Fathom*, Autumn 2013.

7. Ibid.

8. Orianna Zill and Lowell Bergman, "The Black Peso Money Laundering System," *Frontline*, PBS.

9. Mary Anastasia O'Grady, "The Iran-Cuba-Venezuela Nexus," *Wall Street Journal*, November 23, 2014.

10. Linette Lopez, "A Suspected Terrorist and Drug Trafficker Just Became Venezuela's Vice President," Business Insider, January 5, 2017.

11. Yossi Melman, "The Prying Game," *Ha'aretz*, July 23, 2006.

12. Amos Harel, "Kais Obeid Plotted to Abduct Other Israelis," *Ha'aretz*, March 24, 2004.

13. Dugald McConnell and Brian Todd, "Venezuela Defends Controversial Flights to Iran and Syria," CNN, August 21, 2010.

14. See Linette Lopez, "A Suspected Terrorist and Drug Trafficker Just Became Venezuela's Vice President," Business Insider, January 5, 2017.

15. Interview, Washington, D.C., March 11, 2017.

16. Shlomo Abromovitz, "Jihad Derekh Ha'Vrid," *Yediot Aharonot Sheva Yamim*, September 25, 1998.
17. See Matthew Levitt, "Hezbollah as a Criminal Organization," Washington Institute for Near East Policy, *Fathom*, Autumn 2013.
18. Interview, Tel Aviv, June 1, 2016.
19. https://www.youtube.com/watch?v=5GfdH9AzAXE.
20. Robin Wright, "The Assad Family: Nemesis of Nine U.S. Presidents," *New Yorker*, April 11, 2017.
21. Yarin Kimor, "Sochnut Hayav Be'Meleyat 30 Le'Moto Shel Meir Dagan Z'l," Israel Channel 1, April 20, 2016.
22. Interview, Tel Aviv, May 29, 2016.
23. https://www.gpo.gov/fdsys/pkg/CHRG-111shrg52925/html/CHRG-111shrg52925.htm.
24. Gareth Smyth, "'A Kind of Death': Life on the US Treasury Blacklist," *Guardian*, May 25, 2016.
25. Ariella Ringel-Hoffman, "Yoter Sodi Me'Ha'Mossad," *Yediot Aharonot—Mosaf Yom Ha'Atzma'ut*, April 20, 1999.
26. http://sawte.com/showthread.php?t=7794.
27. See https://www.gpo.gov/fdsys/pkg/CHRG-111shrg52925/html/CHRG-111shrg52925.htm.
28. See interview, Tel Aviv, June 1, 2016.

Chapter Fourteen: Follow the Money

1. Interview, Tel Aviv, September 29, 2016.
2. Interview, Tel Aviv, May 30, 2016.
3. Matthew Levitt, "Hizbullah Narco-Terrorism: A Growing Cross-Border Threat," IHS Defense, Risk, and Security Consulting, September 2012.
4. Marco Vernaschi, "Guinea Bissau: Hezbollah, al Qaida and the Lebanese Connection," Pulitzer Center on Crisis Reporting, June 19, 2009.
5. Adam Nossiter, "U.S. Sting That Snared African Ex-Admiral Shines Light on Drug Trade," *New York Times*, April 15, 2013.
6. Interview, Tel Aviv, September 30, 2016.

Chapter Fifteen: Malware and Moles

1. "Seeking Spies?," *Newsweek*, January 11, 1993.
2. Ingrid Lunden, "Website Builder Wix Acquires Art Community DeviantArt for $36M," Tech Crunch, February 23, 2017.
3. Interview, Tel Aviv, September 28, 2016.
4. Ron Suskind, *The One Percent Doctrine: Deep Inside America's Pursuit of Its Enemies Since 9/11.* New York: Simon & Schuster, 2006, p. 54.
5. https://www.treasury.gov/about/organizational-structure/offices/Pages/Office-of-Foreign-Assets-Control.aspx.
6. Matthew Levitt and Michael Jacobson, "The Money Trail: Finding, Following, and Freezing Terrorist Finances," The Washington Institute for Near East Policy, Policy Focus No. 89, November 2008, p. 25.

7. https://www.treasury.gov/press-center/press-releases/Pages/tg1057.aspx.

8. Interview, Tel Aviv, September 28, 2016.

9. Kim Zetter, "Flame and Stuxnet Cousin Targets Lebanese Bank Customers, Carries Mysterious Payload," *Wired*, August 9, 2012.

10. See Alex Gibney, Marc Shmuger (producers), *Zero Days* (documentary film), Magnolia Pictures, Germany, 2016.

11. Fahmida Y. Rashid, "Gauss Attack Toolkit Targeting Lebanese Banks Related to Stuxnet, Flame," *Security Week*, August 9, 2012.

12. See Kim Zetter, "Flame and Stuxnet Cousin Targets Lebanese Bank Customers, Carries Mysterious Payload," *Wired*, August 9, 2012.

13. Zvi Bar'el, "Neighbors: The Bomblets Left Behind," *Ha'aretz*, April 7, 2010.

14. Interview, Jerusalem, June 1, 2016.

15. https://www.treasury.gov/press-center/press-releases/Pages/hp73.aspx.

16. Nour Samaha, "Lebanon's Intelligence War," al-Jazeera Online, December 2, 2011.

17. http://docu.nana10.co.il/Article/?ArticleID=1141626.

18. Ibid.

19. Greg Miller, "Hezbollah Damages CIA Spy Network in Lebanon," *Washington Post*, November 21, 2011.

20. Interview, Washington, D.C., May 2, 2017.

21. "Gun Battles Break Out in Beirut," CNN, May 9, 2008.

22. See Zvi Bar'el, "Neighbors: The Bomblets Left Behind," *Ha'aretz*, April 7, 2010.

Chapter Sixteen: Lawyers, Guns, and Money

1. Natalie Schreffler, "North Korea and Hezbollah: A Nexus Worth Fearing?," Penn State International Affairs Review, April 8, 2013.

2. Declaration of Shai U., "Ya'akov Licci Against American Express Bank Ltd.," July 6, 2009.

3. Ibid.

4. Transcript of oral argument, https://www.nycourts.gov/ctapps/arguments/2012/Oct12/Transcripts/101012-183.pdf.

5. "Arab Bank Fined $24m For Laundering," al-Jazeera," August 17, 2005.

6. Aaron D. Pina, "Palestinian Factions," CRS Report for Congress, June 8, 2005.

7. Interview, Tel Aviv, May 29, 2017.

Chapter Seventeen: We Cannot Confirm or Deny

1. Associated Press, JPost.com Staff, "Life for Lebanese Man for Israel Spying," *Jerusalem Post*, August 1, 2009.

2. Conal Urquhart, "Israel Kills Hamas Leader in Syrian Capital," *Guardian*, September 27, 2004.

3. Joel Greenberg, "Palestinian Militant Slain in Damascus," *Chicago Tribune*, September 27, 2004.

4. Adam Goldman and Ellen Nakashima, "CIA and Mossad Killed Senior Hezbollah Figure in Car Bombing," *Washington Post*, January 30, 2015.

5. Jean-Pierre Filiu, *Gaza: A History*, New York: Oxford University Press, 2014, pp. 206–207.

6. Interview, Chief Superintendent "Shimon," Lod, April 17, 2014.

7. Ibid.

8. Ronen Bergman, "The Dubai Job," *GQ*, January 4, 2011.

9. Staff, "An Eye for an Eye: The Anatomy of Mossad's Dubai Operation," *Der Spiegel*, January 17, 2011.

10. Interview, September 26, 2016.

11. Yossi Melman and Dan Raviv, "Israel's Hit Squads," *Atlantic*, February 2010.

12. Eran Zohar, "The Flow of Arms into the Gaza Strip," Australian Institute of International Affairs, October 1, 2015.

13. Lee Smith, "Smugglers Galore: How Iran Arms Its Allies," *Weekly Standard*, December 31, 2012.

14. Staff, "How Israel Foiled an Arms Convoy Bound for Hamas," *Time*, March 30, 2009.

15. Kim Zetter, "Dubai Assassination Followed Failed Attempt by Same Team," *Wired*, January 4, 2011.

16. See Ronen Bergman, "The Dubai Job," *GQ*, January 4, 2011.

17. Ilan Evyatar, "Smoke, Mirrors, Cloaks, and Daggers," *Jerusalem Post Magazine*, September 24, 2010.

18. Robert Fisk, "Passport to the Truth in Dubai Remains Secret," *Independent*, February 17, 2010.

19. Danna Harman, "Dubai Assassination Spotlights Top Cop Skills in a Modern-Day Casablanca," *Christian Science Monitor*, March 19, 2010.

20. Yossi Melman, "Dubai Assassins Used Mossad Methods to Kill Hamas Leader," *Ha'aretz*, February 16, 2010.

21. Ron Ben-Yishai, "Hisool Be'Dubai: Ha'Tzilum, Ha'Tachbulot, Ve'Ma'She'Lo Pursam," Ynet, February 16, 2010.

22. https://www.youtube.com/watch?v=pMnLgV-6cJE.

23. See Danna Harman, "Dubai Assassination Spotlights Top Cop Skills in a Modern-Day Casablanca," *Christian Science Monitor*, March 19, 2010.

24. Ibid.

25. Max Abelson, "New York City's Assassination Connection," *Observer*, March 10, 2010.

26. See Ronen Bergman, "The Dubai Job," *GQ*, January 4, 2011.

27. See Max Abelson, "New York City's Assassination Connection," *Observer*, March 10, 2010.

28. Interview, Ramallah, May 15, 2017.

29. Tom Parfitt, "Chechen Link to Dubai Killing of Sulim Yamadayev," *Guardian*, April 5, 2009.

30. https://www.youtube.com/watch?v=pMnLgV-6cJE.

31. Avi Issacharoff, "Report: Dubai Police Chief Tells Mossad Head to 'Be a Man,'" *Ha'aretz*, February 27, 2010.

32. Rory McCarthy, Richard Norton-Taylor, and Mark Tran, "Gordon Brown Pledges Inquiry as Israel Refuses to Rule Out Mossad Plot in Dubai," *Guardian*, February 17, 2010.

33. See https://www.youtube.com/watch?v=pMnLgV-6cJE.

34. Lesley Stahl, "The Spymaster: Meir Dagan on Iran's Threat," CBS News, *60 Minutes*, March 11, 2012.

35. Robert F. Worth and Isabel Kershner, "Hamas Official Murdered in Dubai Hotel," *New York Times*, January 29, 2010.

Chapter Eighteen: The Final Victories of an Old Soldier

1. Quoted in Drake Baer and Richard Feloni, "15 Teddy Roosevelt Quotes on Courage, Leadership, and Success," Business Insider, February 14, 2016.
2. https://www.youtube.com/watch?v=1w60Oiw0hC0.
3. https://web.archive.org/web/20110723234009/http://www.golani.co.il/Info/hi_show.aspx?id=1195&t=5&levelId=.
4. Micha Livna, "Sakanot Hayav: Shloshim Le'Moto Shel Meir Dagan z'l: Dagan Bein Levanon Le'Mat'kal," Special Broadcast, Israel Channel 1, April 20, 2016.
5. http://www.izkor.gov.il/HalalKorot.aspx?id=510105.
6. See Micha Livna, "Sakanot Hayav: Shloshim Le'Moto Shel Meir Dagan z'l: Dagan Bein Levanon Le'Mat'kal," Special Broadcast, Israel Channel 1, April 20, 2016.
7. http://www.pbs.org/wgbh/pages/frontline/tehranbureau/2010/01/updated-who-murdered-professor-ali-mohammadi.html.
8. Sam Ser, "Did a WikiLeaks Document Doom Iranian 'Mossad Agent'?" *Times of Israel*, May 16, 2012.
9. Aharon Etengoff, "Report: Iranian Stuxnet Expert Assassinated in Tehran," TG Daily, November 29, 2010.
10. William Yong and Robert F. Worth, "Bombings Hit Atomic Experts in Iran Streets," *New York Times*, November 29, 2010.
11. Interview, Tel Aviv, June 1, 2016.
12. Julian Borger, "New Book Claims Mossad Assassination Unit Killed Iranian Nuclear Scientists," *Guardian*, July 11, 2012.
13. Isabel Kershner, "Israeli Strike on Iran Would Be 'Stupid,' Ex-Spy Chief Says," *New York Times*, May 8, 2011.
14. Alex Gibney, Marc Shmuger (producers), *Zero Days* (documentary film), Magnolia Pictures, Germany, 2016.
15. https://www.youtube.com/watch?v=1w60Oiw0hC0.
16. Ibid.
17. https://www.youtube.com/watch?v=UZd_jlHdVRg.
18. Interview, Tel Aviv, September 30, 2017.
19. Carol Morello, "Yitzhak Hofi, Israeli Spy Chief Who Helped in Episodes of War and Peace, Dies at 87," *Washington Post*, September 17, 2014.
20. Interview, Tel Aviv, May 9, 2017.
21. See https://www.youtube.com/watch?v=UZd_jlHdVRg.
22. Ibid.
23. Eric Lichtblau and James Risen, "Bank Data Is Sifted by U.S. in Secret to Block Terror," *New York Times*, June 23, 2006.
24. Ibid.
25. Barton Gellman, Paul Blustein, and Dafna Linzer, "Bank Records Secretly Tapped," *Washington Post*, June 23, 2006.
26. Interview, Tel Aviv, May 27, 2017.
27. http://www.abc.net.au/news/2003-08-15/hambali-arrested-in-thailand-reports/1464988.
28. Phil Hirschkorn, "Lawyer: Detained Pakistani to Face Terrorism Charges," CNN, August 6, 2003.

29. See interview, Tel Aviv, May 27, 2017.

30. Ibid.

31. Ibid.

32. See Eric Lichtblau and James Risen, "Bank Data Is Sifted by U.S. in Secret to Block Terror," *New York Times*, June 23, 2006.

33. Terry Atlas and Andrew Mayeda, "When Money Is a Weapon: How the Treasury Got into the Spy Game," Bloomberg, January 20, 2015.

34. Jonathan Fahey and Chris Kahn, "European Sanctions Have Begun to Block the Iranian Banking System Off from the Rest of the World," Business Insider, March 15, 2012.

Chapter Nineteen: Operation Pegasus

1. Yossi Melman, "Who Is New Mossad Chief Tamir Pardo?," *Ha'aretz*, November 29, 2010.

2. Interview, May 30, 2016.

3. Ulrike Putz, "Sabotaging Iran's Nuclear Program: Mossad Behind Tehran Assassinations, Says Source," *Der Spiegel Online*, August 2, 2011.

4. Chris Kraul and Sebastian Rotella, "Drug Probe Finds Hezbollah Link," *Los Angeles Times*, October 22, 2008.

5. Jo Becker, "Beirut Bank Seen as a Hub of Hezbollah's Financing," *New York Times*, December 13, 2011.

6. Ibid.

7. Chris Kraul and Sebastian Rotella, "Colombia Drug Ring May Link to Hezbollah," *Seattle Times*, October 25, 2008.

8. https://www.youtube.com/watch?v=pjeEbEBfC_Q.

9. Michael Ware, "Los Zetas Called Mexico's Most Dangerous Drug Cartel," CNN, August 6, 2009.

10. Alicia A. Caldwell and Mark Stevenson, "U.S. Intelligence Says Sinaloa Cartel Has Won Battle for Ciudad Juarez Drug Routes," CNS News, April 9, 2010.

11. Joby Warrick, "U.S. Accuses Lebanese Companies of Laundering Money for Hezbollah," *Washington Post*, April 23, 2013.

12. U.S. Attorney's Office, Southern District of New York, "Manhattan U.S. Attorney Announces $102 Million Settlement of Civil Forfeiture and Money Laundering Claims Against Lebanese Canadian Bank," (press release), June 25, 2013.

Chapter Twenty: Money in the Crosshairs

1. Chaim Urinson, "Palestinian Behind Kidnap, Murder of 3 Israeli Teens Gets 3 Life Sentences," *Ha'aretz*, January 6, 2015.

2. Ben Hartman, JPost.com Staff, Lahav Harkov, and Yaakov Lappin, "Listen: Recording of Kidnapped Teen's Distress Call to Police Released," *Jerusalem Post*, July 1, 2014.

3. Jodi Rudoren, "Bedouin Trackers Hunting for Clues to Kidnapped Boys," *New York Times*, June 23, 2014.

4. "Security Forces Find Missing Teens' Bodies in West Bank," Ynet News, June 30, 2014.

5. Isabel Kershner, "Trouble Underfoot on Israeli Kibbutz near the Border," *New York Times*, July 18, 2014.

6. Nir Davori, "Echrai Ha'Ksafim Shel Hamas Husal Be'Tzfon Re'Tzu'at A'aza," *Mako Hadashot*, August 24, 2014.

7. Yossi Melman, "Meet David Cohen: The Jewish 'Sanctions Guru' Appointed Deputy Chief of the CIA," *Jerusalem Post*, January 15, 2015.

8. Jean-Charles Brisard and Damien Martinez, "Islamic State: The Economy-Based Terrorist Funding" Thomson Reuters, October 2014.

9. Matthew Levitt, "Declaring an Islamic State, Running a Criminal Enterprise," *Hill*, July 7, 2014.

10. Matthew Levitt, "Terrorist Financing and the Islamic State," Washington Institute for Near East Policy, Washington, D.C., November 13, 2014.

11. http://www.npr.org/2014/07/21/333537790/after-ultimatum-christians-flee-iraqi-city-en-masse.

12. http://www.catholicworldreport.com/Blog/3264/isis_tags_christian_homes_in_mosul_for_confiscation_as_christians_flee.aspx.

13. https://barnabasfund.org/news/Islamic-State-auctions-seized-Christian-homes-in-Iraq-in-bid-for-cash?audience=AU.

14. Financial Action Task Force, "Financing of the Terrorist Organisation Islamic State in Iraq and the Levant (ISIL)," FATF Report, February 2015.

15. Ana Swanson, "How the Islamic State Makes Its Money," *Washington Post*, November 18, 2015. https://www.washingtonpost.com/news/wonk/wp/2015/11/18/how-isis-makes-its-money/.

16. http://abcnews.go.com/International/us-warplanes-destroy-116-isis-fuel-trucks-syria/story?id=35229047.

17. http://www.iraqoilreport.com/news/armed-intel-u-s-strikes-curtail-oil-sector-17473/.

18. http://www.ibtimes.com/amid-anti-isis-fight-90-islamic-state-oil-destroyed-us-led-coalition-airstrikes-syria-2234357.

19. Ibid.

20. Jim Miklaszewsi and Corky Siemaszko, "Millions in ISIS Cash Destroyed in U.S. Airstrike," NBC News, January 11, 2016.

21. Patrick B. Johnston et al., *Foundations of the Islamic State: Management, Money, and Terror in Iraq, 2005–2010*. Santa Monica, CA: RAND Corporation, 2016.

Afterword

1. Stephanie Clifford, "Arab Bank Liable for Supporting Terrorist Efforts, Jury Finds," *New York Times*, September 22, 2014.

2. Marcy Gordon, "Arab Bank to Pay $24 Million Fine," *Washington Post*, August 18, 2005.

3. See Stephanie Clifford, "Arab Bank Liable for Supporting Terrorist Efforts, Jury Finds," *New York Times*, September 22, 2014.

4. Stephanie Clifford, "Arab Bank Reaches Settlement in Suit Accusing It of Financing Terrorism," *New York Times*, August 14, 2015.

5. Reuters, "Manhattan Jury Finds Palestinian Authority Liable for Terrorist Attacks," *Washington Post*, February 23, 2015.

6. Ibid.

7. Greg Tepper and Ilan Ben Zion, "Ex-Mossad Chief's Health Reportedly in Peril After Liver Transplant in Belarus," *Times of Israel*, October 17, 2012.

8. Interview, May 9, 2017.

9. Amir Tibon, "Netanyahu vs. the Generals," Politico, July 3, 2016.

10. https://www.youtube.com/watch?v=1w60Oiw0hC0.

11. "Ex-Mossad Chief Dagan Laid to Rest with Military Honors," *Times of Israel*, March 20, 2016.

12. https://www.youtube.com/watch?v=Ul42FYUop3Y.

13. Interview, Tel Aviv, September 30, 2016.

INDEX